THEODORE ROETHKE

Modern Critical Views

Continued at back of book

Modern Critical Views

THEODORE ROETHKE

Edited and with an introduction by
Harold Bloom
Sterling Professor of the Humanities
Yale University

CHELSEA HOUSE PUBLISHERS ◊ 1988
New York ◊ New Haven ◊ Philadelphia

Library of Congress Cataloging-in-Publication Data
Theodore Roethke.
  (Modern critical views)
  Bibliography: p.
  Includes index.
  Summary: A collection of eight critical essays on Roethke's
poetry arranged in chronological order of publication.
  1. Roethke, Theodore, 1908–1963—Criticism and
interpretation. [1. Roethke, Theodore, 1908–1963—Criticism
and interpretation.   2. American poetry—History and
criticism] I. Bloom, Harold. II. Series.
PS3535.039Z9 1988 811'.54   87-9345
ISBN 1-55546-287-1 (alk. paper)

Contents

Editor's Note

This book gathers together a representative selection of what I judge to be the most useful criticism so far available upon the poetry of Theodore Roethke. The critical essays are reprinted here in the chronological order of their original publication. I am grateful to Neil Arditi for his assistance in editing this volume.

My introduction offers a reading of Roethke's great sequence, "The Shape of the Fire," which concludes *The Lost Son*. Kenneth Burke, Roethke's friend and canonical critic, begins the chronological sequence with his justly renowned pioneering essay on the roots of Roethke's art, his "vegetal radicalism."

The warm overview of Denis Donoghue helps set Roethke in the context of American poetic tradition, as does the deeply informed tribute by Roy Harvey Pearce to Roethke's almost Blakean and Whitmanian power of sympathy.

The benign influence of Kenneth Burke's criticism on Roethke's work is traced by Brendan Galvin, after which the poet James Dickey celebrates both Roethke, his precursor, and the novelist Allan Seager, Roethke's devoted biographer.

J. D. McClatchy, a distinguished younger poet, analyzes Roethke's intense struggle to leap beyond revelation into a direct sense of the Godhead. The rather Yeatsian and overtly Eliotic sequence, "Meditations of an Old Woman," is seen by Rosemary Sullivan as a vital work, though she admits that the Eliotic elements may seem too obtrusive. Another estimate by a poet, Jay Parini's consideration of Blake's influence upon Roethke, also generously defends Roethke where he seems to me, at least, a touch too derivative and even grandiose.

The self-portrait of Roethke's "North American Sequence," a frankly Whitmanian poem, is examined by Thomas Gardner, who finds it to be characteristic of a contemporary American mode. In this book's final essay, the poet James Applewhite movingly locates Roethke's achievement in the broad context of Romantic tradition, with an emphasis upon Wordsworth in particular as the tradition's strongest founder.

Introduction

Theodore Roethke shares with Elizabeth Bishop and Robert Penn Warren the distinction of having emerged as the strongest survivors of what could be called the middle generation of modern American poets, which included Robert Lowell, John Berryman, Delmore Schwartz, and Randall Jarrell. This generation came after the succession from E. A. Robinson and Frost through Pound, Eliot, Moore, Stevens, Williams, and Crane, and before the group that includes Ashbery, Merrill, Ammons, James Wright, Snyder, Merwin, Hollander, Kinnell, and others. The fate of a middle generation is hard, particularly when its older contemporaries included half a dozen poets of authentic greatness. The shadows of Stevens and of Eliot still hover in Roethke's last poems in *The Far Field* (1964), which seems to me as derivative a volume as his first, *Open House* (1941).

Dead much too soon, at fifty-five, Roethke did not have time to work through to another achievement as original as his best book, *The Lost Son* (1948), published at the crucial age of forty. My own sense of Roethke's eminence is founded almost entirely on *The Lost Son*. Elizabeth Bishop was unwaveringly strong, from first to last, while Warren became a great poet at the age of sixty, and maintained this eminence for fully two decades after. Roethke is upon his heights, in my judgement, only in *The Lost Son*, but the book is so marvelous that it justifies placing Roethke with Bishop and Warren in his own generation.

The Lost Son is alive in every poem, but the most memorable include "Big Wind," "Frau Bauman, Frau Schmidt, and Frau Schwartze," "The Waking," and four remarkable sequences: "The Lost Son," "The Long Alley," "A Field of Light," and perhaps the most distinguished, "The Shape of the Fire." Since "The Shape of the Fire" is the Roethke I love best, I choose it for an introductory commentary here. Resenting insinuations that the sequence was too much influenced by Dylan Thomas, Roethke rather eagerly took up a suggestion of W. H. Auden's, and asserted that Thomas

1

Traherne was his true source. The source sensibly can be found in Walt Whitman, the most benign of influences upon Roethke, and the hidden influence upon Eliot and Stevens, two of Roethke's masters. Unlike say Yeats, whose effect upon Roethke was overwhelming and destructive, Whitman worked deep within Roethke to help bring to birth what was best in Roethke's own imagination.

The shape of the fire is the shape or form of Roethke's inspiration, and is the dominant if implicit trope of the sequence, until it becomes explicit in the sunlight of section 5. I take it that the title helps guide us to the realization that the poem is not about the first or natural birth, but instead concerns the second birth into poetic vision. The painful birth imagery of section 1 is more a farewell to mothering nature than a celebration of her function.

> What's this? A dish for fat lips.
> Who says? A nameless stranger.
> Is he a bird or a tree? Not everyone can tell.

> Water recedes to the crying of spiders.
> An old scow bumps over black rocks.
> A cracked pod calls.

> Mother me out of here. What more will the bones allow?
> Will the sea give the wind suck? A toad folds into a stone.
> These flowers are all fangs. Comfort me, fury.
> Wake me, witch, we'll do the dance of rotten sticks.

> Shale loosens. Marl reaches into the field. Small birds pass over
>   water.
> Spirit, come near. This is only the edge of whiteness.
> I can't laugh at a procession of dogs.

> In the hour of ripeness the tree is barren.
> The she-bear mopes under the hill.
> Mother, mother, stir from your cave of sorrow.

> A low mouth laps water. Weeds, weeds, how I love you
> The arbor is cooler. Farewell, farewell, fond worm.
> The warm comes without sound.

Roethke was reluctant to associate himself with Rimbaud; there is a Notebook comment of 1944 in which he oddly remarks: "The error of Rimbaud: the world is chaotic, therefore I must be." Hart Crane was the

American Rimbaud, as he meant to be; Roethke will not survive a poetic comparison with either. But "The Shape of the Fire" is the most Rimbaldian of Roethke's poems, in its aggressivity and its deep rebellion against nature. The aggressivity subverts the referential aspect of the poem, while the rebellion dissolves any clear sense of a unified subjectivity in Roethke's use of "I." "What's this?" dismisses nature as the "dish for fat lips" that the poem's voice declines to devour. The "nameless stranger," whether bird or tree, is a messenger from beyond nature guiding the poet's Rimbaldian drunken boat over the black rocks of an intransigent nature, to the music of a call from "a cracked pod," also now beyond natural process.

An immense ambivalence in this poet, longing for the maternal even as he is guided out of it, is impelled to fall back on the rejected image of mothering in order to accomplish the new emergence into a vision antithetical to nature's. The prayer to be mothered out of the mother is accompanied by parallel antitheses: a sea nursing the wind, toad folding into a stone, flowers that are fangs, a fury that comforts. Even the contra-natural is viewed dialectically, as the awakening patroness is addressed under the name of witch, and the dance of deliverance from process becomes one of rotten sticks.

If the spirit beckoned near is identified as Whitman's, then the highly Whitmanian affirmation is wholly contextualized: "Weeds, weeds, how I love you." The fat lips of the opening are replaced now by the low mouth lapping water, emblem here of the rebirth into the incarnation of what the eighteenth century called the Poetical Character. Perhaps the most brilliant stroke in section 1 is the final trope, where the soundless warm of the shaping fire replaces the fond warm of what Blake called the state of Generation.

After the relative clarity of this first section, Roethke gives us the most difficult movement, not only of "The Shape of the Fire," but of any poem he ever published. It yields a surreal coherence to repeated rereadings, while defying the heresy of any paraphrase. To me it seems a total success, representing as it does the startled awakening to the poetic condition, a state of origins where every prior expectation has been twisted askew. Eye, ear, nose, foot have relocated themselves, and the nameless stranger of annunciation has been replaced by an hallucinatory listener, Roethke's version of Blake's Idiot Questioner, flat-headed, replete with platitudes and rubber doughnuts, and greeted by the poet with a question one might ask of Satan: "Have you come to unhinge my shadow?"

A poignant tentativeness attends the poet's new state, near allied, as it must have been for Roethke himself, to the disorders of schizophrenia. After a child-like nonsense song of this new innocence, Roethke cries out: "Who waits at the gate?" The answer does not seem to be the abandoned "mother of quartz" with her renewal of the whispers of family romance, but the wasp and other emblems of antithetical redemption of section 3:

> The wasp waits.
>   The edge cannot eat the center.
> The grape glistens.
>   The path tells little to the serpent.
> An eye comes out of the wave.
>   The journey from flesh is longest.
> A rose sways least.
>   The redeemer comes a dark way.

The center, being prolific, will hold against the devouring edge or circumference. If the long journey from flesh to poetic incarnation is longest, this is because, as St. John of the Cross suggested, you must go by a dark way, wherein there is no knowing. Roethke indeed does get back to where he does not know, to the childhood world of section 4: "Death was not. I lived in a simple drowse." Dylan Thomas's "Fern Hill" and much of Traherne are doubtless analogues, but Wordsworth is closer, as James Applewhite has indicated. These intimations of immortality guide us to the fifth and final section, the strongest passage in all of Roethke, an epiphany both Whitmanian and Wordsworthian:

> To have the whole air!—
> The light, the full sun
> Coming down on the flowerheads,
> The tendrils turning slowly,
> A slow snail-lifting, liquescent;
> To be by the rose
> Rising slowly out of its bed,
> Still as a child in its first loneliness;
> To see cyclamen veins become clearer in early sunlight,
> And mist lifting out of the brown cat-tails;
> To stare into the after-light, the glitter left on the lake's surface,
> When the sun has fallen behind a wooded island;
> To follow the drops sliding from a lifted oar,
> Held up, while the rower breathes, and the small boat drifts
>   quietly shoreward;

To know that light falls and fills, often without our knowing,
As an opaque vase fills to the brim from a quick pouring,
Fills and trembles at the edge yet does not flow over,
Still holding and feeding the stem of the contained flower.

Certainly one of the most American of visions, this splendor is extraordinary for its gentle but taut control of the nearly ineffable. What the sequence gives us is truly the shape of the fire, the shape of the movement: to have, to be, to see, to stare, to follow, and at last to know. To know what? A falling, a filling to the brim, a trembling at the edge that will not flow over: these are the shapes of the creative fire transformed into a sustaining light. Roethke concludes with the image of a light still holding and feeding, a mothering light that contains the flower of restored consciousness as its child. The trope, almost Dantesque, achieves an aesthetic dignity worthy of Wordsworth or Whitman, true founders of the tradition that chose Roethke, at his rare best, as its own.

KENNETH BURKE

The Vegetal Radicalism
of Theodore Roethke

Perhaps the best way-in is through the thirteen flower poems that comprise
the first section of *The Lost Son*. The two opening lyrics, "Cuttings," and
"Cuttings (later)," present the vital strivings of coronated stem, severed
from parental stock. Clearly the imagistic figuring of a human situation,
they view minutely the action of vegetal "sticks-in-a-drowse" as

> One nub of growth
> Nudges a sand-crumb loose,
> Pokes through a musty sheath
> Its pale tendrilous horn.

The second of the two (that sum up the design of this particular poetic
vocation) should be cited entire, for its nature as epitome:

> This urge, wrestle, resurrection of dry sticks,
> Cut stems struggling to put down feet,
> What saint strained so much,
> Rose on such lopped limbs to a new life?
>
> I can hear, underground, that sucking and sobbing,
> In my veins, in my bones I feel it,—
> The small waters seeping upward,
> The tight grains parting at last.
> What sprouts break out,

From *The Sewanee Review* 58, no. 1 (January–March 1950). © 1950 by the University of the South.

> Slippery as fish,
> I quail, lean to beginnings, sheath-wet.

Severedness, dying that is at the same time a fanatic tenacity; submergence (fish, and the sheer mindless nerves of sensitive-plants); envagination as a home-coming.

To characterize the others briefly: "Root Cellar" (of bulbs that "broke out of boxes hunting for chinks in the dark," of shoots "lolling obscenely," of roots "ripe as old bait"—a "congress of stinks"); "Forcing House" (a frantic urgency of growth, "shooting up lime and dung and ground bones . . . as the live heat billows from pipes and pots"); "Weed Puller" (the poet "Under the concrete benches, / Hacking at black hairy roots,— / Those lewd monkey-tails hanging from drainholes"); "Orchids" ("adder-mouthed" in the day, at night "Loose ghostly mouths / Breathing"); "Moss-Gathering" (the guilt of moss-gathering); "Old Florist" (genre portrait, lines in praise of a man vowed to the ethics of this vegetal radicalism); "Transplanting" (a companion piece to the previous poem, detailing *operations* in ways that appeal to our *sensations*); "Child on Top of a Greenhouse" (the great stir below, while the young hero climbs, smashing through glass, the wind billowing out the seat of his britches); "Flower-Dump" (the picturesqueness greatly increased by a strong contrast, as the catalogue of the heap and clutter ends on a vision of "one tulip on top / One swaggering head / Over the dying, the newly dead"); "Carnations" (where the theme shifts to talk of "a crisp hyacinthine coolness, / Like that clear autumnal weather of eternity,"—a kind of expression, as we shall later try to indicate, not wholly characteristic of this poet).

From this group we omitted one item, "Big Wind," because we want to consider it at great length. It reveals most clearly how Roethke can endow his brief lyrics with intensity of *action*. Nor is the effect got, as so often in short forms, merely by a new spurt in the last line. No matter how brief the poems are, they progress from stage to stage. Reading them, you have strongly the sense of entering at one place, winding through a series of internal developments, and coming out somewhere else. Thus "Big Wind" first defines the situation (water shortage in greenhouse during storm) with a five-line rhetorical question. Next come fifteen lines describing the action appropriate to the scene, the strained efforts of those who contrive to keep the pipes supplied with hot steam. Then the substance of this account is restated in a figure that likens the hothouse to a ship riding a gale. And after eleven lines amplifying the one turbulent metaphor, there are two final lines

wherein the agitation subsides into calm, with a splendid gesture of assertion. We cite the summarizing image, and its closing couplet:

> But she rode it out,
> That old rose-house,
> She hove into the teeth of it,
> The core and pith of that ugly storm,
> Ploughing with her stiff prow,
> Bucking into the wind-waves
> That broke over the whole of her,
> Flailing her sides with spray,
> Flinging long strings of wet across the roof-top,
> Finally veering, wearing themselves out, merely
> Whistling thinly under the wind-vents;
> She sailed into the calm morning,
> Carrying her full cargo of roses.

The unwinding of the trope is particularly fortunate in suggesting transcendence because the reference to the "full cargo of roses," even as we are
thinking of a ship, suddenly brings before us a vision of the greenhouse
solidly grounded on terra firma; and this shift apparently helps to give the
close its great finality. Thus, though you'd never look to Roethke for
the rationalistic, the expository steps are here ticked off as strictly as in the
successive steps of a well-formed argument. And thanks to the developmental structure of such poems, one never thinks of them sheerly as descriptive:
they have the vigor, and the poetic morality, of action, of form unfolding.

To round out this general sampling, we might consider a poem written
since the publication of *The Lost Son*. It is "The Visitant," and in contrast
with "The Big Wind," which is robust, it possesses an undulance, a
hushedness, a contemplative, or even devotional attitude, that makes of love
an almost mystic presence. Roethke here begins with such a natural scene as
would require a local deity, a genius loci, to make it complete. Hence as the
poem opens, the place described is infused with a numen or pneuma, a
concentration of spirit just on the verge of apparition.

The work is divided into three movements: the first anticipatory, the
third reminiscent, the second leading through a partly secular, yet gently
pious, theophany. The mood is beautifully sustained.

The introductory stanza evokes a secretive spot by a stream, at a time
of vigil ("I waited, alert as a dog") while, with a shift in the slight wind
(figuring also a breath of passion?), "a tree swayed over water." Nine lines

establishing expectancy, a state of suspension as though holding one's breath ("The leech clinging to a stone waited").

The second stanza is of the "coming." We quote it entire:

> Slow, slow as a fish she came,
> Slow as a fish coming forward,
> Swaying in a long wave;
> Her skirts not touching a leaf,
> Her white arms reaching toward me.
>
> She came without sound,
> Without brushing the wet stones;
> In the soft dark of early evening,
> She came,
> The wind in her hair,
> The moon beginning.

The wind is thus there too, so the ambiguities of the advent may now presumably stand also for erotic movements sometimes celebrated by poets as a "dying." The swaying tree of the first stanza has its counterpart in the swaying "fish" of the second.

The third stanza is of the same scene, now retrospectively: The spirit is there still, but only through having been there, as in the first stanza it was there prophetically. Thus, at the end:

> A wind stirred in a web of appleworms;
> The tree, the close willow, swayed.

The peculiar mixture of tension and calm in this poem is of great felicity. The talk of "swaying," the key word repeated in each stanza, has its replica in the cradle-like rhythm. And the whole effect is gratifyingly idyllic, even worshipful.

As a comment on method, we might contrast, "The Visitant" with another poem where Roethke was apparently attempting, in a somewhat "essayistic" manner, to trace the birth of Psyche. It begins

> The soul stirs in its damp folds,
> Stirs as a blossom stirs,
> Still wet from its bud-sheath,
> Slowly unfolding.

Cyclamen, turtle, minnow, child, seed, snail—each in turn is exploited to define how the spirit moves, "still and inward." The lines are the poet's *De*

Anima: and the emergent soul is seen ultimately in terms of an inner Snail-Phallus. As there is a mind's eye, a spirit breath, an inner ear, so he would seem to conceive a kind of transcendent sex-within-sex, the essence of pure snailhood ("outward and inward . . . hugging a rock, stone and horn . . . taking and embracing its surroundings"). But though the poem is almost a review of Roethke's favorite images, it is far less successful in combining Psyche and Eros than "The Visitant." For it is weaker in action, development, being rather a series of repetitive attempts to arrive at the same end from different images as starting point. Roethke could have got to this poem by translating the theories of mystical theology directly into his own impressionistic equivalent. In "The Visitant" he has moved beyond such mere correspondences by introducing a dramatic situation and building around it. A comparison of the two poems shows how the essayistic (that moves toward excellence in Pope) could be but an obstruction to Roethke. (Since this comment was written, the poem has been greatly revised, mainly by omission of about half its original contents. In its final form, there is a progression of but three images [blossom, minnow, snail] culminating in a catachresis ["music in a hood"]. One epithet ["a light breather"] is lifted from the body of the poem to be used as title. And the last six lines diminish gradually from ten syllables to two. The poem has thus finally been assimilated, has been made developmental.)

We have said that the mention of "coolness" and "eternity" was not characteristic of Roethke's language. We meant this statement in the strictest sense. We meant that you will rarely find in his verse a noun ending in "-ness" or "-ity." He goes as far as is humanly possible in quest of a speech wholly devoid of abstractions.

To make our point by antithesis: glancing through Eliot's "Burnt Norton," we find these words:

Abstraction, possibility, speculation, purpose, deception, circulation, arrest, movement, fixity, freedom, compulsion, *Erhebung* without motion, concentration without elimination, completion, ecstasy, resolution, enchantment, weakness, mankind, damnation, consciousness, disaffection, stillness, beauty, rotation, permanence, deprivation, affection, plenitude, vacancy, distraction, apathy, concentration, eructation, solitude, darkness, deprivation, destitution, property, desiccation, evacuation, inoperancy, abstention, appetency, silence, stillness, co-existence, tension, imprecision, temptation, limitation.

If Roethke adheres to his present aesthetic, there are more of such expressions in this one Quartet of Eliot's than Roethke's Vegetal Radicalism would require for a whole lifetime of poetizing.

In one poem, to be sure, they do cluster. In "Dolor," lines detailing the "tedium" of "institutions" (notably the schoolroom), we find, besides these two words: sadness, misery, desolation, reception, pathos, ritual, duplication. But their relative profusion here explains their absence elsewhere, in verse written under an aesthetic diametrically opposed to such motives. (In one place he uses "sweetness" as a term of endearment, yet the effect is more like an epithet than like an abstract noun.)

Accordingly, in the attempt to characterize Roethke's verse, you could profitably start from considerations of vocabulary. The motive that we have in mind is by no means peculiar to this one poet. It runs through modern art generally. And though few of the artists working in this mode are interested in formal philosophy, the ultimate statement of the problem would take us back to some basic distinctions in Immanuel Kant's *Critique of Pure Reason*: notably his way of aligning "intuitions," "concepts," and "ideas."

If you perceive various sensations (of color, texture, size, shape, etc.), you are experiencing what Kant would call "intuitions of sensibility." If you can next "unify" this "manifold" (as were you to decide that the entire lot should be called a "tree"), in this word or name you have employed a "concept of the understanding." "Intuitions" and "concepts," taken together, would thus sum up the world of visible, tangible, audible things, the objects and operations of our sensory experience. And because of their positive, empirical nature, they would also present the sensible material that forms the basis of a poetic image (however "spiritual" may be the implications of the poet's language in its outer reaches).

"Intuitions" and "concepts" belong to Kant's "Aesthetic" and "Analytic" respectively. But there is also a purely "Dialectical" realm, comprising "ideas of reason." This is the world of such invisible, intangible, inaudible things as "principles." The various "isms" would be classed as "ideas of reason." In carrying out an idea, men will at every turn deal with the concrete objects that are represented in terms of "intuitions" and "concepts"; yet the idea itself is not thus "empirical," but purely "dialectical," not available to our senses alone, or to measurement by scientific instruments.

Do not these distinctions of Kant's indicate the direction which poetry might take, in looking for a notable purification of language? If one could avoid the terms for "ideas," and could use "concepts" only insofar as they are needed to unify the manifold of "intuitions," the resultant vocabulary would move toward childlike simplicity. And it would be cleansed of such unwieldy expressions (now wielded by politicos and journalists) as: capitalism, fascism, socialism, communism, democracy (words unthinkable in Roethke's verse, which features rather: cry, moon, stones, drip, toad, bones, snail, fish, flower, house, water, spider, pit, dance, kiss, bud, sheath, budsheath, ooze, slip-ooze, behind which last term, despite ourselves, we irresponsibly keep hearing a child's pronunciation of "slippers").

Kant's alignment was designed primarily to meet the positivistic requirements of modern technological science. And since he himself, in the *Critique of Judgment,* talked of "aesthetic ideas," the issue is not drawn by him with finality. The modern lyric poet of imagistic cast might even with some justice think of himself as paralleling the scientific ideal, when he stresses the vocabulary of concrete things and sensible operations; yet the typical scientist language, with its artificially constructed Greek-Roman compounds, seems usable only in a few sophisticated gestures (as with the ironic nostalgia of a Laforgue). This much is certain, however: Whatever the complications, we can use the Kantian distinctions to specify a possible criterion for a purified poetic idiom. The ideal formula might be stated thus: *A minimum of "ideas," a maximum of "intuitions."* In this form, it can sum up the Roethkean aesthetic. (The concept would be admitted as a kind of regrettable necessity.)

For further placements (as regards the problems of linguistic purity set by urbanization), we might think of Dante's *De Vulgari Eloquentia,* Wordsworth's Preface to the *Lyrical Ballads,* and D. H. Lawrence's cult of the "physical" as contrasted with the "abstract."

Dante introduced the criterion of the *infantile* in the search for a purified poetic idiom. Choosing between learned Latin and the vernacular, he noted that the "vulgar locution" which infants imitate from their nurses is "natural" and "more noble," hence the most fit for poetry. But though he set up the infantile as a criterion for preferring Italian to a learned and "artificial" language, his criteria for the selection of a poetic vocabulary within Italian itself encompassed a quite mature medium. Thus, the ideal speech should be "illustrious, cardinal, courtly, and curial"; and in such a language, one would necessarily introduce, without irony or sullenness, many "ideas of reason." Indeed, what we have called the "infantile" criterion of selection we might rather call a search for the ideal mother tongue (had it not been for the Fall, Dante reminds us, all men would still speak Hebrew, the language of the Garden of Eden). That is, we could stress its *perfection,* its maturity and scope (its "mother wit"), rather than its *intellectual limitations* (though in the first great division of labor, separating those who specialize in being males and those who specialize in being females, the class of womanhood would seem to be the "more noble," so far as concerned its associations with the *medium* of poetry). The ideal language, we might say, was under the sign not of the child but of the Virgin Mother; though even, had the infant Jesus been the ultimate term for the motivation here, his essential kingliness would have been enough to derive the illustrious, cardinal, courtly, and curial from the infantile alone, as so modified.

In any case, as early as Dante's time, though prior to the upsurge of the industrial revolution, the division of labor was sufficiently advanced for him to assert that each kind of craftsman had come to speak a different language in the confusion of tongues caused during work on the Tower. The diversity of languages was thus derived from specialization, quite as with particular technical idioms today—and the higher the specialized activity, Dante says, the more "barbarous" its speech. His principle of selection could thus acquire a new poignancy later, when the learned language he had rejected had become an essential part of the vernacular itself, and when the relation between mother and child is not formally summed up in the infancy of a universal ruler (though, roundabout, in furtive ways, there are the modern mothers who are by implication ennobled, in giving birth to offspring they encourage to be child tyrants).

By the time of Wordsworth's preface, after several centuries of progressively accelerated industrialization, the search for a principle of selection, for a "purified" speech, involves another kind of regression, a romantic reversion, not just to childhood simplicity, but also to "low and rustic life." For in this condition, "the essential passions of the heart . . . can attain their maturity, are less under restraint, and speak a plainer and more emphatic language." Though Wordsworth is talking of the rustic life itself, approaching the problem in terms of language (as Wordsworth's own explicit concern with selection entitles us to do), we should stress rather the *imagery* drawn from "the necessary character of rural occupations." Such imagery, he says, would be "more easily comprehended" and "more durable"; and by it "our elementary feelings" would be "more forcibly communicated," since "the passions of men are incorporated with the beautiful and permanent forms of nature."

Wordsworth is also explicitly considering another threat to poetry, the journalistic idiom which by now has almost become the norm with us, so that poets are repeatedly rebuked for not writing in a style designed to be used once and thrown away. Thus, on the subject of the causes that now act "with a combined force to blunt the discriminating powers of the mind," bringing about "a state of almost savage stupor," Wordsworth writes:

> The most effective of these causes are the great national events
> which are daily taking place, and the increasing accumulation of
> men in cities, where the uniformity of their occupations produces
> a craving for extraordinary incident, which the rapid communi-
> cation of intelligence hourly gratifies.

"The rapid communication of intelligence hourly"; this is Wordsworth's
resonant equivalent for "journalism." In such an expression he does well by
it, even while recognizing its threat to poetic purity as he conceives of such
purity.

He goes on to state his belief that, despite his preference for the ways
of pre-technological nature as the basis for a poet's imagery, "If the time
should ever come when what is now called Science . . . shall be ready to put
on . . . a form of flesh and blood, the Poet will lend his divine spirit to aid
the transfiguration." Maybe yes, maybe no. Though concerned with the
purification of vocabulary for poetic purposes, Wordsworth does not show
(or even ask) how the technological idioms themselves can be likened to the
language learned at the breast.

We should note, however, one major respect in which the terms of the
new technology are in spirit a language close to childhood. For they have the
quality of death rays and rocket ships, and other magical powers the thought
of which can make the child wonder and in his imagination feel mighty.
Indeed, the pageantry of the technological (the new lore of the giant-killers)
can appeal to the infantile, long before there is any concern with such
romances of love as, variously, concern Dante, Wordsworth, and Roethke,
all three. What you put around a Christmas tree reflects no longer the
mystery of the Birth, but the wonders of modern technological production.
So, surprisingly, we glimpse how a poet's nursery language may be more
mature than at first it may seem. It may be no younger than the adolescent
in spirit, though this adolescence is on the side that leans toward the universal sensibility of childhood (and of the maternal) rather than toward the
forensic, abstract, and journalistically "global."

A bridge builder, no matter how special his language, has successfully
"communicated" with his fellows when he has built them a good bridge. In
this respect, the languages of the technological specialties confront a different communicative problem than marks the language of the specialist in
verse. And even if, with Wordsworth, you believed in the ability of poetry
to poetize any conditions that modern technology might bring into being,
you could question whether this result could be got through the Wordsworth
aesthetic. Hence a century later, D. H. Lawrence, whose flower poems could

have been models for Roethke, warns against a kind of *abstraction from the physical* that accompanies the progress of scientific materialism.

The doctrine infuses all of Lawrence's writings. But one can find it especially announced in his essay, "Men Must Work and Women as Well," reprinted in the *Viking Portable*. We think of statements like these: "Mr. Ford, being in his own way a genius, has realized that what the modern workman wants, just like the modern gentleman, is abstraction. The modern workman doesn't *want* to be interested in his job. He wants to be as little interested, as nearly perfectly mechanical, as possible." . . . The trend of our civilization is "towards a greater and greater abstraction from the physical, towards a further and further physical separateness between men and women, and between individual and individual." . . . Such displays even as "sitting in bathing suits all day on a beach" are "peculiarly non-physical, a flaunting of the body in its non-physical, merely optical aspect. . . . He only *sees* his meal, he never *really* eats it. He drinks his beer by idea, he no longer tastes it. . . . Under it all, as ever, as everywhere, vibrates the one great impulse of our civilization, physical recoil from every other being and from every form of physical existence. . . . We can look on Soviet Russia as nothing but a logical state of society established in anti-physical insanity.— Physical and material are, of course, not the same; in fact, they are subtly opposite. The machine is absolutely material, and absolutely anti-physical— as even our fingers know. And the Soviet is established on the image of the machine, 'pure' materialism. The Soviet hates the real physical body far more deeply than it hates Capital. . . . The only thing to do is to get your bodies back, men and women. A great part of society is irreparably lost: abstracted into non-physical, mechanical entities."

One may object to the particulars here; the *tendency* Lawrence discusses is clear enough. And though machinery (as viewed in psychoanalytic terms) may stand for the pudenda, and though the abstractions of technology and finance may even make for a compensatory overemphasizing of the sexual (Love Among the Machines), Lawrence was noting how the proliferation of mechanical means makes for a relative withdrawal, for a turn from intuitive immediacy to pragmatist meditation; hence his crusade against the intellect (and its "ideas").

As a novelist, Lawrence confronted this problem in all its contradictoriness. His crusade against the intellect was itself intellectual, even intellectualistic. Along with his cult of simplicity (which, going beyond Dante's infantile-maternal criterion and Wordsworth's rustic one, became a super-Rousseauistic vision of ideal savagery) there was his endless discussion of the issue. But though few modern novels contain a higher percentage of talk that might fall roughly under the heading of "ideas," (talk under the slogan, Down With Talk), in his verse he sought for images that *exemplified* the state of intuitive immediacy rather than expatiating on the problem of its loss. For whereas the novels dealt with people, the verse could treat of animals and inanimate beings that imagistically figured some generalized or idealized human motive (as with the heroic copulation of whales and elephants, or the social implications in the motions of a snap-dragon). All told, he loquaciously celebrated the wisdom of silent things—for the yearning to see beyond the intellect terminates mystically in the yearning to regain a true state of "infancy," such immediacy of communication as would be possible only if man had never spoken at all (an aim often sought in sexual union, though both sexual barriers and the breaking of those barriers are preponderantly conditioned by the many "ideas of reason" that are the necessary result of language and of the social order made possible by language).

All told, then, we can see in Roethke's cult of "intuitive" language: a more strictly "infantile" variant of the Dantesque search for a "noble" vernacular; a somewhat suburban, horticulturist variant of Wordsworth's stress upon the universal nature of rusticity; and a close replica of Lawrence's distinction between the "physical" and the "abstract."

With "prowess in arms" (*Virtus*) he is not concerned. The long poems, still to be considered, are engrossed with problems of welfare (*Salus*), though of a kind attainable rather by persistent dreamlike yielding than by moralistic "guidance of the will." As for *Venus*, in Roethke's verse it would seem addressed most directly to a phase of adolescence. The infantile motif serves here, perhaps, like the persuasive gestures of sorrow or helplessness, as appeal to childless girls vaguely disposed toward nursing. The lost son's bid for a return to the womb may thus become transformed into a doting on the erotic imagery of the "sheath-wet" and its "slip-ooze." And in keeping, there is the vocabulary of flowers and fishes (used with connotations of love), and of primeval slime.

We have considered representative instances of Roethke's poetic manner. We have viewed his choice of terms from the standpoint of three motivational orders as described by Kant. And we noted three strategic moments in the theory of poetic selectivity (Dante on the infantile, Wordsworth on the rustic, Lawrence on the physical). Now let us ask what kind of selectivity is implicit in Roethke's flower images (with their variants of the infantile, rustic, and physical).

In particular, what is a greenhouse? What might we expect it to stand for? It is not sheer nature, like a jungle; nor even regulated nature, like a formal garden. It is not the starkly unnatural, like a factory. Nor is it in those intermediate realms of institutional lore, systematic thanatopses, or convenient views of death, we find among the reliques of a natural history museum. Nor would it be like a metropolitan art gallery. It is like all these only in the sense that it is a museum experience, and so an aspect of our late civilization. But there is a peculiar balance of the natural and the artificial in a greenhouse. All about one, the lovely, straining beings, visibly drawing sustenance from ultimate, invisible powers—in a silent blare of vitality—yet as morbid as the caged animals of a zoo.

Even so, with Roethke the experience is not like going from exhibit to exhibit among botanic oddities and rarities. It is like merging there into the life-laden but sickly soil.

To get the quality of Roethke's affections, we should try thinking of "lubricity" as a "good" word, connoting the curative element in the primeval slime. Thus, with him, the image of the mire is usually felicitous, associated with protection and welcome, as in warm sheath-like forms. Only in moments of extremity does he swing to the opposite order of meanings, and think rather of the mire that can hold one a prisoner, sucking toward stagnation and death. Then, for a period of wretchedness, the poet is surprised into finding in this otherwise Edenic image, his own equivalent for Bunyan's slough of despond.

Flowers suggest analogous human motives quite as the figures of animals do in Aesop's fables (except that here they stand for relationships rather than for typical characters). The poet need but be as accurate as he can, in describing the flowers objectively; and while aiming at this, he comes upon corresponding human situations, as it were by redundancy. Here was a good vein of imagery to exploit, even as a conceit: that is, any poet shrewdly choosing a theme might hit upon hothouse imagery as generating principle for a group of poems. Yet in this poet's case there was a further incentive. His father had actually been a florist, in charge of a greenhouse. Hence, when utilizing the resources of this key image for new developments, Roethke could at the same time be drawing upon the most occult of early experiences. Deviously, elusively, under such conditions the amplifying of the theme could also be "regressive," and in-turning.

The duality, in the apparent simplicity, of his method probably leads back, as with the somewhat mystic *ars poetica* of so many contemporary poets, to the kind of order statuesquely expressed in Baudelaire's sonnet, "Correspondances," on mankind's passage through nature as through "forests of symbols," while scents, sounds, and colors "make mutual rejoinder" like distant echoes that fuse "in deep and dusky unity."

In "Night Crow," Roethke states his equivalent of the pattern thus:

> When I saw that clumsy crow
> Flap from a wasted tree,
> A shape in the mind rose up:
> Over the gulfs of dream
> Flew a tremendous bird
> Further and further away
> Into a moonless black,
> Deep in the brain, far back.

One could take it as a particularized embodiment of a general principle, an anecdote of *one* image standing for the way of all such images, which are somehow felt twice, once positivistically, and once symbolically.

In this connection, even one misprint becomes meaningful. In "Weed Puller," he writes of flowers "tugging all day at perverse life." At least, that is the wording presumably intended. The line actually reads: "tugging at preverse life." In Roethke's case, this was indeed a "pre-verse" way of life. In the flowers, their hazards and quixotisms, he was trained to a symbolic vocabulary of subtle human relations and odd strivings, before he could have encountered the equivalent patterns of experience in exclusively human terms. As with those systems of pure mathematics which mathematicians sometimes develop without concern for utility, long before men in the practical realm begin asking themselves the kind of questions for which the inventor of the pure forms has already offered the answers; so, in the flower-stories, the poet would be reverting to a time when he had noted these forms before he felt the need for them, except vaguely and "vatically."

The opposite way is depicted in a drawing (we falsely remembered it as a caricature) printed in *L'Illustration* and reproduced in Matthew Josephson's book on Émile Zola. It is entitled "Zola Studying Railroad Life on a Locomotive; Drawing Made on the Scene, During a Voyage Between Paris and Le Havre, When He Was Seeking the 'Living Documents' for his Novel, *La Bête Humaine*." Zola, standing, stiffly erect, between the cabin and the coal car, dressed in a semi-formal attire that would suit a doctor or a lawyer of that time, is all set to make the trip that would supply him with certain required documentary observations for a "scientific" novel.

What, roughly, then, is the range of meaning in Roethke's flowers? In part, they are a kind of psychology, an empathic vocabulary for expressing rudimentary motives felt, rightly or wrongly, to transcend particular periods of time. Often, in their characters as "the lovely diminutives," they are children in general, or girls specifically. When we are told in "The Waking" that "flowers jumped / Like small goats," there is a gracing of the bestial motive referred to as "the goat's mouth" in the "dance" of "The Long Alley," section 4. The preconscious, the infantile, the regressive, the sexual—but is there not in them a further mystery, do they not also appeal as a pageantry, as "positions of pantomime," their natural beauty deriving added secular "sanctification" from the principle of hierarchy? For the thought of flowers, in their various conditions, with their many ways of root, sprout, and blossom, is like the contemplation of nobles, churchmen, commoners, peasants (a world of masks). In hothouse flowers, you confront, enigmatically, the representation of status. By their nature flowers contribute grace to social magic—hence, they are insignia, infused with a spirit of social ordination. In this respect they could be like Aesop's animals, though only incipiently so. For if their relation to the social mysteries were schematically recognized, we should emerge from the realm of intuitions (with their appropriate "aesthetic ideas") into such "ideas of reason" as a Pope might cultivate ("whatever is, is right . . . self-love, to urge, and reason, to restrain . . . force first made conquest, and that conquest, law . . . order is heaven's first law . . . that true self-love and social are the same"). A Roethke might well subscribe to some such doctrine, notably Pope's tributes to "honest Instinct"—but in terms whereby the assumptions would, within these rules of utterance, be themselves unutterable.

Other of the shorter poems should be mentioned, such as "My Papa's Waltz," which is dashing, in its account of a boy whirled in a dance with his tipsy father; "Judge Not," a more formalistic statement than is characteristic. Some of the short pieces come close to standard magazine verse. "The Waking" risks a simple post-Wordsworthian account of pure joy. And "Pickle Belt," recounting "the itches / Of sixteen-year-old lust," while not of moment in itself, in its puns could be listed with the crow poem, if one were attempting to specify systematically just how many kinds of correspondence Roethke's images draw upon. But mostly, here, we want to consider the four longer pieces: "The Lost Son," "The Long Alley," "A Field of Light," and "The Shape of the Fire."

Roethke himself has described them as "four experiences, each in a sense stages in a kind of struggle out of the slime; part of a slow spiritual progress, if you will; part of an effort to be born." At the risk of brashness, we would want to modify this description somewhat. The transformations seem like a struggle less to be born than to avoid being undone. Or put it thus: The dangers inherent in the regressive imagery seem to have received an impetus from without, that drove the poet still more forcefully in the same direction, dipping him in the river who loved water. His own lore thus threatened to turn against him. The enduring of such discomforts is a "birth" in the sense that, if the poet survives the ordeal, he is essentially stronger, and has to this extent *forged himself* an identity.

The four poems are, in general, an alternating of two motives: regression, and a nearly lost, but never quite relinquished, expectancy that leads to varying degrees of fulfillment. In "Flight," the first section of "The Lost Son," the problem is stated impressionistically, beginning with the mention of death ("concretized," of course, not in the name of "death," which would be at the farthest an abstraction, at the nearest an abstraction personified, but circumstantially: "At Woodlawn I heard the dead cry"). When considering the possible thesaurus of flowers, we were struck by the fact that, in the greenhouse poems, there was no overt reference to the use of flowers for the sick-room and as funeral wreaths. Deathy connotations are implicitly there, at the very start, in the account of the Cuttings, which are dying even as they strain heroically to live. And there is the refuse of "Flower Dump." But of flowers as standing for the final term of human life, we recall no mention. Roethke has said that he conceives of the greenhouse as symbol for "a womb, a heaven-on-earth." And the thought of its vital internality, in this sense, seems to have obliterated any conscious concern with the uses to which the products of the florist's trade are put. In any case his present poem, dealing with a lyric "I" in serious danger, fittingly begins in the sign of death.

The opening stanza, however, contains not merely the theme of death-like stagnation. There is also, vaguely, talk of moving on:

> Snail, snail, glister me forward,
> Bird, soft-sigh me home.

In the society of *this* poet's lowly organisms, there is a curative element, incipiently. And throughout the opening section, with its images of rot and stoppage, there is likewise a watching and waiting. Even a rhetorical *question* is, after all, subtly, in form a *quest*. Hence the call for a sign ("Out of what door do I go, / Where and to whom?"), though it leads but to veiled oracular answers ("Dark hollows said, lee to the wind, / The moon said, back of an eel," etc.), transforms this opening section ("The Flight") into a hunt, however perplexed. Thus the stanza that begins "Running lightly over spongy ground," is followed by one that begins, "Hunting along the river." The section ends on a riddle, in terms contradictory and symbolic, as befits such utterance. The connotations are Sphinxlike, oracular; the descriptions seem to touch upon an ultimate wordless secret. What is the answer? Put all the disjunct details together, and, for our purposes, we need but note that the object of the quest is lubricitous (in the mode of furtive felicity). End of section 1.

Section 2: "The Pit"—nine lines, in very subdued tonality, about roots—in general an amplification of the statement that the poet's search is radical. We cite the passage entire, since it is a splendid text for revealing the ingenuity of Roethke as rhetorician:

> Where do the roots go?
>   Look down under the leaves.
> Who put the moss there?
>   These stones have been here too long.
> Who stunned the dirt into noise?
>   Ask the mole, he knows.
> I feel the slime of a wet nest.
>   Beware Mother Mildew.
> Nibble again, fish nerves.

Considered as topics ("places" in the traditional rhetorical sense), the stanza could be reduced to a set of images that variously repeat the idea of the deep-down, the submerged, the underground. Roots . . . "under the leaves" . . . stones long buried beneath moss . . . the sound of moles burrowing . . . these are details that variously repeat the same theme in the first six lines. The last three, while similar in quality (the dank, hidden, submerged, within), add a further development: the hint of incipience, ambiguously present in lines seven and eight ("I feel" and "Beware"), comes clear in line nine: "Nibble again, fish nerves."

For the moment confining ourselves to the first six: note how this series of lyric is dramatized. Surprisingly, much is done by a purely grammatical resource. Thus, the underlying assertion of the first couplet (this mood is like roots, like under-the-leaves) is transformed into a kind of "cosmic" dialogue, split into an interchange between two voices. The next restatement (it is like moss-covered stones) is broken into the same Q-A pattern, but this time the answer is slightly evasive, though still in the indicative ("These stones have been here too long," a "vatic" way of suggesting that the mood is like stones sunken, and covered heavily). The third couplet (it is like the sound of moles burrowing) is introduced by a slightly longer and more complex form of question. (The first was where-roots-go, the second who-put-moss-there, and the third is who-stunned-dirt-into-noise, a subtly growing series.) Also the answer is varied by a shift into the imperative ("ask the mole").

All this questioning and answering has been as if from voices in the air, or in the nature of things. But the turn in the last three lines is announced by a shift to the lyric "I" as subject. The image of mildew is made not only personal, but "essential," by being named as "Mother Mildew." The indicative in line seven ("I feel") shifts to imperatives in lines eight and nine ("Beware" and "Nibble"); but whereas in the first of these imperatives the topic (mildew) appears as object of the command, in the second the topic ("fish nerves") is given as subject.

Thus, though the stanza is but a series of restatements, it has considerable variety despite the brevity of the lines and despite the fact that each sentence ends exactly at the end of a line. And the grammatical shifts, by dramatizing the sequence of topics, keep one from noting that the stanza is in essence but a series of similarly disposed images (symbolizing what Roethke, in a critical reference, has called "obsessions").

As for the closing line, the more one knows of the fish image in Roethke's verse, the more clearly one will feel the quality of incipience in the nibbling of "fish nerves."

The third section, "The Gibber," might (within the conditions of a lyric) be said to culminate in the *act* that corresponds to the attitude implicit in the opening scene. It is sexual, but reflexively so: the poet is disastrously alone. Listening, "by the cave's door," the poet hears an old call ("Dogs of the groin / Barked and howed,") and sinister things, in the mood of a Walpurgisnacht, call for his yielding in a kind of death). Against a freezing fear, there is a desperate cry for infantile warmth: "I'm cold. I'm cold all over. Rub me in father and mother." The reflexive motif is most direct, perhaps, in the lines: "As my own tongue kissed / My lips awake." The next lines (Roethke has called them a kind of Elizabethan "rant") culminate in a shrilly plaintive inventory of the hero's plight:

All the windows are burning! What's left of my life?
I want the old rage, the lash of primordial milk!
Goodbye, goodbye, old stones, the time-order is going,
I have married my hands to perpetual agitation,
I run, I run to the whistle of money,

the lamentation being summed up, by a break into a different rhythm:

Money money money
Water   water   water.

Roethke's Vegetal Radicalism is not the place one would ordinarily look for comments on the economic motive. Yet you can take it as a law that, in our culture, at a moment of extreme mental anguish, if the sufferer is accurate there will be an accounting of money, too. It will be at least implicit, in the offing—hence with professional utterers it should be explicit. So, the agitation comes to a head in the juxtaposing of two liquidities, two potencies, one out of society, the other universal, out of nature. (And in the typical dichotomy of aestheticism, where the aesthetic and the practical are treated as in diametrical opposition to each other, does not this alignment encourage us to treat art and the rational as antitheses? For if money is equated with the practical and the rational, then by the dialectics of the case art is on the side of an "irrational," nonmonetary Nature.)

After a brief rush of scenic details (cool grass, a bird that may have gone away, a swaying stalk, the shadow of a worm, undirected clouds—all developed by the grammatico-rhetorical method we noted in "The Pit") the section ends on a world of white flashes, which the poet finally characterizes as of the essence of cinder "falling through a dark swirl."

Into the funnel: down the drain. The dream-death. Though the second section was *entitled* "The Pit," here actually is the poem's abysmal moment, after which there must be a turning.

Hence, section 4, "The Return." Recovery in terms of the "father principle." Memory of a greenhouse experience: out of night, the coming of dawn, and the father. After the description of the dark, with the roses likened to bloody clinkers in a furnace (an excellently right transition from the ashes theme at the close of the previous section to the topic of steam knocking in the steam pipes as a heralding of the advent), the movement proceeds thus (note that the theme of white is also kept and appropriately transformed):

> Once I stayed all night.
> The light in the morning came up slowly over the white
> Snow.
> There were many kinds of cool
> Air.
> Then came steam.
>
> Pipe-knock.
> Scurry of warm over small plants.
> Ordnung! ordnung!
> Papa is coming!

We happen to have seen a comment which Roethke wrote on this passage, and we cite it for its great use in revealing his methods:

Buried in the text are many little ambiguities that are not always absolutely necessary to know. For instance, the "pipe-knock." With the coming of steam, the pipes begin knocking violently, in a greenhouse. But "Papa," or the florist, often would knock his own pipe (a pipe for smoking) on the sides of the benches, or the pipes. . . . Then, with the coming of steam (and "papa"— the papa on earth and heaven being blended, of course) there is the sense of motion in the greenhouse—my symbol for the whole of life, a womb, a heaven-on-earth.

Recalling De Quincey's comments on the knocking at the gate after the murder scene in Macbeth, and recalling that we have just been through a "suicide" scene, might we not also include, among the connotations of this sound, the knock of conscience? Particularly in that the return to the paternally (or "super-egoistically") rational is announced in terms of an admonition (*Ordnung! ordnung!*)—and we should note, on the side, as a possible motivating factor in Roethke's avoidance of ideational abstraction, that this German word for order is one of his few such expressions, though here it has practically the force of an imperative verb, as "sweetness," in another context, was not in function an abstract noun but rather a *name,* an epithet of personal endearment. (Roethke has said that he had in mind the father's Prussian love of discipline, as sublimated into the care of flowers; and he wanted to suggest that the child, as a kind of sleepy sentry, "jumped to attention at the approach.")

The final section (sans title) amplifies the subject of illumination (that we have followed from darkness, through "white flashes," to dawn). But its opening suggests its unfinishedness (as with a corresponding mid-stage in Eliot's *Four Quartets*):

> It was beginning winter,
> An in-between time.

And after talk of light (and reflexively, "light within light") the poem ends on his variant of religious patience and vigil, as applied to the problem of super-egoistic rationality:

> A lively understandable spirit
> Once entertained you.
> It will come again.
> Be still.
> Wait.

Again the funnel, in the narrowing-down of the lines. But not, this time, the funnel of darkness that had marked the end of section 3. There has been a coming of light after darkness, a coming of warmth after cold, a coming of steam after powerlessness, a coming of the father and of his super-egoistic knock—and now at the last a more fulsome coming is promised. And within the rules of this idiom, "understandable" is a perfect discovery. It is perhaps the only "intellectualistic" word (the only word for "rational") that would not have jarred in this context.

All four of the long poems follow this same general pattern. Thus, "The Long Alley" begins with a sluggish near-stagnant current (from sources outside the poem we have learned that this brooding, regressive stream is "by the edge of the city"). Direction is slight but it is there:

> A river glides out of the grass. A river or serpent.
> A fish floats belly upward,
> Sliding through the white current,
> Slowly turning,
> Slowly.

But the way out is roundabout, a way in. Next there are apostrophes to an absent "kitten-limp sister," a "milk-nose," a "sweetness I cannot touch," as our hero complains that he needs "a loan of the quick." And the stanza ends narcissistically. In the third section, after a plea again reflexively addressed ("Have mercy, gristle") there is an agitated "dance," a simulated *argutatio lecti* (Catullus 6, 11) conveyed somewhat impressionistically, symbolically, enigmatically. After this "close knock," again struggling toward warmth ("Sweet Jesus, make me sweat," a musically felicitous cry, in that the last word is an umlaut modification of the first: sw—t sw—t), there is a somewhat idealistic vision, a gentle name-calling, in which girls ("tenderest") are "littlest flowers" with "fish-ways," while the talk of light ("drowsing in soft light . . . Light airs! A pierce of angels!") prepares for the closing stanza with its talk of warmth. The progress of the sections might be indicated by these summarizing lines: (1) "My gates are all caves"; (2) "Return the gaze of a pond" (an ingenious inversion of the Narcissus image); (3) "I'm happy with my paws"; (4) "The tendrils have me"; (5) "I'll take the fire."

The shortest of the four long poems, "A Field of Light," begins similarly with "dead water" and evolves into a celebrating of "the lovely diminutives," while the poet walked "through the light air" and "moved with the morning." The mood is most succinctly conveyed, perhaps, in the line: "Some morning thing came, beating its wings." The poem is in three stages: (1) The "dead water," but almost pleasantly, a "watery drowse"; (2) the question-like and questionable act ("Alone, I kissed the skin of a stone; marrow-soft, danced in the sand"); (3) exhilarated sense of promise.

However, despite the alleviation here, in the final poem, "The Shape of the Fire," the entire course is traveled again. Indeed, if we can accept the ingenious suggestion of one commentator (Mr. Bill Brown, a student in a poetry class of Roethke's), the line "An old scow bumps over black rocks" is about as regressive as human memory could be. It suggests to him "the heart-beat of the mother," as the foetus might hear it dully while asleep in the amniotic fluid, the ultimately regressive baptismal water. (Such reminiscence from pre-natal experience would be a purely naturalistic equivalent for the "clouds of glory" that Wordsworth Platonically saw the infant memory "trailing" from its "immortal" past.) In any case, at the very least, the line suggests the state of near-stagnation, a stream so low that a boat of even the shallowest draught scrapes bottom. And after a reflexive section ("My meat eats me," while before this there was but half a being, "only one shoe" and "a two-legged dog"), and a section on vigil ("The wasp waits"), and one to announce awakening promise ("Love, love sang toward," a pleasantly impressionistic idyll of early happiness at the age when childhood was merging into puberty), now the boat can again figure, but transfigured, to assert direction:

> To stare into the after-light, the glitter left on the lake's surface,
> When the sun has fallen behind a wooded island;
> To follow the drops sliding from a lifted oar,
> Held up, while the rower breathes, and the small boat drifts
>   quietly shoreward;
> To know that light falls and fills, often without our knowing,
> As an opaque vase fills to the brim from a quick pouring,
> Fills and trembles at the edge yet does not flow over,
> Still holding and feeding the stem of the contained flower.

Thus, at the end, the cut flower with which the book began. And though the image of the gliding boat (as contrasted with the bottom-scraping one) has moved us from stagnation to felicity (here is a resting on one's oars, whereas Shelley's enrapt boats proceed even without a rower), note that the position of the poet in the advancing craft is backward-looking. Still, there is testimony to a delight in seeing, in contrast with Baudelaire's poem on Don Juan crossing the Styx, similarly looking back: Charon steered the craft among the shades in torment,

> Mais le calme héros, courbé sur sa rapière,
> Regardait le sillage et ne daignait rien voir.

As for all the possible connotations in light, as used in the final illumination of the Roethke poem, spying, we may recall that the last line of the second section was: "Renew the light, lewd whisper."

All told, to analyze the longer poems one should get the general "idea" (or better, mood or *attitude*) of each stanza, then note the succession of images that actualize and amplify it. Insofar as these images are of visible, tangible things, each will be given its verb, so that it have sufficient incidental vividness. But though, in a general way, these verbs will be, either directly or remotely, of the sort that usually goes with the thing (as were dogs to bark, or pigs to grunt), often there may be no verb that, within the conditions of the poem, the noun objectively requires.

For instance, at the beginning of "The Shape of the Fire," there is a line "A cracked pod calls." As an image, the cracked pod belongs here. It is dead, yet there is possibility of a new life in it. Hence, topically, the line might have read simply "A cracked pod." Similarly, there is the line, "Water recedes to the crying of spiders." If spiders stand in general for the loathsome, the line might be translated formalistically: "The principle of fertility is overcome by the principle of fear." However, though pods may rattle, and spiders may weave or bite or trap flies, pods don't call and spiders don't cry.

In considering this problem most pedestrianly, we believe we discovered another rhetorical device which Roethke has used quite effectively. That is, whenever there is no specific verb required, Roethke resorts to some word in the general category of *communication*. Thus, though "shale loosens" and "a low mouth laps water," a cracked pod calls, spiders and snakes cry, weeds whine, dark hollows, the moon and salt say, inanimate things answer and question and listen or are listened to. To suggest that one thing is of the same essence as another, the poet can speak of their kissing, that is, being in intimate communion (a device that has unintended lewd overtones at one point where the poet, to suggest that he is of the essence of refuse, says, "Kiss me, ashes," a hard line to read aloud without disaster, unless one pauses long on the comma). The topic is clouds? Not clouds that billow or blow, but would just *be*? The line becomes: "What do the clouds *say*?"

There are possible objections to be raised against this sort of standard poetic personifying, which amounts to putting a communicative verb where the copula is normally required, or perhaps one could have no verb at all. But it does help to suggest a world of natural objects in vigorous communication with one another. The very least these poetic entities do is resort to "mystic participation." The poet's scene constitutes a society of animals and things. To walk through his idealized Nature is to be surrounded by figures variously greeting, beckoning, calling, answering one another, or with little groups here and there in confidential huddles, or strangers by the wayside waiting to pose Sphinxlike questions or to propound obscure but truth-laden riddles. One thus lives as though ever on the edge of an Ultimate Revelation. And as a clear instance of the method as a device for dramatization, consider a passage in "The Lost Son," which, topically considered, amounts to saying, "This is like dying in a weedy meadow, among snakes, cows, and briars," but is transformed by communicative verbs thus:

> The weeds whined,
>   The snakes cried,
> The cows and briars
> Said to me: Die.

Somewhat incongruously, we have expressed the underlying statement in terms of simile. Yet similes are very rare in Roethke. The word "like" appears, unless we counted wrong, but three times in the four long poems; "as," used as a synonym for "like," occurs not much oftener. Indeed, one way to glimpse the basic method used here is to think, first, of simile, next of metaphor, and then (extrapolating) imagine advancing to a further step. Thus, one might say, in simile, "The toothache is like a raging storm," or metaphorically, "The raging tooth." Or "beyond" that, one might go elliptically, without logical connectives, from talk of toothache to talk of ships storm-tossed at sea. And there one would confront the kind of *ars poetica* in which Roethke is working.

The method may be further extended by the use of a word in accordance with pure pun-logic. Thus, if in "reach" you hear "rich," you may say either "reach me" or "rich me" for the reach that enriches. ("Rich me cherries a fondling's kiss.")

Much of this verse is highly auditory, leaving implicit the kind of tonal transformations that Hopkins makes explicit. And often the ellipses, by weakening strictly logical attention, induce the hearer to flutter on the edge of associations not surely present, but evanescently there, and acutely evocative (to those who receive poetry through ear rather than eye).

Surely, in a poem still to be considered, "God, give me a near" is a barely audible extending of the sense in "God, give me an ear" (here the tonal effect is surest if approached through visual reading); and in the same poem, "tree" and "time" have been "irresponsibly" transposed, with suggestive effects, thus: "Once upon a tree / I came across a time." "The ear's not here / Beneath the hair" (in the opening stanza of section 2, "The Shape of the Fire") is tonal improvising, which leads one vaguely to think of the ear as surrogate for a different order of receptacle. And in the lines immediately following ("When I took off my clothes / To find a nose, / There was only one / For the waltz of To, / The pinch of Where"), besides "to" in the sense of "toward," there are suggestions of "two" (here present in its denial, but the meaning most prominent to an auditor who does not have the page before him), while there are also connotations of "toe" as in toe dance (which in turn stirs up a belfry of bat-thoughts when we consider the narcissistic nature of this particular "toe dance," recall similarly the "last waltz with an old itch" in "The Long Alley," and then flutter vaguely in the direction of the infantile "polymorphous perverse" as we think of the briskly and brilliantly conveyed corybantics in the brief lyric, "My Papa's Waltz," the account of a child snatched up and whirled riotously in a dance by his tipsy father). And since "t" is but an unvoiced "d," we believe that, on the purely tonal level, "God" may be heard in "gate." In any case, in "The Long Alley" there are but three lines elliptically separating "this smoke's from the glory of God" and "My gates are all caves."

Though Roethke's lines often suggest spontaneous simplicity, and though the author has doubtless so cultivated this effect that many lines do originally present themselves in such a form, on occasion the simplicity may be got only after considerable revision. Thus, in an early vision of "The Shape of the Fire," there had been a passage:

> The wind sharpened itself on a rock. It began raining.
> Finally, having exhausted the possibilities of common sense,
> I composed the following.

"It began raining" was later changed to "Rain began falling." An earlier version had been, "It rains offal," but this, though more accurate, had to be abandoned presumably because of its closeness to "It rains awful." Eventually the reference to rain was dropped completely—for if the essence of this rain (its quality as motive) could not be specified, the reference was perhaps better omitted. The second and third lines were changed to: "Finally, to interrupt that particular monotony, / I intoned the following." Both versions thus sounded self-conscious and formalistic, whereas the final version is naively vatic:

> The wind sharpened itself on a rock;
> A voice sang:

The "I" of the versifier at work has been replaced by a cosmically communicating "voice."

Stanley Kunitz, reviewing *The Lost Son and Other Poems* in *Poetry*, justly observes:

The sub-human is given tongue; and what the tongue proclaims is the agony of coming alive, the painful miracle of growth. Here is a poetry immersed in the destructive element. It would seem that Roethke has reached the limits of exploration in this direction, that the next step beyond must be either silence or gibberish. Yet the daemon is with him, and there is no telling what surprises await us.

Reverting, in this connection, to our talk of intuitions, concepts, and ideas, and recalling the contrast between the vocabulary of these poems and that of Eliot's *Quartets,* we might put the matter thus, in seeking to characterize Roethke's "way":

There is a realm of motives local to the body, and there is a possible ultimate realm, of motives derived from the Ground of All Existence, whatever that may be. In between, there are the motives of man-made institutions, motives located generally in the terminologies of technology, business, politics, social institutions, and the like. Here are many titular words, abstractions, "ideas of reason," to name the realm midway between the pains, pleasures, appetites of the individual body and the Universal Ground.

Since the body emerges out of nature, its language seems closer to the ultimate realm of motives than do the abstractions of politics. However, the pleasures, pains, fears, and appetites of the body are all, in subtle ways, moulded by the forms of the political realm; hence what we take as "nature" is largely a social pageant in disguise. But the vocabulary of traffic regulation is alien to the "noble" speech of childhood emerging from infancy. (Parker Tyler, so often excellent in his insights, convincingly points to the "aristocratic" element in Charlie Chaplin's child-motif. And Nietzsche, in his *Genealogy of Morals,* might better be talking of a child when he cites, as his example of the aristocrat, the person whose resentment "fulfils and exhausts itself in an immediate reaction, and consequently instills no *venom,*" while this resentment "never manifests itself at all in countless instances," since "strong natures" cannot "take seriously for any length of time their enemies, their disasters, their *misdeeds,*" and forgive insult simply because they forget it.)

In any case, as tested by the simplicity of the "natural" vocabulary, the forensic sub-Ciceronian speech is "barbaric." And though we may, by roundabout devices, disclose how politics, through the medium of family relations, affects the child's experiences at the very start of life, the *ideas* are certainly not there—hence the "purest" vocabulary is that of the emotionally tinged perceptions (the "intuitions of sensibility").

But how much of human motivation is the poet to encompass in his work? Or, next, how much is he to encompass *directly, explicitly,* and how much by *implication,* by resonances derived from sympathetic vibrations in the offing? There comes a time, in life itself, when one flatly confronts the realm of social hierarchy (in the scramble to get or to retain or to rewardingly use money, position, prestige). Will one, then, if a poet, seek to discuss these motives just as flatly in his poetic medium? Or will he conceive of poetry by antithesis (as so many of our poets, now teaching poetry, place it in direct antithesis to their means of livelihood, hence contending that the "aesthetic" is precisely what the "didactic" is not).

It is not for critics, in their task of characterization, to legislate for the poet here. It is enough to note that there are several methods of confronting the problem, and that Roethke's work has thoroughly and imaginatively exemplified one of them. He meets, in his way, the problem which Eliot met in another by expanding his poetry to encompass theological doctrine, and thereby including a terminology which, within the Roethke rules, would be ungainly (unless used ironically—and children don't take to irony). Eliot added winds of doctrine. Roethke "regressed" as thoroughly as he could, even at considerable risk, toward a language of sheer "intuition."

However, our use of the Kantian pattern will deceive us, if we conclude that such intuitions really do remain on the level of "sensation." For not only do they require the "concept" (as a name that clamps intellectual unity upon a given manifold of sensations); they also invoke motives beyond both sense and understanding: we go from intuitions of a sensory sort to intuitions of a *symbolic* sort (as with the motives of the "unconscious" which make variously for fusion, confusion, diffusion). In scholastic usage, by "intuition" was meant the recognition that something is as it is. The term was not restricted merely to sense perception. Not only would color, sound, or odor be an intuition; but there would be intuition in the recognition that two and two make four, or that a complex problem is solvable in a certain way, or that a science rests on such and such principles. Applied to modern poetizing, the word might also be used to name a situation when the poet chooses an expression because it "feels right," though he might not be able to account for the choice rationalistically. The judgment would rely on such motives as are, under favorable circumstances, disclosable psychoanalytically, or may be idealistic counterparts of hierarchic motives (a "beauty" involving *social* distinction between the noble and the vulgar, mastery and enslavement, loveliness and crassness); and there may also be included here responses to the incentives of pun-logic.

Thus, if in one context the image of a flower can stand for girlhood in general, and if in other contexts a fish can have similar connotations, in still other contexts flower and fish can be elliptically merged (for reasons beyond the fact that the one can be plucked and the other caught), producing what we might call a "symbolic intuition" atop the purely sensory kind. Or we might consider such idealistic mergers a symbolist variant of the "aesthetic idea" (as distinguished from "ideas of reason" in the more strictly rationalist sense). They are "fusions" if you like them, "confusions" if you don't, and "diffusions" when their disjunction outweighs their conjunction. And they are a resource of all our "objectivist" poets who use "positive" terms to elicit effects beyond the positive. Particularly we are in a purely idealistic (rather than positivistic) order of intuitions when we extend the motifs, going from fish to water and from flower to warmth or light, and hence from water to motions that are like pouring, or from flowers to motions that are like swaying (so that a sudden influx of birds might be a symbol descending through the fish-water-girl line, or a swaying tree might descend through the flower-warmth-girl side of the family, the two branches being reunited if the tree is swaying over water, after talk of a swaying fish).

This is the liquescent realm in which Roethke operates. But by eschewing the "rationality" of doctrine (a "parental principle" which one may situate in identification with father governments or mother churches, or with lesser brotherhoods themselves authoritatively endowed), the poet is forced into a "regressive" search for the "super-ego," as with talk of being "rubbed . . . in father and mother." Eliot could thus "rub" himself in dogma, borrowed from the intellectual matrix of the church. But Roethke, while avidly in search of an essential parenthood, would glumly reject incorporation in any cause or movement or institution as the new parent (at least so far as his poetic idiom is concerned). Hence his search for essential motives has driven him back into the quandaries of adolescence, childhood, even infancy. Also, as we have noted elsewhere, the search for essence being a search for "first principles," there is a purely technical inducement to look for definition in terms of one's absolute past; for a *narrative* vocabulary, such as is natural to poetry, invites one to state essence (priority) in *temporal* terms, as with Platonist "reminiscence"—an enterprise that leads readily to "mystic" intuitions of womb heaven and primeval slime.

The battle is a fundamental one. Hence the poems give the feeling of being "eschatological," concerned with first and last things. Where their positivism dissolves into mysticism, they suggest a kind of phallic pantheism. And the constant reverberations about the edges of the images give the excitement of being on the edge of Revelation (or suggest a state of vigil, the hope of getting the girl, of getting a medal, of seeing God). There is the pious awaiting of the good message—and there is response to "the spoor that spurs."

Later poems repeat the regressive imagery without the abysmal anguish. Thus, in "Praise to the End!" our hero, expanding in a mood of self-play ("What a bone-ache I have . . . Prickle-me . . . I'm a duke of eels . . . I'll feed the ghost alone. / Father, forgive my hands . . . The river's alone with its water. / All risings / Fall") follows with snatches of wonder-struck childhood reminiscence mixed with amative promise:

> Mips and ma the mooly moo,
> The like of him is biting who,
> A cow's a care and who's a coo?—
> What footie does is final.

He ends by asking to be laved in "ultimate waters," surrounded by "birds and small fish." And a line in the opening ("stagnation") section of "The Long Alley" ("My gates are all caves") is now echoed in an altered form happy enough to serve in the upsurge of the final stanza: "My ghosts are all gay." Along with the nursery jingles, some lines are allowed to remain wholly "unsimplified":

> It's necessary, among the flies and bananas, to keep a
>   constant vigil,
> For the attacks of false humility take sudden turns for the
>   worse.

"Where Knock Is Open Wide" is a placid depiction of childhood sensibility and reverie, in a post-Blake, post-Crazy Jane medium close to the quality of Mother Goose, with many "oracular" lines, in Sibylline ways near to the sound of nonsense. The poem progresses thus: thoughts about a kitten (it can "bite with its feet"); lullaby ("sing me a sleep-song, please"); dreams; the parents; an uncle that died ("he's gone for always . . . they'll jump on his belly"); singing in infancy; an owl in the distance; "happy hands"; a walk by the river; a fish dying in the bottom of a boat ("he's trying to talk"); the watering of roses ("the stems said, Thank you"). But "That was before. I fell! I fell!" Thereafter, talk of "nowhere," "cold," and "wind," the death of birds, followed by a paradigm of courtship: "I'll be a bite. You be a wink. / Sing the snake to sleep." And finally: "God's somewhere else. / . . . Maybe God has a house. / But not here."

The title, though borrowed, is extremely apt in suggesting the kind of motivation which Roethke would reconstruct for us. Recall, for instance, Coleridge's distinction between "motive" and "impulse" (a distinction later revised somewhat in his theological writings, but clearly maintained while his reasoning was in accordance with the aesthetic of "The Eolian Harp"). By "motives" Coleridge meant such springs of action as derive from "interests." Bentham's utilitarian grounds of conduct, for instance, would be "motives." But "impulse" is spontaneous, a response free of all *arrière-pensée,* all ulterior purpose. Here, the answer would be as prompt as the call, would be one with the call. In the world of the adult Scramble, such a state of affairs would indeed be a happy hunting ground for hunters—and whoever is in fear of loss must, at the startling knock on the door, hasten to hide the treasure before opening. However, in the theme of childhood reverie, as ideally reconstructed, the poet can contemplate an Edenic realm of pure impulsiveness.

Yet perhaps it is not wholly without *arrière-pensée.* For is the motivation here as sheerly "regressive" as it may at first seem? Is not this recondite "baby-talk" also, considered as rhetoric, one mode of lover-appeal? And considering mention of the wink and the bite in connection with talk of the fall, might we not also discern an outcropping of double meanings, whether intended or not, in reference to a "mooly man" who "had a rubber hat" and "kept it in a can"? The cloaking of the utterance in such apparent simplicity may not prevent conception of an adult sort here, particularly as the lines are followed immediately by talk of "papa-seed."

What next? The placid evocations of childhood might well be carried further (the period of anguished evocations has presumably been safely weathered). Further readings in mystic literature could lead to more developments in the materializing of "spirit" (as in "The Visitant"). But a turn toward the doctrinaire and didactic (the socially "global" as against the sensitively "ultimate") would seem possible only if all this poet's past methods and skills were abandoned.

There is another already indicated possibility, however, which we might define by making a distinction between "personification" and "personalization." And we might get at the matter thus:

Though Roethke has dealt always with very concrete things, there is a sense in which these very concretions are abstractions. Notably, the theme of sex in his poems has been highly generalized, however intensely felt. His outcries concern erotic and auto-erotic motives generically, the Feminine as attribute of a class. Or, though he may have had an individual in mind at the moment, there is no personal particularization in his epithets, so far as the reader is concerned. He courts Woman, as a Commoner might court The Nobility (though of course he has his own "pastoral" variants of the courtly, or coy, relation).

But because his imagism merges into symbolism, his flowers and fishes become Woman in the Absolute. That is what we would mean by "personification."

By "personalization," on the other hand, we would mean the greater *individualizing* of human relations. (Not total individualizing, however, for Aristotle reminds us that poetry is closer than history to philosophy, and philosophy seeks high generalization, whereas historical eras, in their exact combination of events, are unique.) In any case, we have seen one recent poem in which Roethke has attempted "personalization" as we have here defined it: "Elegy for Jane (My student, thrown by a horse)." Though not so finished a poem as "The Visitant," it conveys a tribute of heart-felt poignancy, in a pious gallantry of the quick confronting the dead, and ending:

> If only I could nudge you from this sleep,
> My maimed darling, my skittery pigeon.
> Over this damp grave I speak the words of my love:
> I, with no rights in this matter,
> Neither father nor lover.

Perhaps more such portraits, on less solemn occasions, will be the Next Phase? Meanwhile, our salute to the very relevant work that Roethke has already accomplished, both for what it is in itself, and for its typicality, its interest as representative of one poetic way which many others are also taking, with varying thoroughness.

DENIS DONOGHUE

Theodore Roethke

There is a poem called "Snake" in which Theodore Rocthke describes a young snake turning and drawing away and then says:

> I felt my slow blood warm.
> I longed to be that thing,
> The pure, sensuous form.
>
> And I may be, some time.

To aspire to a condition of purity higher than any available in the human world is a common urge. Poets often give this condition as a pure, sensuous form, nothing if not Itself and nothing beyond itself. But it is strange, at first sight, that Roethke gives his parable in the image of a snake, because snakes tend to figure in his poems as emblems of the sinister. In "Where Knock Is Open Wide" one of the prayerful moments reads: "I'll be a bite. You be a wink. / Sing the snake to sleep." In "I Need, I Need" the term "snake-eycs" is enough to send its owner packing. And there is this, in "The Shape of the Fire":

> Up over a viaduct I came, to the snakes and sticks of another
>   winter,
> A two-legged dog hunting a new horizon of howls.

But this is at first sight, or at first thought, because Roethke more than most poets, sought a sustaining order in the images of his chaos, and only those images would serve. If you offer a dove as answer to a snake, your answer

From *Connoisseurs of Chaos*. © 1964, 1984 by Denis Donoghue. Columbia University Press, 1984.

is incomplete, an order not violent enough. Hence when the right time came, in "I'm Here," Roethke would find that a snake lifting its head is a fine sight, and a snail's music is a fine sound, and both are joys, credences of summer. As Roethke says in "The Longing," "The rose exceeds, the rose exceeds us all."

But he did not sentimentalize his chaos. He lived with it, and would gladly have rid himself of it if he could have done so without an even greater loss, the loss of verifiable life. When he thought of his own rage, for instance, he often saw it as mere destructiveness. In one of his early poems he said: "Rage warps my clearest cry / To witless agony." And he often resorted to invective, satire, pseudonymous tirades, to cleanse himself of rage and hatred. In one of those tirades he said, "Behold, I'm a heart set free, for I have taken my hatred and eaten it." But "Death Piece" shows that to be released from rage is to be—quite simply—dead. And the price is too high. This is one of the reasons why Roethke found the last years of W. B. Yeats so rewarding, because Yeats made so much of his rage, in the *Last Poems, The Death of Cuchulain,* and *Purgatory.* In one of his own apocalyptic poems, "The Lost Son," Roethke says, "I want the old rage, the lash of primordial milk," as if to recall Yeat's cry, "Grant me an old man's frenzy." And in "Old Lady's Winter Words" he says: "If I were a young man, / I could roll in the dust of a fine rage"; and in "The Sententious Man": "Some rages save us. Did I rage too long? / The spirit knows the flesh it must consume." Hence Roethke's quest for the saving rage. Call it—for it is this—a rage for order. He was sometimes tempted to seal himself against the rush of experience, and he reminds himself in "The Adamant" that the big things, such as truth, are sealed against thought; the true substance, the core, holds itself inviolate. And yet man is exposed, exposes himself. And, in a sense, rightly so. As Yeats says in the great "Dialogue of Self and Soul":

> I am content to live it all again
> And yet again, if it be life to pitch
> Into the frog-spawn of a blind man's ditch.

In "The Pure Fury" Roethke says, "I live near the abyss." What he means is the substance of his poetry. The abyss is partly the frog-spawn of a blind man's ditch, partly a ditch of his own contriving, partly the fate of being human in a hard time, partly the poet's weather. As discreetly as possible we can take it for granted, rehearsing it only to the extent of linking it with the abyss in other people. Better to think of it as the heart of each man's darkness. In "Her Becoming" Roethke speaks of it in one aspect:

> I know the cold fleshless kiss of contraries,
> The nerveless constriction of surfaces—
> Machines, machines, loveless, temporal;
> Mutilated souls in cold morgues of obligation.

And this becomes, in the "Fourth Meditation," "the dreary dance of opposites." (But so far it is common enough.)

It is still common enough when Roethke presents it through the ambiguities of body and soul. In "Epidermal Macabre" Roethke, like Yeats in *The Tower,* wishes the body away in favor of a spirit remorselessly sensual:

> And willingly would I dispense
> With false accouterments of sense,
> To sleep immodestly, a most
> Incarnadine and carnal ghost.

Or again, when the dance of opposites is less dreary, Roethke accepts with good grace the unwinding of body from soul:

> When opposites come suddenly in place,
> I teach my eyes to hear, my ears to see
> How body from spirit slowly does unwind
> Until we are pure spirit at the end.

Sometimes the body is "gristle." In "Praise to the End!" Roethke says, "Skin's the least of me," and in the "First Meditation" it is the rind that "hates the life within." (Yeats's "dying animal" is clearly visible.) But there were other moments, as there were in Yeats. In "The Wraith" the body casts a spell, the flesh makes the spirit "visible," and in the "Fourth Meditation" "the husk lives on, ardent as a seed."

Mostly in Roethke the body seems good in itself, a primal energy. And when it is this it features the most distinctive connotations of the modern element: it is a good, but ill at ease with other goods. Above all, it does not guarantee an equable life in the natural world. More often than not in these poems man lives with a hostile nature, and lives as well as he can. In "I Need, I Need" intimations of waste, privation, and insecurity lead to this:

> The ground cried my name:
> Good-bye for being wrong.
> Love helps the sun.
> But not enough.

"I can't marry the dirt" is an even stronger version, in "Bring the Day!" echoing Wallace Stevens's benign "marriage of flesh and air" while attaching to it now, as courageously as possible, the bare note, "A swan needs a pond"; or, more elaborately in another poem, "A wretch needs his wretchedness." The aboriginal middle poems have similar cries on every page: "These wings are from the wrong nest"; "My sleep deceives me"; "Soothe me, great groans of underneath"; "Rock me to sleep, the weather's wrong"; "Few objects praise the Lord."

These are some of Roethke's intimations of chaos. They reach us as cries, laments, protests, intimations of loss. Most of Roethke's later poems are attempts to cope with these intimations by becoming—in Stevens's sense—their connoisseur. In "The Dance" Roethke speaks of a promise he has made to "sing and whistle romping with the bears"; and whether we take these as animals or constellations, the promise is the same and hard to keep. To bring it off at all, Roethke often plays in a child's garden, especially in poems like "O Lull Me, Lull Me," where he can have everything he wants by having it only in fancy. "Light fattens the rock," he sings, to prove that good children get treats. "When I say things fond, I hear singing," he reports, and we take his word for it; as we do again when we acknowledge, in a later poem, that "the right thing happens to the happy man." Perhaps it does. But when Roethke says, "I breathe into a dream, / And the ground cries," and again, "I could say hello to things; / I could talk to a snail," we think that he protests too much, and we know that his need is great. Roethke is never quite convincing in this note, or in the hey-nonny note of his neo-Elizabethan pastiche. Even when he dramatizes the situation in the "Meditations of an Old Woman" the answers come too easily. In two stanzas he has "the earth itself a tune," and this sounds like a poet's wishful dreaming. Roethke may have wanted the kind of tone that Stevens reached in his last poems, an autumnal calm that retains the rigor and the feeling but banishes the fretful note, the whine, the cry of pain. But Stevens earned this. And Yeats earned it too, in poems like "Beautiful Lofty Things." Roethke claimed it without really earning it. Here is a stanza from "Her Becoming":

> Ask all the mice who caper in the straw—
> I am benign in my own company.
> A shape without a shade, or almost none,
> I hum in pure vibration, like a saw.
> The grandeur of a crazy one alone!—
> By swoops of bird, by leaps of fish, I live.
> My shadow steadies in a shifting stream;
> I live in air; the long light is my home;
> I dare caress the stones, the field my friend;
> A light wind rises: I become the wind.

And here is Stevens, in a passage from "The Course of a Particular":

> The leaves cry. It is not a cry of divine attention,
> Nor the smoke-drift of puffed-out heroes, nor human cry.
> It is the cry of leaves that do not transcend themselves,
> In the absence of fantasia, without meaning more
> Than they are in the final finding of the air, in the thing
> Itself, until, at last, the cry concerns no one at all.

How can we compare these two passages except to say that Stevens speaks with the knowledge that there have been other days, other feelings, and the hope that there will be more of each, as various as before? Roethke speaks as if the old woman were now released from time and history and the obligations of each, released even from the memories that she has already invoked. There is too much fantasia in Roethke's lines, and this accounts for a certain slackness that fell upon him whenever he tried too hard to be serene. Stevens's poem is, in the full meaning of the word, mature; Roethke's is a little childish, second-childish. Stevens would affirm, when affirmation seemed just, but not before. Roethke longed to affirm, and when the affirmation would not come he sometimes—now and again—dressed himself in affirmative robes.

But only now and again. At his best he is one of the most scrupulous of poets. In "Four for Sir John Davies," for instance, the harmony between nature and man that Davies figured—the orchestra, the dance, the music of the spheres—is brought to bear upon the poem, critically and never naïvely or sentimentally. The divinely orchestrated universe of Davies's poem is more than a point of reference but far less than an escape route. For one thing, as Roethke says, "I need a place to sing, and dancing-room," and for another, there is no dancing master, and for a third, there isn't even at this stage a dancing partner. So he must do the best he can in his poverty. And if his blood leaps "with a wordless song," at least it leaps:

> But what I learned there, dancing all alone,
> Was not the joyless motion of a stone.

But even when the partner comes and they dance their joy, Roethke does not claim that this makes everything sweet or that nature and man will thereafter smile at each other. In the farthest reach of joy he says:

> We danced to shining; mocked before the black
> And shapeless night that made no answer back.

The sensual cry is what it is, and there are moments when it is or seems to be final, but man still lives in the element of antagonisms. In *Four Quartets* the "daunsynge" scene from Sir Thomas Elyot testifies to modes of being, handsome but archaic; it answers no present problem. Nor does Sir John Davies, who plays a similar role in Roethke's sequence. And even before that, in "The Return," man in the element of antagonisms feels and behaves like an animal in his self-infected lair, "With a stump of scraggy fang / Bared for a hunter's boot." And sometimes he turns upon himself in rage.

When Roethke thinks of man in this way, he often presents him in images of useless flurry. Like Saul Bellow's Dangling Man, he is clumsy, ungainly, an elephant in a pond. Roethke often thinks of him as a bat—by day, quiet, cousin to the mouse; at night, crazy, absurd, looping "in crazy figures." And when the human situation is extreme, Roethke thinks of man as a bat flying deep into a narrowing tunnel. Far from being a big, wide space, the world seems a darkening corridor. In "Bring the Day!" Roethke says, "Everything's closer. Is this a cage?" And if a shape cries from a cloud as it does in "The Exorcism," and calls to man's flesh, man is always somewhere else, "down long corridors." (Corridors, cages, tunnels, lairs—if these poems needed illustration, the painter is easily named: Francis Bacon, keeper of caged souls.)

In "Four for Sir John Davies" the lovers, Roethke says, "undid chaos to a curious sound," "curious" meaning careful as well as strange and exploratory. In this world to undo chaos is always a curious struggle, sometimes thought of as a release from constriction, a stretching in all directions, an escape from the cage. In "What Can I Tell My Bones?" Roethke says, "I recover my tenderness by long looking," and if tenderness is the proof of escape, long looking is one of the means. In *King Lear* it is to see feelingly. In some of Roethke's poems it is given as, quite simply, attention. In "Her Becoming" Roethke speaks of a "jauntier principle of order," but this is to dream. What he wants, in a world of cages and corridors, is to escape to an order, an order of which change and growth and decay are natural mutations and therefore acceptable. In many of the later poems it will be an order of religious feeling, for which the punning motto is, "God, give me a near."

The first step, the first note toward a possible order, is to relish what can be relished. Listening to "the sigh of what is," one attends, knowing, or at least believing, that "all finite things reveal infinitude." If things "flame into being," so much the better. "Dare I blaze like a tree?" Roethke asks at one point, like the flaming tree of Yeats's "Vacillation." And again Roethke says, "What I love is near at hand, / Always, in earth and air." This is fine, as far as it goes, but it is strange that Roethke is more responsive to intimations of being when they offer themselves in plants than in people; and here, of course, he differs radically from Yeats. In the first version of "Cuttings" he is exhilarated when "the small cells bulge," when cuttings sprout into a new life, when bulbs hunt for light, when the vines in the forcing house pulse with the knocking pipes, when orchids draw in the warm air, when beetles, newts, and lice creep and wriggle. In "Slug" he rejoices in his kinship with bats, weasels, and worms. In "A Walk in Late Summer" being "delights in being, and in time." In the same poem Roethke delights in the "midnight eyes" of small things, and in several poems he relishes what Christopher Smart in *Jubilate Agno* calls "the language of flowers." Everywhere in Roethke there is consolation in the rudimentary when it is what it is, without fantasia. It is a good day when the spiders sail into summer. But Roethke is slow to give the same credences to man. Plants may be transplanted, and this is good, but what is exhilarating reproduction in insects and flowers is mere duplication in people. Girls in college are "duplicate gray standard faces"; in the same poem there is talk of "endless duplication of lives and objects." Man as a social being is assimilated to the machine; the good life is lived by plants. In the bacterial poems, weeds are featured as circumstance, the rush of things, often alien but often sustaining. "Weeds, weeds, how I love you," Roethke says in "The Shape of the Fire." In the "First Meditation," "On love's worst ugly day, / The weeds hiss at the edge of the field." In "What Can I Tell My Bones?" "Weeds turn toward the wind weed-skeletons," presumably because "the dead love the unborn." But in "Praise to the End!" when the water's low and romping days are over, "the weeds exceed me."

There are two ways of taking this, and Roethke gives us both. Normally we invoke the rudimentary to criticize the complex: the lower organism rebukes the higher for falling short of itself, as body rebukes the arrogance of vaunting mind or spirit. This works on the assumption that what is simple is more "natural" than what is complex, and that lower organisms have the merit of such simplicity. Or, alternatively, one can imply that the most exalted objects of our human desire are already possessed, in silence and grace, by the lower organisms. Roethke often does this. In "The Advice," for instance, he says:

> A learned heathen told me this:
> Dwell in pure mind and Mind alone;
> What you brought back from the Abyss,
> The Slug was taught beneath his Stone.

This is so presumably because the slug had a teacher, perhaps the dancing master who has retired from the human romp. Roethke doesn't commit the sentimentality of implying, however, that all is sweetness and light in the bacterial world, and generally he avoids pushing his vegetal analogies too far. In his stronger poems the bacterial is featured as a return to fundamentals, a syntax of short phrases to represent the radical breaking-up that may lead to a new synthesis. In grammatical terms, we have broken the spine of our syntax by loading it with our own fetishes. So we must begin again as if we were learning a new language, speaking in short rudimentary phrases. Or, alternatively, we learn in simple words and phrases, hoping that eventually we may reach the light of valid sentences. In this spirit Roethke says, in a late poem, "God bless the roots!—Body and soul are one!" The roots, the sensory facts, are beneath or beyond doubt; in "The Longing" Roethke says, "I would believe my pain: and the eye quiet on the growing rose." Learning a new language in this way, we must divest ourselves at this first stage of all claims to coherence, synthesis, or unity. This is the secular equivalent of the "way of purgation" in *Four Quartets,* and it serves a corresponding purpose, because here too humility is endless. If our humility is sufficient, if we attend to the roots, to beginnings, we may even be rewarded with a vision in which beginning and end are one, as in the poem "In Evening Air":

> Ye littles, lie more close!
> Make me, O Lord, a last, a simple thing
> Time cannot overwhelm.
> Once I transcended time:
> A bud broke to a rose,
> And I rose from a last diminishing.

We can see how this goes in the first stanzas of "Where Knock Is Open Wide":

> A kitten can
> Bite with his feet;
> Papa and Mama
> Have more teeth.

We can take this as pure notation, the primitive vision linking things that to the complex adult eye seem incommensurate. But the adult eye is "wrong," and it must go to school again if it is ever to say, "I recover my tenderness by long looking." Roethke's lines are "intuitions of sensibility," the ground of our beseeching, acts of the mind at the very first stage, long before idea, generalization, or concept. And this is the only way to innocence—or so the poem suggests. Then he says in the second stanza:

> Sit and play
> Under the rocker
> Until the cows
> All have puppies.

Here the aimlessness of the kitten stands for the innocence of game and apprehension. The play is nonchalant, and it conquers time by the ease of its reception. Time is measured by the laws of growth and fruition, not by the clock. In this sense it is proper to say, as Roethke does in the next stanza:

> His ears haven't time.
> Sing me a sleep-song, please.
> A real hurt is soft.

In Christopher Smart's "A Song to David" (the source of the title of the present poem) stanza 77 includes the lines:

> And in the seat to faith assigned
> Where ask is have, where seek is find,
> Where knock is open wide.

The cat's ears haven't time because they don't ask for it. If time is for men the destructive element, that is their funeral, and mostly their suicide. "Sing me a sleep-song, please" is a prayer to be released from time. "A real hurt is soft" is an attempt to render human pain as pure description, to eliminate self-pity. And the appropriate gloss is the second stanza of "The Lost Son"— "Fished in an old wound, / The soft pond of repose"—to remind us that the primitive vision is at once harsh and antiseptic. (Roethke himself sometimes forgot this.) Hence these intuitions of rudimentary sensibility are exercises, akin to spiritual exercises, all the better if they are caustic, purgative, penitential. The exercises are never finished, because this is the way things are, but once they are well begun the soul can proceed; the energy released is the rage for a sustaining order.

The search for order begins easily enough in Roethke. Sometimes, as we have seen, it begins in celebration, relishing what there is to relish. Or again it may begin by sounding a warning note. The early poem "To My Sister" is a rush of admonition designed for survival and prudence. "Defer the vice of flesh," he tells her, but on the other hand, "Keep faith with present joys." Later, Roethke would seek and find value in intimations of change and growth, and then in love, normally sexual love. Many of the love poems are beautiful in an Elizabethan way, which is one of the best ways, and whether their delicacy is entirely Roethke's own or partly his way of acknowledging the delicacy of Sir Thomas Wyatt is neither here nor

there. Some of the love poems are among Roethke's finest achievements. I
would choose "The Renewal," "I Knew a Woman," "The Sensualists,"
"The Swan," "She," and "The Voice"—or this one, "Memory":

> In the slow world of dream,
> We breathe in unison.
> The outside dies within,
> And she knows all I am.
>
> She turns, as if to go,
> Half-bird, half-animal.
> The wind dies on the hill.
> Love's all. Love's all I know.
>
> A doe drinks by a stream,
> A doe and its fawn.
> When I follow after them,
> The grass changes to stone.

Love was clearly a principle of order in Roethke's poems, but it never
established itself as a relation beyond the bedroom. It never became dialogue or *caritas*. Outside the bedroom Roethke became his own theme, the
center of a universe deemed to exist largely because it had such a center.
This does not mean that the entire universe was mere grist to his mill; he is
not one of the predatory poets. But on the other hand, he does not revel in
the sheer humanity of the world. Indeed, his universe is distinctly under-
populated. Even Aunt Tilly entered it only when she died, thereby inciting
an elegy. This is not to question Roethke's "sincerity"; poems are written
for many reasons, one of which is the presence of poetic forms inviting
attention. But to indicate the nature of Roethke's achievement it is necessary
to mark the areas of his deepest response and to point to those areas that he
acknowledged more sluggishly, if at all. I have already implied that he
responded to the human modes of being only when a specific human relation touched him and he grasped it. He did not have that utter assent to
other people, other lives, that marks the best poetry of William Carlos
Williams or Richard Eberhart, the feeling that human life is just as mirac-
ulous as the growth of an orchid or the "excess" of a rose. Indeed, one might
speculate along these lines: that Roethke's response to his father and mother
and, in the love poems, to his wife was so vivid that it engrossed all other
responses in the human world. It set up a monopoly. And therefore flowers
and plants were closer to him than people.

Even when he acknowledged a natural order of things, Roethke invari-

ably spoke of it as if it did not necessarily include the human order or as if
its inclusion of that order were beside the point. The natural order of things
included moss growing on rock, the transplanting of flowers, the cycle of
mist, cloud, and rain, the tension of nest and grave, and it might even
include what he calls, rather generally, "the wild disordered language of the
natural heart." But the question of the distinctively human modes of life was
always problematic. In Roethke's poems human life is endorsed when it
manages to survive a storm, as in "Big Wind," where the greenhouse—
Roethke's symbol for "the whole of life"—rides the storm and sails into the
calm morning. There is also the old florist, standing all night watering the
roses, and the single surviving tulip with its head swaggering over the dead
blooms—and then Otto.

To survive, to live through the weeds—in Roethke's world you do this
by taking appropriate security measures. Property is a good bet. In "Where
Knock Is Open Wide" there is a passage that reads:

> That was before. I fell! I fell!
> The worm has moved away.
> My tears are tired.
>
> Nowhere is out. I saw the cold.
> Went to visit the wind. Where the birds die.
> How high is have?

The part we need is the last line, "How high is have?" This virtually identifies security with property. In several poems Roethke will pray for a close
relation to God, and this will rate as security, but in the meantime even
property in a material sense will help. And because he lived in our own
society and sought order from the images of his chaos, security and property
normally meant money. In "The Lost Son," for instance, there is this:

> Good-bye, good-bye, old stones, the time-order is going.
> I have married my hands to perpetual agitation,
> I run, I run to the whistle of money.
>
> Money money money
> Water water water.

And even if he wrote two or three poems to make fun of this, the fact
remains: property and the fear of dispossession, money and the lack of it,
were vivid terms in his human image. Property was money in one's purse,
more reliable than most things—more reliable than reason, for instance.

In his search for a viable and live order Roethke used his mind for all it was worth, but he would not vote for reason. He did not believe that you could pit the rational powers against the weeds of circumstance and hope to win. When he spoke of reason it was invariably Stevens's "Reason's click-clack," a mechanical affair. In one poem Roethke says, "Reason? That dreary shed, that hutch for grubby schoolboys!" Indeed, reason normally appears in his poems, at least officially, as a constriction. Commenting on his poem "In a Dark Time," Roethke said that it was an attempt "to break through the barriers of rational experience." The self, the daily world, reason, meant bondage; to come close to God you had to break through. These things were never the medium of one's encounter with God, always obstacles in its way. For such encounters you had to transcend reason; if you managed it, you touched that greater thing that is the "reason in madness" of *King Lear*. The good man takes the risk of darkness. If reason's click-clack is useless, there remains in man a primitive striving toward the light. Nature, seldom a friend to man, at least offers him a few saving analogies, one being that of darkness and light. Much of this is given in the last stanzas of "Unfold! Unfold!":

> Sing, sing, you symbols! All simple creatures,
> All small shapes, willow-shy,
> In the obscure haze, sing!

> A light song comes from the leaves.
> A slow sigh says yes. And light sighs;
> A low voice, summer-sad.
> Is it you, cold father? Father,
> For whom the minnows sang?

> > A house for wisdom; a field for revelation.
> > Speak to the stones, and the stars answer.
> > At first the visible obscures:
> > Go where light is.

To go where light is: the object is self-possession, sometimes featured as a relation to the world:

> > I lose and find myself in the long water;
> > I am gathered together once more;
> > I embrace the world.

To be one's own man, to come upon "the true ease of myself," to possess oneself so fluently as to say, "Being, not doing, is my first joy"— these are definitive joys when "the light cries out, and I am there to hear."

If it requires "the blast of dynamite" to effect such movements, well and good. At any cost Roethke must reach the finality in which, as he says in "Meditation at Oyster River," "the flesh takes on the pure poise of the spirit." (This is his version of Yeats's "Unity of Being.") Hence he admires the tendrils that do not need eyes to seek, the furred caterpillar that crawls down a string, anything that causes movement, gives release, breaks up constriction. In the natural world there is growth, the flow of water, the straining of buds toward the light. And in the poet's craft these move in harmony with the vivid cadence, fluency, Yeats's "tact of words," the leaping rhythm.

For the rest, Roethke's symbolism is common enough. The life-enhancing images are rain, rivers, flowers, seed, grain, birds, fish, veins. The danger signals are wind, storm, darkness, drought, shadow. And the great event is growth, in full light. "The Shape of the Fire" ends:

> To have the whole air!
> The light, the full sun
> Coming down on the flowerheads,
> The tendrils turning slowly,
> A slow snail-lifting, liquescent;
> To be by the rose
> Rising slowly out of its bed,
> Still as a child in its first loneliness;
> To see cyclamen veins become clearer in early sunlight,
> And mist lifting out of the brown cattails;
> To stare into the after-light, the glitter left on the lake's
>   surface,
> When the sun has fallen behind a wooded island;
> To follow the drops sliding from a lifted oar,
> Held up, while the rower breathes, and the small boat drifts
>   quietly shoreward;
> To know that light falls and fills, often without our knowing,
> As an opaque vase fills to the brim from a quick pouring,
> Fills and trembles at the edge yet does not flow over,
> Still holding and feeding the stem of the contained flower.

The flower, contained, securely held in a vase filled with water and light—with this image we are close to the core of Roethke's poetry, where all the analogies run together. The only missing element is what he often called "song," the ultimate in communication, and for that we need another poem, another occasion. One of his last poems, a love poem, ends:

> We met to leave again
> The time we broke from time;
> A cold air brought its rain,
> The singing of a stem.
> She sang a final song;
> Light listened when she sang.

If light listens, if light attends upon a human event, then the event is final. Kenneth Burke has pointed out that Roethke tends to link things, whenever there is a choice, by means of a word in the general vocabulary of communication. We need only add this, that when the relation is as close as a relation can be, the participants "sing," and there is singing everywhere, singing and listening. "The light cries out, and I am there to hear."

Pushed to their conclusion, or followed to their source, these analogies would run straight to the idea of God, or rather to the image of God. And taking such stock in the symbolism of creation and light, Roethke could hardly have avoided this dimension. Nor did he. One of his last and greatest poems is called "The Marrow":

> The wind from off the sea says nothing new.
> The mist above me sings with its small flies.
> From a burnt pine the sharp speech of a crow
> Tells me my drinking breeds a will to die.
> What's the worst portion in this mortal life?
> A pensive mistress, and a yelping wife.
>
> One white face shimmers brighter than the sun
> When contemplation dazzles all I see;
> One look too close can make my soul away.
> Brooding on God, I may become a man.
> Pain wanders through my bones like a lost fire;
> What burns me now? Desire, desire, desire.
>
> Godhead above my God, are you there still?
> To sleep is all my life. In sleep's half-death,
> My body alters, altering the soul
> That once could melt the dark with its small breath.
> Lord, hear me out, and hear me out this day:
> From me to Thee's a long and terrible way.
>
> I was flung back from suffering and love
> When light divided on a storm-tossed tree;

Yea, I have slain my will, and still I live;
I would be near; I shut my eyes to see;
I bleed my bones, their marrow to bestow
Upon that God who knows what I would know.

The first stanza is all alienation—from nature and man and the self. The second is preparation for prayer, a relation with God as the light of light, source of the sun. The third is the prayer itself to the ground of all beseeching. In the fourth and last stanza the loss of selfhood is associated with the breakup of light on a storm-tossed tree, the emaciation of the human will; and then the last gesture—the voiding of the self, restitution, atonement (a characteristic sequence in late Roethke).

From the poems I have quoted, it might seem that Roethke was concerned with only one thing—himself. And this is true. But in his case it does not mean what it usually does. It does not mean that he is thrilled by his own emotions or that he spends much time in front of his mirror. The saving grace in Roethke, as in Whitman, is the assumption that he is a representative instance, no more if no less. When Roethke searches for value and meaning he assumes that this is interesting insofar as it is representative and not at all interesting when it ceases to be so. This is the source of Roethke's delicacy, as of Whitman's. When he says, in "I Need, I Need," "The Trouble is with No and Yes," or when he says, in "The Pure Fury," "Great Boehme rooted all in Yes and No," he advances this choice as a universal predicament rather than a proof of his own tender conscience. Again, in "The Waking" and other poems of similar intent, when he says, "I learn by going where I have to go," he is not claiming this as a uniquely sensitive perception; the line points to areas of feeling important because universal. And when he says, "Light takes the Tree; but who can tell us how?" the question is given with notable modesty, although indeed Roethke could have staked a higher claim for it, since it is the basis of several of his own religious poems. The motto for this delicacy in Roethke is a line from "The Sententious Man": "Each one's himself, yet each one's everyone." And there is the "Fourth Meditation" to prove that Roethke was never really in danger of solipsism.

With these qualifications, then, it is permissible to say that he was his own theme and to consider what this means in the poems—with this point in mind, however, that Whitman's equations were not available to Roethke. Roethke was not content to think of the self as the sum of its contents, even if he had Yeats to tell him that a mind is as rich as the images it contains. He would try to accumulate property, but only because he thought of property as a protective dike; behind the dike; one could live. But he never thought of this as having anything to do with the "nature" of the self. The self was problematic, but not a problem in addition. In one of his last and most beautiful poems, "In a Dark Time," he said:

> A man goes far to find out what he is—
> Death of the self in a long, tearless night,
> All natural shapes blazing unnatural light.
>
> Dark, dark my light, and darker my desire.
> My soul, like some heat-maddened summer fly,
> Keeps buzzing at the sill. Which I is *I*?

That is still the question. In the early poems Roethke held to the common romantic idea of "the opposing self," the self defined by its grappling with the weeds of circumstance; hence, as Hopkins said, "Long Live the Weeds." Much later, Roethke was to consider this more strictly, notably in a poem like "The Exorcism," where he asks in a beguiling parenthesis, "(Father of flowers, who / Dares face the thing he is?)" And this question is joined to several bacterial images of man partaking uneasily of several worlds, beasts, serpents, the heron and the wren. In "Weed Puller" man is down in a fetor of weeds, "Crawling on all fours, / Alive, in a slippery grave."

Many of the middle poems feature a declared loss of self, often given as division, absence. In "Where Knock Is Open Wide" Roethke says:

> I'm somebody else now.
> Don't tell my hands.
> Have I come to always? Not yet.
> One father is enough.
>
> Maybe God has a house.
> But not here.

There is a similar feeling in "Sensibility! O La!" and in "The Shimmer of Evil" perhaps the most explicit of all versions is, quite simply, "And I was only I"—which leads almost predictably but nonetheless beautifully to "There was no light; there was no light at all." The later poems tend to reflect upon the nature of the self by listing its demands; behind the love poems there is the assertion that "we live beyond / Our outer skin" even when the body sways to music. And much of this feeling culminates in the lovely "Fourth Meditation," which begins with many intuitions of sensibility and goes on to this:

But a time comes when the vague life of the mouth no longer
    suffices;
The dead make more impossible demands from their silence;
The soul stands, lonely in its choice,
Waiting, itself a slow thing,
In the changing body.

> The river moves, wrinkled by midges,
> A light wind stirs in the pine needles.
> The shape of a lark rises from a stone;
> But there is no song.

This is a later version of the predicament, loss of self, which cries through
the middle poems. In "The Lost Son" he says:

> Snail, snail, glister me forward,
> Bird, soft-sigh me home.
> Worm, be with me.
> This is my hard time.

And a few lines later we read: "Voice, come out of the silence. / Say something." But there is no song in that "kingdom of bang and blab." In Roethke's
poems song is proof that infinity clings to the finite. In "Old Lady's Winter
Words" he says, "My dust longs for the invisible." What he wants is given
in phrase, image, and rhythm: "the gradual embrace / of lichen around
stones"; "Deep roots"; and, quite directly:

> Where is the knowledge that
> Could bring me to my God?

The only knowledge is reason in madness.

Theodore Roethke was a slow starter in poetry. He survived and grew
and developed without attaching himself to schools or groups. He was never
a boy wonder; he was never fashionable as the Beat poets were fashionable;
most of the currents of easy feeling left him untouched, unmoved. He never
set up shop as a left-wing poet or a right-wing poet or a Catholic poet or a
New England poet or a Southern poet or a California poet. He never claimed
privilege in any region of feeling. This was probably as good for his poetry
as it was bad for his fame. He made his way by slow movements, nudgings
of growth, like his own plants and flowers. But he grew, and his poems got
better all the time—so much so, that his last poems were his greatest
achievements, marvelously rich and humane.

Along the way he was helped by friends, often poets like Louise Bogan

and Marianne Moore, but this is another story, not mine to tell. He was,
however, helped also by other writers, earlier poets, and some of this story
may be told, and the telling should disclose something of the poetry. Clearly,
he was a careful, scrupulous poet. There are lines and phrases here and there
that show that he was prone to infection, picking up things from lesser
poets, like Dylan Thomas, and keeping them beyond the call of prudence.
But the poets who really engaged him were those who offered him a challenge, a mode of feeling, perhaps, that he himself might not possess, or
possessed without knowing that he did. The Elizabethan song-poets, and
especially John Donne, challenged him in this way, and his own love poems
reflect not only their own feeling but the strenuous competition of the
Elizabethan masters. And then there were poets like Davies and Smart who
disclosed certain modes of feeling and belief that were not so deeply a
personal challenge but a measure of time in which we live. And there were
the great modern masters whom he could hardly have avoided hearing. He
learned a lot from T. S. Eliot—mainly, I think, how to be expressive while
holding most of his ammunition in reserve. And this often comes through
the verse as a cadence, as in this passage from "I'm Here":

> At the stream's edge, trailing a vague finger;
> Flesh-awkward, half-alive,
> Fearful of high places, in love with horses;
> In love with stuffs, silks,
> Rubbing my nose in the wool of blankets;
> Bemused; pleased to be;
> Mindful of cries,
> The meaningful whisper,
> The wren, the catbird.

Consider the rhetoric of the short phrase, at once giving and taking; Eliot is
a great master in these discriminations. Think of this passage in "East
Coker":

> In the middle, not only in the middle of the way
> But all the way, in a dark wood, in a bramble,
> On the edge of a grimpen, where is no secure foothold,
> And menaced by monsters, fancy lights,
> Risking enchantment.

Other cadences Roethke got from other poets—from Hopkins, notably, especially from "The Wreck of the Deutschland," which Roethke uses
in the poem about the greenhouse in a storm, "Big Wind":

> But she rode it out,
> That old rose-house,
> She hove into the teeth of it,
> The core and pith of that ugly storm.

From Joyce Roethke learned one kind of language for the primitive, the rudimentary, the aboriginal, especially the Joyce of the *Portrait of the Artist as a Young Man,* bearing hard on the first chapter; and *Finnegans Wake* showed him one way of dealing with the unconscious. And there is Wallace Stevens. Roethke disapproved of Stevens's procedures in argumentative theory, but in fact he learned some fundamental lessons from Stevens. When he says, "I prefer the still joy," he is Stevens's pupil, conning a lesson he could well have done without. And I think he found in Stevens a justification of, if not an incitement to, his own propensity for the "pure moment." In one of his later poems he says, "O to be delivered from the rational into the realm of pure song." And if pure song is pure expression or pure communication, it is also close to Stevens's "hum of thoughts evaded in the mind." Stevens seems to me to be behind those poems in which Roethke longs for essence, for an essential "purity," or finds it in a still moment. He records it in a passage like this, for instance, from the "First Meditation":

> There are still times, morning and evening:
> The cerulean, high in the elm,
> Thin and insistent as a cicada,
> And the far phoebe, singing,
> The long plaintive notes floating down,
> Drifting through leaves, oak and maple,
> Or the whippoorwill, along the smoky ridges,
> A single bird calling and calling;
> A fume reminds me, drifting across wet
>   gravel;
> A cold wind comes over stones;
> A flame, intense, visible,
> Plays over the dry pods,
> Runs fitfully along the stubble,
> Moves over the field,
> Without burning.
>   In such times, lacking a god,
>   I am still happy.

And Stevens is behind those poems in which Roethke presents the "single man" who contains everything:

> His spirit moves like monumental wind
> That gentles on a sunny blue plateau.
> He is the end of things, the final man.

When Whitman comes into the later poems, such as "Journey to the Interior," he shows Roethke how to deal with natural forms without hurting them, so that "the spirit of wrath becomes the spirit of blessing"; or how to give one thing after another without lining them up in symbolist rivalry, so that he can say "Beautiful my desire, and the place of my desire"; or how to preserve one's own integrity even when beset by "the terrible hunger for objects." But Whitman was a late consultant to Roethke. Much earlier, and toward the end of his poetic life, he attended upon Yeats's poems and contracted debts handsomely acknowledged in the "In Memoriam" and again in "The Dance." To Roethke—or so it seems from the poems—Yeats stood for the imperious note, concentration, magnificent rhetoric clashing against the bare notation, the dramatic play of self and soul.

> What's madness but nobility of soul
> At odds with circumstance? The day's on fire!
> I know the purity of pure despair,
> My shadow pinned against a sweating wall.
> That place among the rocks—is it a cave,
> Or winding path? The edge is what I have.

It peters out somewhat. Yeats would not have praised the last line. But the rest is very much in Yeats's shadow, particularly the Yeats of "Coole Park and Ballylee, 1931." The dramatic occasion; the landscape, moralized with a large showing; the poet, finding correspondences and emblems in herons, wrens, swans; nature with her tragic buskin on—these are the Yeatsian gestures. And, to take them a little further, Roethke knows that if he proposes to learn a high rhetoric he must do it in earnest. So he begins with the magisterially rhetorical question, then the short declaration, not yet intimate, "The day's on fire!" and only then the despair. And even now it is given as knowledge rather than romantic exposure, so that even the shadow, the other self, is presented as an object of contemplation before the poet acknowledges the feeling as his own in "a sweating wall."

One of the odd things in this list of relationships, however, is that it is quite possible to think of Roethke as one of the best modern poets without troubling about the fact that he was, after all, an American poet. When reading Stevens or Frost or Williams or Robert Lowell we are constantly aware that we are reading American poets; but this is not an insistent element in Roethke. Indeed, it is quite clear that he bears no special relation to either of the dominant traditions in American poetry—New England and the South. Temperamentally he is not too far away from such writers as Hawthorne, Melville, or James. Like them, in his quite different way, he was concerned with the wounded conscience, the private hazard. But while it is obviously proper in some sense to relate the poems of Robert Lowell to this tradition, it has little bearing on Roethke's work. And the tradition of the South can be ruled out. This suggests that the discussion of American literature in terms of these two traditions may by now have lost much of its force. To think of the New England tradition as scholastic, autocratic, and logical, and the Southern tradition as humanistic, Ciceronian, grammatical, and rhetorical is fine as far is it goes, but its relevance clearly fades in regard to poets like Roethke. This may well be the point to emphasize, that Roethke and many of the poets of his generation took their food wherever they could find it. Yeats could well be more useful to them than, say, Hawthorne, because they saw their problems as being human, universal, in the first instance, and American problems only by application and inference. Roethke committed himself to his own life. He thought of it as a human event of some representative interest. And he set himself to work toward lucidity and order without turning himself into a case study entitled "The Still Complex Fate of Being an American." This is one aspect of Roethke's delicacy. Contemporary American poets, for the most part, are not going his way; they insist upon their complex fate and would not live without it. But Roethke's way of being an American is an eminently respectable way, and part of his achievement is that he makes it available to others.

"The Far Field" is a distinguished example of this delicacy. It has four unequal sections. The first is a dream of journeys, journeys without maps, featuring imprisonment, attenuation of being, the self "flying like a bat deep into a narrowing tunnel" until there is nothing but darkness. It is life in a minor key, diminished thirds of being. The second stanza translates these into major terms, images of force, aggression, suffering, death, dead rats eaten by rain and ground beetles. But the poet, meditating upon these images, thinks of other images, of life, movement, freedom, everything he means by "song." And these natural configurations lead to thoughts of life as cycle, evolution and return, proliferations of being, the whole process of life, which the poet calls "infinity"; what Wallace Stevens in "The Bouquet" calls "the infinite of the actual perceived, / A freedom revealed, a realization touched, / The real made more acute by an unreal." In the third section the

poet feels a corresponding change in himself, a moving forward, a quickening, and as he commits himself to earth and air he says, "I have come to
a still, but not a deep center." Naturally it feels like a loss, another dimi-
nution of being, even if the sense of life-ordained process is strong. And this
feeling leads straight into the fourth and last section:

> The lost self changes,
> Turning toward the sea,
> A sea-shape turning around,—
> An old man with his feet before the fire,
> In robes of green, in garments of adieu.
>
> A man faced with his own immensity
> Wakes all the waves, all their loose wandering fire.
> The murmur of the absolute, the why
> Of being born fails on his naked ears.
> His spirit moves like monumental wind
> That gentles on a sunny blue plateau.
> He is the end of things, the final man.
>
> All finite things reveal infinitude:
> The mountain with its singular bright shade
> Like the blue shine on freshly frozen snow,
> The after-light upon ice-burdened pines;
> Odor of basswood on a mountain-slope,
> A scent beloved of bees;
> Silence of water above a sunken tree:
> The pure serene of memory in one man,—
> A ripple widening from a single stone
> Winding around the waters of the world.

Roethke says: "The end of things, the final man,"; Stevens asserts in "The
Auroras of Autumn":

> There is nothing until in a single man contained,
> Nothing until this named thing nameless is
> And is destroyed. He opens the door of his house
> On flames. The scholar of one candle sees
> An Arctic effulgence flaring on the frame
> Of everything he is. And he feels afraid.

The difference is that Stevens identifies the man with his imagination, and
his imagination with his vision—and insists upon doing so. And the imag-

ination feeds upon as much reality as it can "see" and values only that; what it can't see won't hurt or help it. The scholar has only this one candle. Roethke's man is not a scholar at all, or if he is, he is an amateur, perhaps a mere teacher. His imagination is partly his memory, which offers hospitality to sights, sounds, and smells, and partly his conscience, and partly his feeling for modes of being that he cannot command, directions that he cannot chart. Hence his poems are the cries of their occasions, but rarely cries of triumph. This is what makes his later poems the noble things they are, stretching of the spirit without fantasia or panache. "Which is the way?" they ask, and if they include God in their reply they do so with due deference, knowing that one can be "too glib about eternal things," too much "an intimate of air and all its songs."

Another way of putting it is that the poems, especially the middle poems, are cries of their occasions, sudden, isolated cries. The later poems turn cries into prayers, praying for a world order, a possible world harmony of which the cries are part, like voices in polyphony. The self in exposure is monotone; a sustaining society is polyphony; God is the Great Composer. The poet's ideal is the part song, music for several instruments, what the Elizabethans called "broken music." In "In Evening Air" Roethke says, "I'll make a broken music, or I'll die." In such poems as "The Marrow" and "In a Dark Time" he made a broken music at once personal and—in Stevens's sense—noble. And then, alas, he died.

ROY HARVEY PEARCE

Theodore Roethke:
The Power of Sympathy

For Robert Estrich
"What you survived I shall believe . . ."

At the end of Wallace Stevens's "The Noble Rider and the Sounds of
Words" there is a passage which may serve as prolegomenon to the poetics
of our recent past:

> The mind has added nothing to human nature. It is a violence
> from within that protects us from a violence without. It is the
> imagination pressing back against the pressure of reality. It seems,
> in the last analysis, to have something to do with our self-
> preservation; and that, no doubt, is why the expression of it, the
> sound of its words, helps us live our lives.

Using the passage, one can trace some of the relationships between the work
of the great elder modernists (Stevens and his generation) and of the poets
who come immediately after. The work of the former defines the poet's
vocation according to an extreme choice, whereby he may attend either to
the violence without or to the violence within. Only thus may he master the
ways of violence with sensibility and learning; only thus transform violence
into process, that process of art which form charts for us. Stevens himself is
preeminently the poet of the opposing self; Eliot is the poet of the opposing
other. And the poets of the generations after Eliot and Stevens, necessarily
mindful of their elders' ways, have as necessarily accepted their elders'

From *Theodore Roethke: Essays of the Poetry,* edited by Arnold Stein. © 1965 by
the University of Washington Press.

definition of the poet's vocation: how, through the exercise of his craft, to contain violence, whatever its origin and end, so as to make it a source of power.

At bottom, then, the issue for the poet is the issue for modern man in all his capacities and institutions: power. The commonplace is nonetheless true for being a commonplace. The conditions of modern life have at once created and tapped sources of a force so great that it must inevitably issue as violence. For the poet what threatens is an entropy of the sensibility as it manifests itself in language. And yet he has access to the sensibility only through language. If language—either as he knows it within or as he knows it without—runs mad with the terror of that to which it refers, the poet must yet live with it, live through it. He needs power; so he must put himself vitally in touch with violence. The touch is everything. He knows that violence cannot be attenuated, much less done away with. But it can be transformed into power, so then to bring into consonance the life of the spirit and the life of society—the self alone and the self as other coordinate with other, perhaps higher, selves.

Theodore Roethke's achievement takes on its special meaning from the fact that he single-mindedly searched out violence in its very sources and strove mightily to find such modes of order as would transform it into power—the power of sympathy, the means to reach across the gulf which separates the sources of the violence within from those of the violence without. The paradigm for his poetry is this: violence transformed into power through order. The structure and technique of the poems enact the transformation, and would create a kind of spiritual exercise whereby the reader might learn the lessons of the poet's life.

For in Roethke's work the poet's life is always insistently there. Sometimes it is too much so, to be sure, and the exercise leads to no end but wonderment about the poet as private person. In such cases, the process limits rather than transforms, leading to curiosity rather than self-knowledge. Roethke himself seems to have known this. And as he put his poems into volumes, he tried consistently to eliminate from his collections verses in which the requisite transformative factor, for whatever reason, is absent. "Feud," for example, put into *Open House* but not subsequently reprinted, begins:

> Corruption reaps the young; you dread
> The menace of ancestral eyes;
> Recoiling from the serpent head
> Of fate, you blubber in surprise.

> Exhausted fathers thinned the blood,
> You curse the legacy of pain;
> Darling of an infected brood,
> You feel disaster climb the vein.

The manner is not really Roethke's, we may decide, but, say, Allen Tate's. Still, what is lacking in (not wrong with) the poem—when viewed in the light of the poems as Roethke selected and ordered them in *Words for the Wind*—is a means of involving the reader directly in the lucubrations of the speaker. The reader is that "you," and finds himself accused, but as the later Roethke might have decided, not sufficiently tutored into an understanding of the accusation. "Feud" ends:

> You meditate upon the nerves,
> Inflame with hate. This ancient feud
> Is seldom won. The spirit starves
> Until the dead have been subdued.

The violence remains without, to be stoically resisted, perhaps conquered— in any case, not understood. The violence within—which empowers the resisting—is controlled and focused by rhetoric, and someone else's at that. "Feud" is a considerable poem, and persuasive. The later Roethke—I daresay the authentic Roethke—wanted to do more than persuade. The authentic Roethke, as he sought to define himself, is not he who, in language on loan, would persuade the living that they must subdue the dead. For a poem like "Feud" rather commemorates than celebrates, rather neutralizes violence than transforms it, rather shuns power than seeks it. The authentic Roethke came to be the celebrant of the transformation of violence into power.

It is this growing sense of his own vocation, I think, which led Roethke not to put into his volumes his poems about life in mental hospitals—for example, "Lines upon Leaving a Sanitarium" (1937), "Meditation in Hydrotherapy" (1937), and "Advice to One Committed" (1960). The last named begins:

> Swift's servant beat him; now they use
> The current flowing from a fuse,
> Or put you on a softer diet;
> Your teeth fall out—but you'll be quiet;
> Forget you ever were someone—
> You'll get ten minutes in the sun.

There is a fine Swiftian quality to such poems. But they are too neat. They are objectively rather than subjectively personal, and (when viewed in the

light of what Roethke came to demand of his verse) just will not do. "The
Return" (1946), however, Roethke did put into *The Lost Son* and kept in
The Waking and *Words for the Wind:*

> I circled on leather paws
> In the darkening corridor,
> Crouched closer to the floor,
> Then bristled like a dog.
>
> As I turned for a backward look,
> The muscles in one thigh
> Sagged like a frightened lip.
>
> A cold key let me in
> That self-infected lair;
> And I lay down with my life,
> With the rags and rotting clothes,
> With a stump of scraggy fang
> Bared for a hunter's boot.

The importance of specific occasion and locale here is diminished exactly as
the significance of the experience is increased; such details as we are given
are internalized into a sequence of metaphors which urge us to participate
in the poem and to use it as a means of defining our own return to the
mental hospitals—if such are meant here—which we perforce make out of
our lives. The violence of the controlling metaphor—marked by "circled,"
"crouched," "bristled," "sagged," "self-infected," and "bared"—such violence is countered, then transformed, by that "And I lay down with my life."
For it is the power of lying down—but still *with* one's life—which finally
dominates and teaches us to defy the hunter's boot. The difference between
"Advice to One Committed" and "The Return" is the difference between
death-in-life and life-in-death.

For violence leads to death—alternatively to the death of the self at the
hands of the other, or the death of the other at the hands of the self. This
Roethke saw and felt and understood more deeply and with greater intelligence than any poet of our time. He sought to find a means of refusing the
either/or option which his culture offered him. The design of *Words for the
Wind* and *The Far Field* manifests that search. In choosing earlier poems to
reprint, in adding new poems, in grouping them, he mapped out his quest so
as to make it his readers'. He rejected not only such "autobiographical"
poems as I have cited but a number of wonderfully funny poems attacking
persons who threatened—not so much himself as what he increasingly stood

for. Also, he rejected a number of poems bitingly observant of modern urban life. One guesses that he was overreacting to his own aggressiveness, as though it too were a form of violence which threatened. (Although he had some of this cake and ate it too: in the pieces he published under the pseudonym "Winterset Rothberg.") He would—as he depicted the growth of the poet's mind—observe violence, and carefully annotate it; and he would turn it only upon himself. Thus he discovered the nature and working of violence, studied the transformative role of order, and found the power to become a poet.

The first poem in *Words for the Wind* is the title poem from *Open House*. Preserving it, and the four which immediately follow, Roethke preserves himself as public spokesman. "Open House" is, in contrast to the bulk of the poems, somewhat "rhetorical." Its general mode is like that of "Feud"—persuasive. Moreover, it rather declares than develops:

> My secrets cry aloud.
> I have no need for tongue.
> My heart keeps open house,
> My doors are widely swung.
> An epic of the eyes
> My love, with no disguise.

So many figurations—each to be accepted or declined separately, but each leading to the closing lines:

> I stop the lying mouth:
> Rage warps my clearest cry
> To witless agony.

Roethke was to reverse the order described here: to transform agony, by virtue of the transformation no longer witless, into a clearest cry, hence to transcend rage. Doing so, he was to move beyond rhetoric into the actual processes of consciousness.

He had to begin at the beginning—with primitive things. For him, understanding the natural order of primitive things came to be a means to and model for understanding all in the natural order, himself included, which is beyond the primitive. What the natural order contains, and therefore manifests, is growth—what seems to be violence but is not, for it is directed toward an end, as power must be if it is truly to be power. And in the rest of the poems kept from *Open House* the poet is caught in the excitement of his own crashing-through to the edge of just this insight. After a "Mid-Country Blow," he writes: "When I looked at the altered scene, my

eye was undeceived, / But my ear still kept the sound of the sea like a shell."
"The Heron" is described with the greatest exactitude as he moves; and
then "A single ripple starts from where he stood." Roethke would be following, tracing out, that single ripple the rest of his life. But in these poems
it is enough—more would be at this stage too much—that he see it at only
the outset; that in "No Bird" he define one dead as being beyond the
"breeze above her head" and the "grasses [which] whitely stir"; that (re-
versing a figure from Marvell) he proclaim "Long live the weeds that
overwhelm / My narrow vegetable realm!" Wonderment is enough—the
wonderment of the lovely "Vernal Sentiment": "I rejoice in the spring, as
though no spring ever had been." Intermixed as it is with such poems, the
declarative "Open House," like others of its kind in the *Words for the Wind*
sequence after which it is named, gains a vitality which is not its own when
it is taken separately. "Night Journey," which concludes the sequence, details a cross-country train trip, with its myriad revelations:

> Bridges of iron lace,
> A suddenness of trees,
> A lap of mountain mist.

Because he can see in such things the kind of vitality and growth revealed to
him in the more telling poems of the sequence, Roethke is justified at the end
in returning to his declarative mode: "I stay up half the night / To see the
land I love."

Inevitably (so the design of *Words for the Wind* indicates), Roethke's
journey was—as he said in so many words in the title of a late poem—into
the interior. First the interior was that of the natural order, and then his
own, to the degree that he was part of the natural order. The design of
Words for the Wind, as it emerges at this stage, is the design of another *Song
of Myself*, or another *Prelude*—as in later poems. Roethke himself makes
quite clear, perhaps having discovered only later that the design, worked out
retrospectively, had a certain necessity of its own. At this point, having
discovered the vitality, violence, and power of the natural order, he was
obliged to understand it. He had, then, to move away from the rather safe
and simplistic forms of *Open House* to forms adequate to the understanding
he would achieve: a structure of verse which would articulate the essential
facts and qualities of its primitive realm and, at the same time, be expressive
of the act of articulation itself. Roethke's was to be a lover's battle with his
world; victory would result only if it were fought to a draw. The risks, in the
context of modernist verse, were great: to dare the heresy of the pathetic
fallacy and that of imitative form. And there were failures, to be sure. One

takes them as the price paid for successes. And, because one can be doubly retrospective, one looks ahead to the poems beyond those from *The Lost Son,* which make up the second sequence in *Words for the Wind.*

At this stage, Roethke is surest of himself in his greenhouse poems. He seems wholly to comprehend the natural order and those, including himself, who are close to it. At first glance, the effect of the poems is to impute human qualities to the natural world; at second glance, once the poems have had their way, the effect is to discover those qualities in great and complex detail. There is then established a new order of understanding: that such qualities, precisely as they are human, are derived from the natural order. A kind of underground dialectic is everywhere at work, an argument generated by the organization and movement of the poems.

> Sticks-in-a-drowse droop over sugary loam,
> Their intricate stem-fur dries;
> But still the delicate slips keep coaxing up water;
> The small cells bulge.
>
> ("Cuttings")

"Sticks-in-a-drowse" and "coaxing" register human qualities; but "intricate" and "delicate" (such commonplace descriptive words they are) work to qualify and classify the implied anthropomorphic claim, and to establish a more-than-analogical relationship between perceiver and things perceived. The act of perception, when it is expressed, is one with the growth, the vital principle, of the things perceived. Thus, in "Cuttings, *later*" the poet can say that he knows exactly what is going on here, knows it unmediated:

> This urge, wrestle, resurrection of dry sticks,
> Cut stems struggling to put down feet,
> What saint strained so much,
> Rose on such lopped limbs to a new life?
>
> I can hear, underground, that sucking and sobbing,
> In my veins, in my bones I feel it,—
> The small waters seeping upward,
> The tight grains parting at last.
> When sprouts break out,
> Slippery as fish,
> I quail, lean to beginnings, sheath-wet.

The natural world is not the emblem of self-knowledge and self-realization, but the source and occasion of their being. One sees, one hears, one knows, and one is. Or at least, one begins to be.

The poet discovers this in others—the subjects of "Old Florist" and "Frau Bauman, Frau Schmidt, and Frau Schwartze," for example. But most of all, he discovers it in himself—as a "Weed Puller"

> down in that fetor of weeds,
> Crawling on all fours,
> Alive, in a slippery grave;

and in "Moss-Gathering," when

> afterwards I always felt mean, jogging back over the
>   logging road,
> As if I had broken the natural order of things in that
>   swampland;
> Disturbed some rhythm, old and of vast importance,
> By pulling off flesh from the living planet;
> As if I had committed, against the whole scheme of life, a
>   desecration.

The "natural order of things" and the "scheme of life," then, must be his central subject. The papa who, in all his power, waltzes so surely; the boy, at sixteen, itching with the lust of good smells in the pickle factory; the mother, dwelling in "That fine fuming stink of particular kettles"—these he must understand because they are closest to the "natural order of things" and the "scheme of life." Yet their world, with all its unself-conscious spontaneity, is lost to him. And, as I have pointed out, he must begin at the beginning, studying "The Minimal," the "lives on a leaf," which are "Cleaning and caressing, / Creeping and healing."

He concludes the poems kept from *The Lost Son* with another one in his declarative mode. By now, however, that mode has been qualified and accommodated to the mode which is dominant in *The Lost Son*.

> Dark water, underground,
> Beneath the rock and clay,
> Beneath the roots of trees,
> Moved into common day,
> Rose from a mossy mound
> In mist that sun could seize.
>
> The fine rain coiled in a cloud
> Turned by revolving air
> Far from that colder source
> Where elements cohere

Dense in the central stone.
The air grew loose and loud.

Then, with diminished force,
The full rain fell straight down,
Tunneled with lapsing sound
Under even the rock-shut ground,
Under a river's source,
Under primeval stone.

                              ("The Cycle")

Surely, we are to recall the end of *The Waste Land* here. And Roethke is
initiating a grand dialogue with one of his modernist masters. He too would
Give, Sympathize, Control—come to know the sources of power, in order at
once to make proper obeisance to them and to share in them. The rain that
comes to save his land, however, comes from underground, and returns
there, only again and again to move through, in the title of the poem, "The
Cycle." The poet, in short, must discover his own cycle, his own underground, his own relationship to the source under the primeval stone.

In *Words for the Wind* Roethke puts into the section called "Praise to
the End" not only poems from the volume of that name but the closing
sequence of *The Lost Son*. This sequence does indeed belong where he
places it; for, like the sequence kept from *Praise to the End!*, it most fully
manifests the violence of Roethke's journey into the interior—beyond childhood with its order (of a sort), beyond the order of the natural world, to the
swirling, threatening, inchoate sources of his very being. The Wordsworthian
title of the section, and the *Prelude* passage from which the title comes, are
helpful, in that they sum up and categorize Roethke's effort here:

How strange, that all
The terrors, pains, and early miseries,
Regrets, vexations, lassitudes interfused
Within my mind, should e'er have borne a part,
And that a needful part, in making up
The calm existence that is mine when I
Am worthy of myself! Praise to the end!

Writing a kind of apologia for those poems which comprise the "Praise to
the End" section, Roethke explained:

The method is cyclic. I believe that to go forward as a spiritual
man it is necessary first to go back. Any history of the psyche (or

allegorical journey) is bound to be a succession of experiences, similar yet dissimilar. There is a perpetual slipping-back, then a going-forward; but there is *some* "progress." Are not some experiences so powerful and so profound (I am not speaking of the merely compulsive) that they repeat themselves, thrust themselves upon us, again and again, with variation and change, each time bringing us closer to our own most particular (and thus most universal) reality? We go, as Yeats said, from exhaustion to exhaustion. To begin from the depths and come out—that is difficult; for few know where the depths are or can recognize them; or, if they do, are afraid.

We need guidance like this, if only to prepare ourselves for the exhaustion which is our proper due.

The style of these poems is regressive, but out of the regression there comes a certain progression, a deepening of one's sense of the fact, the factuality, of consciousness itself. The poems seem to anticipate the effort to comprehend them, and to defy it; yet the thrust of defiance is itself a thrust *toward* the reader and on his behalf—so, paradoxically, a crucial factor in his mode of comprehension. The language is most often that of the earliest stages of childhood, thus only barely language; it is charged with the force of the primary process of consciousness and so threatens always to disintegrate. Roethke is closest to the entropy of sensibility here. That infantile amnesia which psychoanalysis has discovered for us is broken through, or almost. And yet, as Roethke claims, these are "traditional" poems. The tradition is that deepest in the sensibility of individual men; it is a composite of their childhood experiences, experiences so deeply lived through as to seem the experience of the world from which, as children, they could not yet properly differentiate themselves. Coming at this point in the sequence of Roethke's poems, they establish the conditions under which it is possible to see how, in autobiographical fact, a man is part of the natural order in general and of his own natural order in particular. The literary source of the language is appropriately traditional too, as Roethke noted: "German and English folk literature, particularly Mother Goose; Elizabethan and Jacobean drama, especially the songs and rants; the Bible; Blake and Traherne; Dürer." What the poems demand of a reader is a willing suspension of adult consciousness, and yet a firm and controlled sense of oneself in the act of willing that suspension—which is, indeed, in recording the growth of his poet's mind, what they must have demanded of Roethke.

In a sense, they are not poems, but rather pre-poems; so that the reader, working through them, must bring his own capacities as protopoet most actively to bear on them. In effect, the reader *completes* them. One can hardly talk about these poems, or in terms of them. One can only try to talk through them—which perhaps is a way, a way we too much neglect, of learning, all over again, to talk. Thus the first section of the first poem in the six-poem sequence which begins "Praise to the End," "Where Knock Is Open Wide":

> A kitten can
> Bite with his feet;
> Papa and Mamma
> Have more teeth.
>
> Sit and play
> Under the rocker
> Until the cows
> All have puppies.

His ears haven't time.
Sing me a sleep-song, please.
A real hurt is soft.

> Once upon a tree
> I came across a time,
> It wasn't even as
> A ghoulie in a dream.
>
> There was a mooly man
> Who had a rubber hat
> And funnier than that,—
> He kept it in a can.
>
> What's the time, papa-seed?
> Everything has been twice.
> My father is a fish.

Let us say that this is an entrance-into-the-world poem. For the child, cause and effect are not "rationally" related—thus it is the knock, not the door, which opens wide on this experience; the kitten's scratches with his feet are in effect identical with teeth-bites; and if time is measured by gestation and birth, it is no matter that cows don't have puppies. When the father will not listen, it is his ears, not his larger self, that decline. And in the deepest world of once-upon, the distinction between time and place is of no significance.

Papa generates, therefore must be seed, therefore has a sense of time. Like papa, like son; therefore everything has been twice. And further, in this world, papa is primeval, is therefore a fish, swimming through time. What intrudes itself everywhere is the adult world, which threatens the world of the child, precisely as it promises so much to that world. A real hurt is in fact a hurt, as the child's world is threatened; but it is at the same time soft, as it is a hurt from the adult world which promises so much.

We can read such verse only in this way. Even as in its art Roethke's poem gets us to consent to the world it establishes, we report the news of that world back to the one in which we actually live. We do the world of these verses wrong if we translate it into a language appropriate to ours. Rather we must incorporate it, incorporate its style of apperception and knowing, into our own. Thus the way of exhaustion, the slipping-back so as to go forward, progress.

The progress in the "Praise to the End" sequence is not linear, but rather consists of an increased complexity of the modes of consciousness, an increased capacity to comprehend the world at once in its primeval and in its "civilized" states. "Where Knock Is Open Wide" ends:

> I'm somebody else now.
> Don't tell my hands.
> Have I come to always? Not yet.
> One father is enough.
>
> Maybe God has a house.
> But not here.

"Bring the Day!", the third poem, ends:

> O small bird wakening,
> Light as a hand among blossoms,
> Hardly any old angels are around any more.
> The air's quiet under the small leaves.
> The dust, the long dust, stays.
> The spiders sail into summer.
> It's time to begin!
> To begin!

"O Lull Me, Lull Me," the sixth and last poem of the sequence, ends:

> Soothe me, great groans of underneath
> I'm still waiting for a foot.

> The poke of the wind's close,
> But I can't go leaping alone.
> For you, my pond,
> Rocking with small fish,
> I'm an otter with only one nose:
> I'm all ready to whistle;
> I'm more than when I was born;
> I could say hello to things;
> I could talk to a snail;
> I see what sings!
> What sings!

From establishing a sense of place, to a sense of the origin of things, to a sense of proper relationship with things—not separated in natural, organic fact, but only in degree and quality of understanding. The effect is of a man finding and piecing together his knowledge of himself, which is a product of his knowledge of the natural order. Power, then—as we had always known but yet had to discover on our own—is knowledge.

Prefaced by the sequence which I have just discussed, "The Lost Son" serves all the more to celebrate that power. Fleeing from his father, the son turns from a knowledge so violent in its destructiveness as, at the outset, to be beyond comprehension. The poet himself seems to be fleeing from Eliot; for there are here too a number of significant echoes. The boy, in any case, flees from "the kingdom of bang and blab" down to a river teeming with primeval creatures; he descends into a pit, where he can "feel the slime of a wet nest"; his world is now one terrifying gibber into whose "dark swirl" he falls. And then, at last, he returns to his father—but now with strength to endure. He can assent to his father's "Ordnung! Ordnung!" to the degree that he understands that the words are necessary, because natural. It is winter; and he lives on, fortified by his memories of what he has learned on his flight—of the spirit within and without himself which he has discovered. In the last poem of the sequence, there is a shift to the second person, where before the first has been used—as though the poet were now sufficiently in possession of himself to achieve a certain objectivity:

> A lively understandable spirit
> Once entertained you.
> It will come again.
> Be still.
> Wait.

At the end, there is a recollection of "Ash-Wednesday." The tranquility in which the recollection comes, however, results from a confrontation, and containment, of the violence within, not—as with Eliot—the violence without.

And the rest of the poems in the "Praise to the End" sequence give analogues of and variations upon this theme. The poem whose title is given to the section celebrates, for the first time in the volume, the power of sexuality. "I'm awake all over:," the poet writes, and continues:

> I've crawled from the mire, alert as a saint or a dog;
> I know the back-stream's joy, and the stone's eternal pulseless
>   longing.
> Felicity I cannot hoard.
>
> . . . .
>
> I believe! I believe!—
> In the sparrow, happy on gravel;
> In the winter-wasp, pulsing its wings in the sunlight;
> I have been somewhere else; I remember the sea-faced uncles.
> I hear, clearly, the heart of another singing,
> Lighter than bells,
> Softer than water.
>
> Wherefore, O birds and small fish, surround me.
> Lave me, ultimate waters.
> The dark showed me a face.
> My ghosts are all gay.
> The light becomes me.

These lines mark the poet's sense of his freedom ever after to know, and so to be, himself. Now he is empowered to live in the most possible of all best worlds. Out of the underground dialectic there has emerged a knowledge which is knowing.

Knowing himself in his world, he may know others in theirs and so demonstrate that the two worlds are one. The rest of the poems collected in *Words for the Wind* (about one half the volume) are such demonstrations. They show a degree of formal, "willed" control—a capacity to tighten and loosen movement as syntax will allow it—quite beyond that of the earlier poems. Such poems—even, as regards substance, the most intimate of them— have a certain "public" quality, the assured decorum of the poet as his own kind of noble lord. Consequently, they also have the quality of a certain careless ease. It is the case of the poet as Young Prospero. Only, having read the poems which come before, we know that we are yielding not to the poet's magic but to his wholly earned and deserved authority, an authority which manifests itself as the poet's style. Such authority, indeed, enables him to address himself to subjects nominally banal and commonplace and to rediscover their abiding power for us.

The poems record the visitations of spirits other than the poet's own, his definition of the losses which he must encounter day-to-day, rollicking memories of earlier days, his nursery-rhymed farewell-and-hail to childhood, and, above all, the infinite possibilities of love. Love, indeed, is the essential substance of them all. It is by now, and at long last, the love which can be given and can be received. Love in these poems is different from love in the earlier poems, precisely as its necessary condition is now both giving and receiving. Consciously, willfully to give and to be given to: this initiates the dialectic of relationship to the other which now moves the poems and gives them the formal control which everywhere characterizes them. Their argument is that in love the flesh becomes spirit; that only in time is love possible; that only in love, so known, is eternity to be glimpsed:

> Let seed be grass, and grass turn into hay:
> I'm martyr to a motion not my own;
> What's freedom for? To know eternity.
> I swear she cast a shadow white as stone.
> But who would count eternity in days?
> These old bones live to learn her wanton ways:
> (I measure time by how a body sways).
>
> ("I Knew a Woman")

> Dream of a woman, and a dream of death:
> The light air takes my being's breath away;
> I look on white, and it turns into gray—
> When will that creature give me back my breath?
> I live near the abyss. I hope to stay
> Until my eyes look at a brighter sun
> As the thick shade of the long night comes on.
>
> ("The Pure Fury")

Just beyond this world, there is a dark world, transcendent, to be discovered. But meantime, there is yet this world, which love makes go round. Roethke, at this stage, was willing to write poem after poem on that truism—in order to bring it back into the life of modern poetry. The pattern and plot that love gives to human life would restore it to its place in the natural order. In "The Waking," he says:

> Great Nature has another thing to do
> To you and me; so take the lively air,
> And, lovely, learn by going where to go.

And in his great sequence, "Four for Sir John Davies," he celebrates (as the Renaissance poet had done before him) the idea of order. For Roethke order is cosmic because sexual, and sexual because cosmic: "The body and the soul know how to play / In that dark world where gods have lost their way." There is then that dark world (elsewhere Roethke calls it an abyss) which threatens, because it awaits. But

> The world is for the living. Who are they?
> We dared the dark to reach the white and warm.
> She was the wind when wind was in my way;
> Alive at noon, I perished in her form.
> Who rise from flesh to spirit know the fall:
> The word outleaps the world, and light is all.
>
> ("The Vigil")

This world and the abyss, light and darkness, love and death—the motifs are common enough, as is our sense of their paradoxical coexistence. Roethke's way with the commonplace is to penetrate into its very commonality: to see it in the natural order, to turn inward and backward upon himself and establish his truest involvement in that order, and then to turn outward, to look forward, to fare forward, and, through an understanding of his relation with all that constitutes the other, to affirm that involvement. His reordering of Eliot's formula is this: sympathize, control, give. He would abolish nothing, transmute nothing—but accept everything, and understand as much of it as he can, love even that which he cannot understand. His verse, then, comes to be a vehicle for understanding—and love its principal mode. "Being, not doing, is my first joy," he came to write in a late poem, "The Abyss," even as he felt himself caught up in "The burning heart of the abominable."

In one of the last poems in *Words for the Wind*, a dying man speaks:

> "A man sees, as he dies,
> Death's possibilities;
> My heart sways with the world.
> I am that final thing,
> A man learning to sing."
>
> ("His Words")

Roethke's reply is: "A breath is but a breath: I have the earth; / I shall undo all dying by my death," and

The edges of the summit still appal
When we brood on the dead or the beloved;
Nor can imagination do it all
In this last place of light: he dares to live
Who stops being a bird, yet beats his wings
Against the immense immeasurable emptiness of things.
("They Sing, They Sing")

This side of the abyss, the dark world, the edges of the summit—so far Roethke, in *Words for the Wind,* charted the journey of his soul. Behind him lay another abyss, into which he had plunged, another dark world, into which he had journeyed, another summit, over which he had leaped. And he had reported fully on his adventures. The reports are poems; and they are so often major poems because they are reports become interpretations, characterized by self-conscious didacticism and a use of traditions and conventions magisterial enough to transfigure, yet not to distort, the experiences on which they center. It is the poems, not the poet, which are transfiguring and transfigured. Roethke seems to have been overwhelmingly aware of the dangers for the modern poet who would risk the personal heresy. Reading the poems, one sees him courting that heresy, as it were employing it against itself. For underpinning the mere person there is the authentic person. I take Roethke's life-work to have been directed toward enlarging and deepening the sense of the authentically personal. On the whole, recent poets who have been of this persuasion have from the outset worked to resist threats to their own sacred selves; theirs has been the violence within fighting the violence without. Roethke rapidly gave up such a sense of his mission; and taught himself (somehow) that first he must learn not to resist himself. Everything followed.

It did not follow as far as it should have. It did not follow as his work promises it would. Our tragedy is that, dying, Roethke did not come to write the poems which would have undone death—I mean the component of death as in his poems he came more and more to acknowledge its immitigable existence. His poems controlled, they sympathized. They only began, at the end, fully to give. They controlled the wide and deep areas of the personal, the widest and deepest, I am persuaded, in the work of any contemporary American poet. And they demonstrated again and again how we have access to those areas only through sympathy—the power of human sympathy as it at first derives and then differentiates itself from the power which maintains the natural order of things. Roethke began to learn, and to make poems which teach, that out of the power of sympathy there comes the power to give, thus to be given to. He began to comprehend the full range of the other, that chain of being which moves from the minimal to God.

The poems in *The Far Field* indicate the distance he had come. Many of the love poems are centered on the consciousness of woman, an "I" different enough from the center of consciousness of the earlier love poems to manifest not only the power of sympathy but of identity with another. In the process, the poet's separate identity is not lost but, for the sake of the poems and the world they create, put aside. The feminine speaker in these poems has little to do with the exacerbated speculations of the masculine speaker of the earlier ones. As the poet gives her to us, we sense that she has always been steadily enough in touch with her interior past (the past of "Where Knock Is Open Wide" and the rest) to have let herself live, and give, fully in the presence of others:

> We are one, and yet we are more,
> I am told by those who know,—
> At times content to be two.
>   ("The Young Girl")

> Before this longing,
> I lived serene as a fish,
> At one with the plants in the pond,
> The mare's tail, the floating frogbit,
> Among my eight-legged friends,
> Open like a pool, a lesser parsnip,
> Like a leech, looping myself along,
> A bug-eyed edible one,
> A mouth like a stickleback,—
> A thing quiescent!

> But now—
> The wild stream, the sea itself cannot contain me.
>   ("Her Longing")

And the poet, as the masculine speaker in some of the poems, has learned too, because he has discovered his beloved as she is necessarily part of the order of great nature:

> My lizard, my lively writher,
> May your limbs never wither,
> May the eyes in your face
> Survive the green ice

Of envy's mean gaze;
May you live out your life
Without hate, without grief,
And your hair ever blaze,
In the sun, in the sun,
When I am undone,
When I am no one.
("Wish for a Young Wife")

He learns that he must some day be no one. And he knows his own temporal oneness all the more specifically, as he knows that of those who people his world—Aunt Tilly whom he celebrates in an "Elegy"; the Heroic "Otto" and all those who have inhabited "my father's world,— / O world so far away! O my lost world!"; and, simply enough, his "Chums":

Some are in prison; some are dead;
And none has read my books,
And yet my thoughts turn back to them.

What matters is that such memories no longer threaten. Again, he can write of the dark world, but now with the control which comes from loving understanding. Indeed, now he is ready to establish the crucial identification for the American poet:

Be with me, Whitman, maker of catalogues:
For the world invades me again,
And once more the tongues begin babbling.
And the terrible hunger for objects quails me.

This passage is from a poem I have already cited, "The Abyss." The manner, the structure, and the movement are superficially like such terrified poems as "Where Knock Is Wide Open." But there is now available to the poet a capacity for objectification, itself a product of a capacity for meditation— meditation outward, as it were. "Too much reality can be a dazzle, a surfeit," he writes, and follows this with: "Too close immediacy an exhaustion." He is free, however, to move through the abyss of exhaustion to the peace beyond, which is the peace of acceptance.

I thirst by day. I watch by night.
I receive! I have been received!
I hear the flowers drinking in their light,
I have taken counsel of the crab and the sea-urchin.

Again the order of nature—now most surely an ordering, so that the conclusion must come:

> I am most immoderately married:
> The Lord God has taken my heaviness away;
> I have merged, like the bird, with the bright air,
> And my thought flies to the place by the bo-tree.
>
> Being, not doing, is my first joy.

There are two grand efforts toward synthesis in *The Far Field*. Per-
fected achievements in themselves, the two poems are nonetheless
prolegomena toward poems which Roethke did not live to write, toward a
synoptic vision of the condition of modern man which at the end was yet
beyond him. In the "North American Sequence," the poet is first the explorer of the natural order; then a part of it; then an explorer into the
interior of his own experience, so conceived; then the poet who can "embrace the world"; then the poet who realizes that "He is the end of things,
the final man"; then he who has been given—or, in his struggle, has given
himself—unmediated vision into the very center of being. The argument of
the "North American Sequence" works to unify, and to make all of a piece,
the world which has invaded the poet, so as to allow him to invade it. The
experience would not seem to be ecstatic; for nothing has been cast off. On
the contrary, everything has been grasped at once and together, gloriously;
and such unification has become the very process of summing-up. The poet
(his mentor is still Whitman) discovers that he is part of that sum, that
sacred sum. Thus, at the end:

> Near this rose, in this grove of sun-parched, wind-warped
>   madronas,
> Among the half-dead trees, I came upon the true ease of
>   myself,
> As if another man appeared out of the depths of my being,
> And I stood outside myself,
> Beyond becoming and perishing,
> A something wholly other,
> As if I swayed out on the wildest wave alive,
> And yet was still.
> And I rejoiced in being what I was:
> In the lilac change, the white reptilian calm,
> In the bird beyond the bough, the single one
> With all the air to greet him as he flies,
> The dolphin rising from the darkening waves;

> And in this rose, this rose in the sea-wind,
> Rooted in stone, keeping the whole of light,
> Gathering to itself sound and silence—
> Mine and the sea-wind's.
>
> ("The Rose")

The compulsion here, as so often in Roethke's later work, is toward the sacred. The underground dialectic, at once empowered and constrained by the poet's dedication to the ordering of nature, has evolved an idea of God. The "Sequence, Sometimes Metaphysical" treats of that idea. In "In a Dark Time" (as in the last poem in the "North American Sequence") the poet encounters himself as one object among many. They constitute "A steady storm of correspondences," and in their storming put to the deepest doubt his sense of the order of nature—as though the order of nature, if only one knows it unmediated, as it really is, might negate itself, and issue into the ultimate entropy. His doubt now is like that which came to him when he confronted for the first time the possibility of his own authentic existence and that of the persons, places, and things which constituted his world:

> Dark, dark my light, and darker my desire.
> My soul, like some heat-maddened summer fly,
> Keeps buzzing at the sill. Which I is *I*?
> A fallen man, I climb out of my fear.
> The mind enters itself, and God the mind,
> And one is One free in the tearing wind.

The logic here is keen. Encountering himself as object, man fights through his terror and so rises from his fallen state. He knows once and for all that the price he has to pay for discovering God as object is the same as that he has had to pay for encountering as object any of the forms of the other: the old divisive agony of meditation. Yet now he has the strength, the power, to will himself into understanding and to make whole what has been divided— himself. So doing, he brings God into his "mind." But now he knows that it is he who has found God, he who has redeemed Him, and made manifest His freedom in that "tearing wind."

Such, I take it, is the central motif in the "Sequence, Sometimes Metaphysical." The "Godhead above my God" whom the poet addresses in "The Marrow" is the source of the power which the poet has always sought; finding it, he will have found the means to redeem the God below:

> I was flung back from suffering and love
> When light divided on a storm-tossed tree;

> Yea, I have slain my will, and still I live;
> I would be near; I shut my eyes to see;
> I bleed my bones, their marrow to bestow
> Upon the God who knows what I would know.

The other poems in the sequence are less "metaphysical" than these two, perhaps; but they nonetheless celebrate those moments of meditation, with its burdens of divisiveness, which are the necessary consequences of the poet's search for, and likewise the necessary antecedents of, his discovery of the sacred. For always he demands—"More! O More! visible." He goes on in this poem:

> Now I adore my life
> With the Bird, the abiding Leaf,
> With the Fish, the questing Snail,
> And the Eye altering all;
> And I dance with William Blake
> For love, for Love's sake;
>
> And everything comes to One,
> As we dance on, dance on, dance on.
>   ("Once More, the Round")

I have said that the poems in *The Far Field* indicate how far Roethke had come. They may also indicate how far he might have gone. In the note of explanation he wrote for John Ciardi's anthology, *Mid-Century American Poets* (1950), Roethke concluded: "The next phase? Something much longer: dramatic and *playable*. Pray for me." He did not live long enough to reach that phase. In his last poems, he did discover one of the necessary means to the dramatic: a full sense of the other. But the discovery was longer in the making, and surely more painful, than he seems to have imagined it would be. For whatever reason, he could not undertake the compulsive twentieth-century quest for identity via the route of alienation—which, we are told, is in our time the only proper route for the man of high imagination. His was the way of sympathy, and he kept to it as long as he lived. In his work, there are many moments of alienation; but they are associated with violence, and he works to transform the violence into power, thus alienation into identification.

Had he lived longer, he might have written a poem of power and identification, a *Jerusalem* for our age. Truly, his beginning was in his end. Even his discovery of God, the ultimate other, could promise him no respite. For God had to be fought toward, and the fighting-toward threatened always to be a fighting against: if not against God, against man. But Roethke was always bound not to be against. . . . The ordering of the "Sequence, Sometimes Metaphysical" registers just this movement, and proves it out. Thus I suggest that perhaps Roethke would have turned to Blake as his great model. (He was always nobly blatant in his study of models.) Calling to mind Blake's *Tiriel,* he pleads with Mnetha (whom Foster Damon calls Blake's Athena), mother of Har (whom Damon calls poetry degenerated), in "The Long Waters" section of the "North American Sequence." And he associates himself with Blake in "Once More, the Round," the last poem in the "Sequence, Sometimes Metaphysical." Perhaps, then, his vision would have become as large as Blake's; and, like Blake, he would have been able to put into his poems the awareness of the concrete and particular conditions of modern life, the biting hatred of abusers of power, even the wonderful comedy which, as he selected his poems for *Words for the Wind,* for the most part he set aside. A Blakean poem—narrative, prophetic, lyric, diatribic—we may guess, was his life's project, as was his life. For him the world was first I, then (from the minimal to God) thou—but not yet, as with Blake, he, she, or they. Learning the lessons of his work, we can say only that in our time, the world (too much with us) is inhabited by third persons, fearing to be first, therefore unable to reach toward the second.

To have revealed the sacredness of the second person, of all persons (and places and things) as they in truth are second—this is Roethke's achievement. And more than that: to have made known that our world of third persons is one in which the power of sympathy, if it exists outside the order of nature, becomes one of violence, now murderous, now suicidal, now both; to have transformed suicide into a means of rebirth and rediscovery; to have "undone" death, and to have dared to "do" love. Freed in the process, Roethke might have indeed become his own kind of Blake.

In a posthumously published piece (*Encounter,* December 1963)—it was intended to be one of the Winterset Rothberg" tirades—Roethke, in fact, wrote in the mode of Blake's *Descriptive Catalogues.* He addressed his "more tedious contemporaries":

Roaring asses, hysterics, sweet-myself beatniks, earless wonders happy with effects a child of two could improve on: verbal delinquents; sniggering, mildly obscene souser-wowsers, this one writing as if only he had a penis, that one bleeding, but always in waltz-time; another intoning, over and over, in metres the experts have made hideous; the doleful, almost-good, overtrained technicians—what a mincing explicitness, what a profusion of adjectives, what a creaking of adverbs!

He went on in this vein, and at length, telling the violent truth. Yet at the end, in Blake's manner, he shifted to verse, characterized by his immense power of sympathy.

> Was it reading you I first felt, full in my face, the hot blast and
>   clatter of insane machinery?
> Yet heard,
> Beneath the obscene murderous noise of matter gone mad,
> Whose grinding dissonance threatens to overwhelm us all,
> The small cry of the human?
>
> I, the loneliest semi-wretch alive, a stricken minor soul,
> Weep to you now;
> But I've an eye to your leaping forth and fresh ways of wonder;
> And I see myself beating back and forth like stale water in a
>   battered pail;
> Are not you my final friends, the fair cousins I loathe and love?
> That man hammering I adore, though his noise reach the very
>   walls of my inner self;
> Behold, I'm a heart set free, for I have taken my hatred and eaten
>   it,
> The last acrid sac of my rat-like fury;
> I have succumbed, like all fanatics, to my imagined victims;
> I embrace what I perceive!
> Brothers and sisters, dance ye,
> Dance ye all!

To have heard always the small cry of the human and to have amplified it and extended its range—that, as things came to stand with Roethke, had to be enough.

BRENDAN GALVIN

Kenneth Burke and Theodore Roethke's "Lost Son" Poems

One of the most interesting and productive friendships between two writers in recent years was that of Theodore Roethke and Kenneth Burke. It began in 1943, when Roethke joined the faculty of Bennington College. Burke spent a part of each week teaching there, and the remainder at his home in Andover, New Jersey. At Bennington he lived in a small upstairs room in Shingle Cottage, while Roethke occupied the floor below. Thus, it was almost inevitable that they should have gotten together often, and that Roethke would show his poems to the critic-novelist-poet who was ten years his senior, just as he had done earlier with Rolfe Humphries, Stanley Kunitz, and others whose critical abilities he respected.

As Allan Seager points out in *The Glass House: The Life of Theodore Roethke*, Burke increased Roethke's intellectual capacity more than any other teacher the poet had come in contact with. Burke is enormously learned, and by the time he and Roethke met had already completed four books of criticism, *Counter-Statement* (1931), *Permanence and Change* (1935), *Attitudes toward History* (1937), and *The Philosophy of Literary Form* (1941), a collection of short stories, *The White Oxen* (1924), a novel, *Towards a Better Life* (1932), and was at work on *A Grammar of Motives* (1945).

Roethke had published his first collection of poems, *Open House*, in 1941, and by 1943 the gestation period for what were to become his greenhouse poems was under way. In 1944 he published only one poem, "Night Crow," and in 1945, none at all. Then in 1946 he published "Carnations,"

From *Northwest Review* 11, no. 3 (Summer 1971). © 1971 by the University of Oregon.

"Child on Top of a Greenhouse," "Fruit Bin," "Moss-Gathering," "Old Florist," and "Weed Puller," all of which are concerned with the greenhouse memories of his childhood, and which differ from the conventionally rhymed and metered poems in *Open House* in that they reject these traditional modes for more open, unrhymed forms and more personal subjects. Roethke's prose piece, "Some Remarks on Rhythm," provides a rationale for these techniques:

> There are areas of experience in modern life that simply cannot be rendered by either the formal lyric or straight prose. We need the catalogue in our time. We need the eye close on the object, and the poem about the single incident—the animal, the child. We must permit poetry to extend consciousness as far, as deeply, as particularly as it can, to recapture, in Stanley Kunitz's phrase, what it has lost to some extent to prose. We must realize, I think, that the writer in freer forms must have even greater fidelity to his subject matter than the poet who has the support of form. He must keep his eye on the object, and his rhythm must move as a mind moves, must be imaginatively right, or he is lost.

Seager believes that the new subjects and techniques were stimulated by Roethke's leaving Pennsylvania State College and going to Bennington, and that he may have "half-consciously" wished the change, since leaving old haunts and habits could have meant for him a loosening up of patterns of thought and feeling. Certainly changes occurred, as the most superficial comparison of *Open House* and Roethke's second book, *The Lost Son and Other Poems,* published in 1948, will show. That Kenneth Burke was instrumental in bringing these changes about, particularly with regard to Roethke's "Lost Son" sequence, is the burden of this essay.

II

One day in 1945, Burke has reported in the Seager biography, he came into Roethke's rooms and Roethke read him two of the "greenhouse poems." "And I said, 'Boy, you've hit it!' And I kept demanding more. As far as I know Ted's gong struck then, when he hit that greenhouse line."

Roethke's letters of this period, collected in *Selected Letters of Theodore Roethke,* edited by Ralph J. Mills, Jr., contain valuable information relative to his relationship with Burke. One dated February 27, 1945, shows that Burke had seen "The Lost Sons" in an unfinished stage, for Roethke says, "I'm going to expand the central section of that, I think." Burke offered to "run interference" for these poems, in other words to use his influence in attempting to get them published in magazines, a tactic which Roethke wasn't above, as some of his letters indicate. One written just before Christmas 1945, again refers to "The Lost Son" and shows the extent of Burke's involvement with it: "Here it is, with I think all the changes you suggested, plus some more. I think it's tightened up; is done. And I hope you do. But if for any reason you feel dubious about it, give up the project and return." The "project," as this letter indicates, refers to the offer to run interference for the poem.

At some point during the composition of the "Lost Son" group, quite probably with "The Lost Son" itself, Burke may have explained via his literary theories the subconscious motivations and images in the poems, thus affording Roethke the conscious knowledge of what he was doing. Knowing this, it is possible that Roethke then deliberately reactivated the situation which is variously repeated in each poem in the sequence. As he said in "Open Letter," an introduction to a selection of his poems,

> Are not some experiences so powerful and so profound (I am not speaking of the merely compulsive) that they repeat themselves upon us, again and again, with variation and change, each time bringing us closer to our own most particular (and thus most universal) reality?

This has its corollary in Burke's *The Philosophy of Literary Form:*

> When an artist hits upon some ... basic situation, he can reindividuate it in many different concrete embodiments, with a strong predisposing factor of appeal already there before he begins.

Another letter, probably written in March 1946, shows Roethke's familiarity with Burke's theories:

> I was struck by the fact that some of your points I have down in notebooks as observations of my own. One belief: "One must go back to go forward." And by back I mean down into the consciousness of the race itself not just the quandries [sic!] of adolescence, damn it . . . I suppose at this point you will say that any regression does go back or repeat what has happened before and not merely in the individual man.

The paragraph following this gives an idea of what Roethke was doing at this time:

It's always seemed to me that many of these blood-thinkers or intuitives aren't or weren't tough enough. They just fart around with the setting sun like William Wordsworth or if they do get down in the subliminal depths they get punchy or scared and bring nothing back from the snakepit (or hen-house).

Evidently Roethke was worried that he might be borrowing too much from Burke, and in a letter to him dated May 2, 1946, explains that he doesn't want to appear to be hanging on Burke's coat-tails, although apparently this hadn't kept him from reading Burke's work. But in October of the same year he is writing to Burke, "I've tried to follow out your ideas for titles for the sections of #2 [presumably 'The Long Alley'] and given the whole a name, too. Let me know whether you like when you have time."

During this period William Carlos Williams was also a recipient of Roethke's work-in-progress. On May 8, 1946, Roethke wrote him from Saginaw, Michigan:

Here's a long one [probably "The Lost Son"] which I think is the best I've done so far. It's written, as you'll see right away, for the ear and not the eye. It's written to be heard, And if you don't think it's got the accent of native American speech, your name ain't W. C. Williams, I say belligerently. In a sense, it's your poem— yours and K. Burke's. He's been enthusiastic about it even in its early version. My real point, I suppose, is that I'm doing not one of these but several: with the mood or the action on the page, not talked-about, not the meditative T. S. Eliot kind of thing.

When *The Lost Son and Other Poems* appeared on March 11, 1948, it was dedicated to Burke and Williams, showing who Roethke thought had exerted the strongest influences on it.

Burke's essay on the poems of this period, "The Vegetal Radicalism of Theodore Roethke," which first appeared in the Winter 1950, issue of *Sewanee Review,* makes no claim to any influence on its author's part, though it does indicate that he was privy to Roethke's private meanings. Twenty years later it is still the authoritative gloss to the "lost son" poems.

One needn't delve too deeply to see where the affinity between Burke and Roethke begins. As early as November 1935, Roethke had had the first of a series of mental breakdowns which were to plague him periodically all his life. Also, in his early poems there emerges a growing awareness of his family, his past—especially the childhood past, and the greenhouse about which that past revolves, as subjects for poems. On this matter a note from

Burke's *Permanence and Change* is instructive: "Once a set of new meanings is firmly established, we can often note in art another kind of regression: the artist is suddenly prompted to review the memories of his youth because they combine at once the qualities of strangeness and intimacy."

Again, turning to *The Philosophy of Literary Form,* and keeping Roethke's difficulties in mind, we read that

> the poet will naturally tend to write about that which most deeply engrosses him—and nothing more deeply engrosses a man than his *burdens,* including those of a physical nature, such as disease. We win by capitalizing on our debts, by turning our liabilities into assets, by using our burdens as a basis of insight. And so the poet may come to have a "vested interest" in his handicaps; these handicaps may become an integral part of his method; and in so far as his style grows out of a disease, his loyalty to it may reinforce the disease. . . . [However,] the true locus of assertion is not in the disease, but in the *structural powers* by which the poet encompasses it.

This is particularly interesting in Roethke's case, since shortly after Christmas 1945, several of his friends saw that he was again unwell, and convinced him to enter Albany (New York) General Hospital, where he was given shock treatments. A few weeks later he entered a nursing home, from which he was released in late January 1946. Seager sees the possibility that this episode "was beneficial to the composition of *The Lost Son* and not a purely morbid or destructive period." The autumn of 1945 had been a particularly feverish period of creativity for Roethke. Drawing on a recent book, Polish psychiatrist Casimierz Dabrowski's *Positive Disintegration,* Seager tries to show how a person may benefit from his neurosis or psychosis. He summarizes Dabrowski's theory as follows:

> Personality . . . develops primarily through dissatisfaction with and the fragmentation of one's existing psychic structure. Stimulated by a lack of harmony in the self and in adaptation to the strains of the external environment, the individual "disintegrates." Anxiety, neurosis, psychosis may be *symptoms* of the disintegration and they mark a retrogression to a lower level of psychic functioning. Finally reintegration occurs at a higher level and the personality evolves to a new plateau of psychic health. Dabrowski points out that these new integrations at "higher" levels seem to happen to people of high intelligence and marked creative powers.

But is this not the same thing that Burke said, in other words, in the passage quoted above? Expanding on that passage, he writes:

> Critical and imaginative works are answers to questions posed by the situation in which they arose. They are not merely answers, they are *strategic* answers, *stylized* answers. For there is a difference in style or strategy, if one says "yes" in tonalities that imply "thank God" or in tonalities that imply "alas!" So I should propose an initial working distinction between "strategies" and "situations," whereby we think of poetry . . . as the adopting of various strategies for the encompassing of situations. These strategies size up the situations, name their structure and outstanding ingredients, and name them in a way that contains an attitude towards them.

He goes on to say that these situations are real and that the strategies for handling them have public content. Such strategies have universal relevance because the situations which they encompass overlap from individual to individual, and from historic period to historic period. One can easily see the appeal that such notions would have to a man with Roethke's troubles. We shall attempt to discover the situations he had to cope with in the "lost son" poems, and the strategies he employed in doing so.

III

"The Lost Son" itself is the best locus from which to analyze these poems because it was the first of them Roethke wrote, and because its five titled sections provide a structure which is used, with various modifications, throughout the sequence.

Here the protagonist ransacks the past in an effort to cope with a present fraught with spiritual crises. Of the First Section, "The Flight," Roethke has said in "Open Letter":

> [It] is just what it says it is: a terrified running away—with alternate periods of hallucinatory waiting (the voices, etc.); the protagonist so geared-up, so over-alive that he is hunting, like a primitive, for some animistic suggestion, some clue to existence from the subhuman. These he sees and yet does not see: they are almost tail-flicks, from another world, seen out of the corner of the eye. In a sense he goes in and out of rationality; he hangs in the balance between the human and the animal.

This running away is also a quest for a stable identity. Burke says in *Attitudes Toward History,* "Vagueness of identity is often symbolized by travel." The situation, as the first lines indicate, is the presence and fear of death. At a cemetery ("Woodlawn"), the dead cry.

This cry is often related with the boy's dead father, and is a threat to his existence. In another of the sequence, "I Need, I Need," where the protagonist is younger than he is here, the following occurs:

> Stop the larks. Can I have my heart back?
> Today I saw a beard in a cloud.
> The ground cried my name:
> Good-bye for being wrong.
> Love helps the sun.
> But not enough.

Here the beard represents the dead father, who again cries out to the son. He is angry, and has died because the son has committed some crime ("for being wrong."), has possibly caused the father's death in some way. "Love helps the sun. / But not enough," may be read in two ways. First, if the sun is taken in its traditional role as symbol of the father in his masculinity, then the son's love placates the father, but cannot return him to life. Secondly, if one reads "sun" punningly as "son," then the *mother's* love helps the child to get along in a world to which he must continually adjust, while it is not enough, at the same time, because the balance provided by the masculine love of the father is missing. Another example: in "Give Way, Ye Gates" he hears "the ghost of some great howl / Dead in a wall."

"The Lost Son" continues with images of stasis:

> I was lulled by the slamming of iron,
> A slow drip over stones,
> Toads brooding in wells.

And in a prime example of the pathetic fallacy, the son believes part of nature to be against him: "All the leaves stuck out their tongues."

At this point he realizes that this stasis is in itself a form of death, that somehow he must act to discover a solution to his problem, must shake "the softening chalk" of his bones. What follows is a prayer to the small things of creation, with whom he feels a kinship:

> Snail, snail, glister me forward,
> Bird, soft-sigh me home,
> Worm, be with me.
> This is my hard time.

Roethke's own comment on this petition helps explain his attitude. It should be borne in mind that his character is very close to being a mouthpiece for the poet himself.

> If the dead can come to our aid in a quest for identity, so can the living—and I mean *all* living things, including the subhuman. This is not so much a naive as a primitive attitude: animistic, maybe. Why not? Everything that lives is holy: I call upon these holy forms of life. One could even put this theologically: St. Thomas says, "God is above all things by the excellence of His nature; nevertheless, He is in all things as causing the being of all things." Therefore, in calling upon the snail, I am calling, in a sense, upon God.
>
> ("On 'Identity' ")

Here we have an example of what, in *The Philosophy of Literary Form*, Kenneth Burke calls magic, or verbal coercion. "If magic says, '*Let there be* such and such,' religion says, '*Please do* such and such.' The decree of magic, the petition of prayer." In effect, then, what the boy is doing is enlisting the aid of God, through His small creatures, in his quest for meaning and identity. More specifically, he is asking to be moved out of his static state "forward" and "home,"—the latter implying a social identity.

Prayer also occurs in "A Field of Light":

> Angel within me, I asked
> Did I ever curse the sun?
> Speak and abide.

By substitution, we may read "curse the father" for "curse the sun." In "I Cry, Love! Love!", the small creatures are again petitioned: "Mouse, mouse, come out of the ferns, / And small mouths, stay your aimless cheeping."

In stanzas two and three of "The Lost Son" the inertia continues. Stanza two, with its fishing imagery, signifies a search into the past ("an old wound"). But the past yields no answers, "Nothing nibbled my line, / Not even the minnows came." In stanza three the boy sits in an empty house. Again, nothing happens. In both of these stanzas the word "I," which would signify some definite identity, is missing.

Other poems of this sequence contain similar conditions of inanition. Part 1 of "A Field of Light," for instance, ends on this note: "I was there alone / In a watery drowse." In "Unfold! Unfold!" we read, "Alone, in a sleep-daze, I stared at billboards." Often this drowse is a temptation to remain mindless rather than continue the quest necessary for survival.

In stanzas four and five of "The Flight," realizing that this passive attitude won't help, the lost son again tries to petition God through the minimal creatures:

> Voice, come out of the silence.
> Say something.
> Appear in the form of a spider
> Or a moth beating the curtain.
>
> Tell me:
> Which is the way I take;
> Out of what door do I go.
> Where and to whom?

As Burke says in his *Sewanee Review* essay, "Even a rhetorical *question* is, after all, subtly, in form a *quest*. Hence the call for a sign, . . . though it leads but to veiled oracular answers, . . . transforms this opening section . . . into a hunt, however perplexed."

These veiled replies occur in the next stanza, where "dark hollows" say "lee to the wind," the moon says "back of an eel," and the salt says, "look by the sea." The answer cannot be gotten merely by the questioner's weeping and feeling sorry for himself. He must become an active seeker, and the voices in this cosmic dialogue imply that the solution to his situation isn't to be found on the social level: "You will find no comfort here, / In the kingdom of bang and blab."

Stanzas seven and eight depict a period of active, frenzied hunting after some clue. This activity is intensified in the first of these by the searcher's running past a number of objects, named one per line. In stanza eight he arrives at a river bank, an area marked by heat, slime and decay. "The Flight" ends with a riddle, as Burke has pointed out, which is contradictory and sphinx-like, as are the oracular pronouncements of the dark hollows, moon, and salt. But, he says, "Put all the disjunct details together," and "the object of the quest is lubricitous (in the mode of furtive felicity)." Here, Burke is characteristically having fun with the multiple meanings of "lubricitous," which can mean oily, unstable, lewd, capable of arousing lasciviousness, etc.

Certainly rat, leg, nose, mouse, and otter have phallic connotations, and the next to last stanza hints at masturbation:

> Take the skin of a cat
> And the back of an eel,
> Then roll them in grease,—
> That's the way it would feel.

This calls to mind the "pulling off flesh from the living planet" of another greenhouse poem, "Moss-Gathering," which action takes place in a similar swampy area as that at the end of "The Flight":

> But something always went out of me when I dug loose those
>   carpets
> Of green, or plunged to my elbows in the spongy yellowish
>   moss of the marshes:
> And afterwards I always felt mean, jogging back over the
>   logging road,
> As if I had broken the natural order of things in that
>   swampland;
> Disturbed some rhythm, old and of vast importance,
> By pulling off flesh from the living planet;
> As if I had committed, against the whole scheme of life, a
>   desecration.

As Roethke has testified in commenting on "Praise to the End!", "Onanism equals death." Whether what happens here is furtively felicitous or not, the passage is full of subconscious ("Just under the water, / It usually goes.") sexual impulses.

In *Attitudes Toward History* Burke notes the incestuous ingredients of the pit, with its "ambivalence of womb and 'cloaque,' the latter aspect tending to draw in also ingredients of 'purification by decay.' " Section 2 of "The Lost Son" is actually called "The Pit," and is made up of a series of submerged womb images, actually the kind of "slippery grave" of Roethke's "Weed Puller";

> The indignity of it!—
> With everything blooming above me,
> Lilies, pale-pink cyclamen, roses
> Whole fields lovely and inviolate,—
> Me down in that fetor of weeds,
> Crawling on all fours,
> Alive, in a slippery grave.

As Burke has pointed out, the first six lines of "The Pit" repeat the deep-down theme in a series of questions and answers, a kind of cosmic dialogue such as appears in "The Flight." "The image of mildew is made not only personal, but 'essential,' by being named as 'Mother Mildew,' " he says. Again the notion of a rebirth is underscored, but the protagonist is fearful of the incipient rebirth, since he is told (or tells himself) to "beware

Mother Mildew." The epithet "fish nerves" emphasizes his stage of evolution at this point. In "Open Letter" Roethke has described this section as "a period of physical and psychic exhaustion" where "other obsessions begin to appear (symbolized by mole, nest, fish)."

"The Pit" represents also a powerful death wish, a temptation to remain at this womb-like stage of existence, and may be compared with the passivity at the beginning of "The Flight." Either the lost son tells himself to "nibble again," or he is told by one of the cosmic voices. In this babble and muddle of statements, one can never be sure. In any event, he doesn't succumb to the fear of a painful rebirth.

Variations on this "pit" theme occur in "A Field of Light," which begins:

> Came to lakes; came to dead water,
> Ponds with moss and leaves floating,
> Planks sunk in the sand.

The following passage from the same poem comes extremely close to repeating the imagery of "The Pit":

> Under, under the sheaves,
> Under the blackened leaves,
> Behind the green viscid trellis,
> In the deep grass at the edge of field,
> Along the low ground dry only in August.

Opening sections of "The Shape of the Fire," "Bring the Day!", "Unfold! Unfold!", and "O, Thou Opening, O" contain similar images of slime, with its attendant animals, the rats, moles, fish, snails, frogs, and so on.

Roethke has said of section 3 of "The Lost Son," "The Gibber," that the obsessions of "The Pit" begin to take hold there, and "again there is a frenetic activity, then a lapsing back into almost a crooning serenity." (in "Open Letter") The title, which means "gibberish," and the short lines and heavy rhymes of the first three stanzas, convey the intensity of the speaker's activity. Evidently he has escaped from the pit, for he listens "at the wood's mouth, / By the cave's door" to a familiar noise, the howling of "dogs of the groin," the sexual urge. The sun, symbol of the father, is against him, and the moon, or mother, rejects him, as does the natural world:

> The weeds whined,
> The snakes cried,
> The cows and briers
> Said to me: Die.

The young man's sexual activities are again *contra naturam,* and his alienation is complete. Burke believes that the "frenetic activity" in these stanzas ends "in the act that corresponds to the attitude implicit in the opening scene. It is sexual, but reflexively so: the poet is disastrously alone."

What follows is a slower movement, the "lapsing back into almost a crooning serenity" mentioned above. Karl Malkoff has pointed out that "Hath the rain a father?" is taken from Job 38:28, as is the imagery of the entire passage, and also the questions about the origins of life found in "The Pit." "The alienation of Job from his father is an important symbol of the poem's meaning; the protagonist's father appears here in his most frightening aspect" (*Theodore Roethke: An Introduction to the Poetry*). "Father Fear," whose "look drained the stones" represents not only the young man's father, but the angry God of Job as well. As in later sections of the poem, and in other poems in the sequence, the lost son merges his father with an alternately benevolent and protective, alternately angry and dangerous, God.

In this stanza new imagery is introduced: "All the caves are ice. Only the snow's here, / I'm cold. I'm cold all over. Rub me in father and mother." In Burke's *Attitudes Toward History* one reads that

> "ice" tends to emphasize castration and frigidity. (Severe mountains, winter, Arctic exploration, death of the individual or the world by cold. . . .) The mountain contains incestuous ingredients (the mountain as mother, with frigidity as symbolic punishment for the offense).

Once again, then, the incest motif occurs, explaining the presence of the angry God-father figure.

In "Give Way, Ye Gates," there is a similar situation, with its final line indicating the punishment for incestuous crimes:

> Mother of blue and the many changes of hay,
> This tail hates a flat path.
> I've let my nose out;
> I could melt down a stone,—
>
> . . . .
> We're king and queen of the right ground.
> I'll risk the winter for you.

What follows is "the ghost of some great howl / Dead in a wall," the wrath of the father. That this is a masturbation fantasy is evident from the line "We'll swinge the instant!", with its play on the several meanings of "swinge" (to thrash or punish, thump, singe) all pertinent. Also, consider the end of the stanza:

> In the high-noon of thighs,
> In the springtime of stones,
> We'll stretch with the great stems.
> We'll be at the business of what might be
> Looking toward what we are.

Here the commercial, "business" aspect, which will be discussed at length further on, is mentioned, as well as the reflexive, narcissistic character of "looking toward what we are."

Returning to "The Lost Son," the following three stanzas, again the short-lined stanzas, detail what is probably an erotic dream which "is rendered in terms of balked sexual experience," according to "Open Letter."

> What gliding shape
> Beckoning through halls,
> Stood poised on the stair,
> Fell dreamily down?
>
> From the mouths of jugs
> Perched on many shelves,
> I saw substance flowing
> That cold morning.
>
> Like the slither of eels
> That watery cheek
> As my own tongue kissed
> My lips awake.

Again, in the last two lines, the narcissistic note is sounded.

In the next stanza, which is a kind of Elizabethan rant, and whose purpose is hinted at in the question "Is this the storm's heart?", the images are of fire ("Do the bones cast out their fire?"; "All the windows are burning!"), ice ("Let the gestures freeze.") and growth from rot ("Is the seed leaving the old bed? These buds are live as birds.") We have already seen Burke's discussion of decay and ice as images of purification. Of the third image found here, fire, he says:

> Purification by fire, "trial by fire," probably suggests "incest-awe." (As in some mystics' dream of "the sun death," where one is both welcomed into the sun and consumed by it. The sun was

originally a female, the goddess of fertility as preserved in the German "Frau Sonne.")

(Attitudes Toward History)

Mingled fire and ice imagery also occurs in "Bring the Day!": "I'm a biscuit. I'm melted already. / The white weather hates me."

The young man's isolation is emphasized again in this part of "The Lost Son" by the lack of compassion he sees in the social order:

> Where, where are the tears of the world?
> Let the kisses resound, flat like a butcher's palm;
> Let the greatness freeze; our doom is already decided.

But the following line, "All the windows are burning! What's left of my life?" indicates that a change is taking place. Fearing this change, he again yearns for the safety of the womb, "the lash of primordial milk." But "the time-order is going," the protective and permissive world of childhood is disappearing. In the next four lines, several levels of meaning are intermingled:

> I have married my hands to perpetual agitation,
> I run, I run to the whistle of money.
>
> > Money money money
> > Water water water.

Of this Burke says,

> Roethke's Vegetal Radicalism is not the place one would normally look for comments on the economic motive. Yet you can take it as a law that, in our culture, at a moment of extreme mental anguish, if the sufferer is accurate there will be an accounting of money, too. It will be at least implicit, in the offing— hence with professional utterers it should be explicit. So, the agitation comes to a head in the juxtaposing of two liquidities, two potencies, one out of society, the other universal, out of nature.

One of Burke's earlier observations on alienation and economics may have given rise to Roethke's lumping them together in "The Lost Son," though certainly the economic problem was real enough to him:

> An increasing number of people become alienated by material dispossession. And an increasing number who still share some

material advantages from the ailing economic structure become spiritually alienated as they lose faith in the structure's "reason-ableness." One may be materially or spiritually alienated, or both.

(*The Philosophy of Literary Form*)

Of course "I have married my hands to perpetual agitation" may be inter-preted on both sexual and commercial levels, and one should also note "John-of-the-thumb's jumping; / Commodities, here we come!" in "Sensi-bility! O La!"

After a brief period of calm, characterized by imagery of the natural world, flashes of white light follow, and in his overaliveness the lost son associates himself with the natural world ("I've more veins than a tree"), and falls "through a dark swirl," a near-blackout, as Roethke says in "Open Letter." Burke sees this as the poem's actual abysmal moment, after which a rebirth ensues.

Section 4, "The Return," brings the lost son back to the greenhouse of childhood. What has gone before is treated as if it were a dream, for the first stanza describes not only the trip to the greenhouse, but recapitulates the night journey of sections 1 through 3:

> The way to the boiler was dark,
> Dark all the way,
> Over the slippery cinders
> Through the long greenhouse.

The roses, which "kept breathing in the dark," mirror his ability to do the same, to stay alive in spite of the fears and ordeals of the slimy pit, to be capable of regeneration.

In stanza three the theme of light is carried over from the end of "The Gibber":

> There was always a single light
> Swinging by the fire-pit,
> Where the fireman pulled out roses,
> The big roses, the big bloody clinkers.

Here the natural world of the flowers contains analogies with the human world, since they too survive a fire-pit (an image which combines two of the three purifying agents in "The Gibber").

Light is again prevalent in the next stanza, with the coming of day opposed to all the previous imagery of darkness.

Once I stayed all night.
The light in the morning came slowly over the white
Snow.
There were many kinds of cool
Air.
Then came steam.

This passage, with its tone of rational observation, should be compared with the shorter, choppier lines of the previous sections as well as with the rant in part 3, for coupled with the changes in imagery are changes in the young man's feelings, as shown in this new tone. The coolness of the air, and the coming of the comforting steam, also bring "Papa."

Pipe-knock

Scurry of warm over small plants.
Ordnung! ordnung!
Papa is coming!

Roethke's statement on this action is extremely important to a reading of the poem:

Buried in the text are many little ambiguities, not all of which are absolutely essential to the central meaning of the poem. For instance, the "pipe-knock." With the coming of steam, the pipes begin knocking violently, in a greenhouse. But "Papa," or the florist, as he approached, often would knock the pipe he was smoking on the sides of the benches, or on the pipes. Then, with the coming of steam and "papa"—the papa on earth and heaven are blended—there is the sense of motion in the greenhouse, my symbol for the whole of life, a womb, a heaven-on-earth.

("Open Letter")

Burke's essay on Roethke's "vegetal radicalism" has an appropriate gloss to this which shows that he had access to the poet's private meanings:

Recalling De Quincey's comments on the knocking at the gate after the murder scene in Macbeth, and recalling that we have just been through a "suicide" scene, might we not also include, among the connotations of this sound, the knock of conscience? Particularly in that the return to the paternally (or "super-ego-istically") rational is announced in terms of admonition (*Ordnung! ordnung!*)—and we should note, on the side, as a possible motivating factor in Roethke's avoidance of ideational abstraction, that this German word for order is one of his few such expressions, though here it has practically the force of an imperative verb, . . . (Roethke has said that he had in mind the father's Prussian love of discipline, as sublimated into the care of flowers; and he wanted to suggest that the child, as a kind of sleepy sentry, "jumped to attention at the approach.")

In *Attitudes Toward History,* written many years before both "The Lost Son" and the *Seeanee Review* essay, Burke had made comments similar to those above. Writing on the punning game, "knock-knock," which became popular during the Depression, he said,

> We recall De Quincey's comments on the way guilt was symbolized in *Macbeth* by the knocking at the gate. Recall also the varient in the Negro spiritual, "Somebody's Knocking at Your Door." We should also recall the "tapping," "gentle rapping" Poe's raven. . . .
>
> In the case of *Macbeth,* the knocking called forth a passage of *lewdness* an expulsion of filth. Sometimes it seems to have frightened Joyce similarly. One finds a kindred manifestation in the naive expulsion of filth in many of our so-called "realistic" novelists. Might there be lurking behind this literary symptom something like the fear that in the child causes evacuation?

Clearly some of this works for the pipe-knock in "The Lost Son," especially when tied up with the German *Ordnung,* which means not only "attention," but "order" and "cleanliness." The rational God-father figure puts everything in the greenhouse in order, and his coming as a kindly God, rather than as Father Fear of "The Gibber," plainly expunges the guilt the son felt earlier. If one wishes to read *ordnung* or order as a pun, then it can also mean "ordure," or manure, with which, according to Roethke, his father as greenhouse keeper was perpetually occupied:

> Fertilizer is a constant problem. My father literally spent weeks scouring the valley contracting with farmers for cowdung. Whether he insisted on a particular breed of cattle, I can't say but even that could be possible. Such were the lengths to which Prussian perfectionism was carried. . . . He insisted on richness, wetness, thick consistency, and above all, age. It got so I thought the only important part of the farm was back of the barn. . . . [The manure machine was] a veritable Roman bath: about forty

by twenty-five feet, with an assembly of pipes, faucets, steam-
gauges, a cat-walk for the attending mixture of the brew, which
was a special, I dare-say, scent formula—such was the nature of
the Roethke's manure, lime, hot water, bone-meal, and God
knows what else. Anyway, it grew roses.

(*The Glass House: The Life of Theodore Roethke*)

Is it any wonder that the son's awe of the father was so great? He was able
to produce roses from filth, a feat which must have made the boy envious
indeed.

That "Papa" is also the sun (cf. "The sun was against me," of part 3),
his influence here clearly reveals:

> A fine haze moved off the leaves;
> Frost melted on far panes;
> The rose, the chrysanthemum turned toward the light.
> Even the hushed forms, the bent yellowy weeds
> Moved in a slow up-sway.

It is on this note, with the flowers moving toward the sun, upward, and the
implied corresponding state of mind in the boy, that this section comes to an
end.

IV

At this point a closer look at the "papa" figure should be taken, since
next to the young protagonist he is the most important and fully-realized
character in the sequence.

Wilhelm Roethke, who had been head forester on the estate of Bismark's
sister, arrived in Saginaw, Michigan, from Germany in 1872. Otto, Theodore
Roethke's father, was still a baby at that time. When Wilhelm had made
enough money from his market garden, he built a greenhouse on his property and began to raise flowers. Two of his three sons, Charles and Otto,
later took over the greenhouse, Charles managing the business end, Otto
growing the flowers.

At its peak, the firm occupied twenty-five acres within the city of
Saginaw, a quarter of a million feet under glass. Otto Roethke lived in a
frame house directly in front of the greenhouse, Charles next door. It was
the largest floral establishment in Michigan, as well as the most complete,
since it had its own icehouse, game preserve, and owned the last stand of
virgin timber in the Saginaw Valley. And Otto's specialities were orchids
and roses, many of which were grown as experiments and never sold.

"Old Florist," from part 1 of *The Lost Son,* conveys Roethke's admiration for his father's green thumb, as does "Transplanting," here quoted in full:

> Watching hands transplanting,
> Turning and tamping,
> Lifting the young plants with two fingers,
> Sifting in a palm-full of fresh loam,—
> One swift movement,—
> Then plumping in the bunched roots,
> A single twist of the thumbs, a tamping and turning,
> All in one,
> A shaking down, while the stem stays straight,
> Once, twice, and a faint third thump,—
> Into the flat-box it goes,
> Ready for the long days under the sloped glass:
>
> The sun warming the fine loam,
> The young horns winding and unwinding,
> Creaking their thin spines,
> The underleaves, the smallest buds
> Breaking into nakedness,
> The blossoms extending
> Out into the sweet air,
> The whole flower extending outward,
> Stretching and reaching.

The observations in this poem show that Roethke saw a good deal of what his father did for a living, and, according to poems like "Moss-Gathering" and "Weed Puller," actually helped out himself.

But in other poems, notably in "My Papa's Waltz," another side of Otto Roethke is revealed. Here he is a figure of terror to his young son:

> The whiskey on your breath
> Could make a small boy dizzy;
> But I hung on like death:
> Such waltzing was not easy.
>
> We romped until the pans
> Slid from the kitchen shelf;
> My mother's countenance
> Could not unfrown itself.

> The hand that held my wrist
> Was battered on one knuckle;
> At every step you missed
> My right ear scraped a buckle.
>
> You beat time on my head
> With a palm caked hard by dirt,
> Then waltzed me off to bed
> Still clinging to your shirt.

And in "Otto," from Roethke's last volume, *The Far Field*, he is pictured as a pillar of strength:

> Once when he saw two poachers on his land,
> He drew his rifle over with one hand;
> Dry bark flew in their faces from his shot,—
> He always knew what he was aiming at.
> They stood there with their guns, he walked toward,
> Without his rifle, and slapped each one hard;
> It was no random act, for those two men
> Had slaughtered game, and cut young fir trees down.
> I was no more than seven at the time.

The Seager biography makes use of several of Roethke's schoolboy essays to get at the root of the poet's feelings toward his father. One, probably written in high school, in which Roethke calls himself "John," shows how sensitive he was to his father's anger:

> Papa and the man were fixing the well. They had the top off. You could lie on your stomach and look very deep into the black water. He thought it would be wonderful to spit down there. He did. It went floating down like foam, then bobbed like a paper boat. Just when he felt so nice and dreamy, Papa grabbed him by the collar and boxed his ears until his head reeled. "You dirty boy!" he yelled. "Schkeckliches Kind!" echoed Bob, the foreman, who always agreed with Papa.

This not only shows what a dreamy child Roethke must have been, but may also be a source for his feeling of having been defiled by life (compare "You dirty boy!").

Again, in an essay which may have been written for a rhetoric course at the University of Michigan, Roethke narrates the story of a fishing trip, this time in the first person. He describes himself as having been very awkward as a child. He was always stumbling, flushing the game too soon, rocking the boat, and asking too many questions, all in the manner of small boys. One day his father forbade him to accompany him on a fishing trip because on the previous day he had knocked the father's hat into the water. The boy, fishing alone in an anchored boat, caught a large pike, which pulled the pole, his father's favorite, out of his hands. He followed the fish about the lake until it tired, and when it did he retrieved both pole and fish. When Otto Roethke returned and saw the size of the pike, he asked how he had caught him, and the young Roethke answered, "Well, I let your pole fall in the water." To this the father's guide responded, "By God, Otto! That's an old trick, throwing your pole in the water. It's the only way to tire a big fish out when you ain't got a reel. There aren't many people would know enough to do that!" This made Otto Roethke proud, and aside from showing that the guide may have shrewdly saved the younger Roethke's skin, this anecdote reveals in its conclusion the boy's overwhelming desire to please his father:

> And that was the sweetest moment in a day filled with glory, far more thrilling than the first tug of the pike, or the horrible first glimpse of him, or the hand-to-hand struggle, or the calm peace that followed. I had been adjudged clever of hand and mind for the first time in my life and I hadn't deserved it.

In his chapter on Roethke's mental difficulties, Seager says that this feeling of unworthiness plagued Roethke all his life. Dr. Ian Shaw, one of the psychiatrists who examined him during his years in Seattle, said that the periods after he had won a prize (and he won many, including a Fulbright, two National Book Awards, two Guggenheim Fellowships, an award from the American Academy of Arts and Letters, and a Pulitzer Prize, among others) were often the worst because his pervading sense of guilt never permitted him to believe that he deserved them.

Returning again to the first piece, which ends with "John" seeing his grandfather's maid in his father's arms, Roethke concluded, "Then he crept out the back door, feeling quite happy. He wouldn't worry any more. He hated Papa." Seager believes that Roethke saw his father as a short-tempered man, and doubted that the man loved him. Thus, the hatred expressed by "John" was probably quite real, and a great source of guilt as well. In April 1923, Otto Roethke died of cancer. Two months before, his brother Charles had committed suicide after financial misdealings which cost the family their greenhouse. Theodore Roethke, not yet fifteen, had lost his whole meaningful world at a time when a boy could still believe that his father was more than a man—perhaps even a God. To the end of his life he was to feel this loss, as these lines from an uncollected poem, "The Old Florist's lament," published in *The Spectator* in 1962 show: "When Otto Roethke went to bed, / That was the end of day."

Who can say how deeply the loss of his father affects a boy of fourteen? There is the possibility that the awakening of sexuality at puberty and the subsequent death of the father were in some way coupled in the boy's mind. Thus the tremendous guilt and the howling ghost in these poems.

V

Of the final section of "The Lost Son," "*It was beginning winter,*" the poet has said in "Open Letter," "Illumination, the coming of light suggested at the end of the last passage occurs again, this time to the nearly grown man. But the illumination is still only partly apprehended; he is still 'waiting.' " This coming of light occurs at "beginning winter, / An in-between time," when the slowly moving light over the snow provides a background for the surviving natural things, the seed-crowns and "bones of weeds" which are emblematic of the young man's own survival. His mind, like the light, also moves, "not alone, / through the clear air, in the silence." This describes a Unity of Being similar to that sought by Yeats.

> Was it light?
> Was it light within?
> Was it light within light?
> Stillness becoming alive,
> Yet still?
>
> A lively understandable spirit
> Once entertained you.
> It will come again.
> Be still.
> Wait.

This conclusion, as "Open Letter" indicates, leaves the lost son still waiting for the "lively understandable spirit" in what is a patient religious vigil for *further* illumination. In other poems in this group, with their further regressions into the dark areas beneath the conscious mind, there are moments of silence and illumination, and some growth of the spirit, but the slipping-back will always be necessary for the going-forward.

VI

In "Main Components of Ritual," from *Attitudes Toward History,* Burke discusses the organization of works of art in a way which will explain the structure of "The Lost Son" and what happens in it. Indeed, the ingredients named by Burke are so similar to those in this sequence of poems as a whole, and so unlike the ingredient in Roethke's earlier poems, that one can hardly doubt that he studied and applied Burke's theories.

Burke begins: "The organization of a work can be considered with relation to a "key" symbol of authority. The work is a ritual whereby the poet takes inventory with reference to the acceptance or rejection of this authority." The symbol of authority in "The Lost Son," as in the other poems of this group, is of course, the father, who by the end of the poem is accepted as the god-like sponsor of growth (of the greenhouse and child both), rather than the angry, inscrutable God of Job, who is capable of destroying his children.

Burke continues: "If the ingredient of acceptance is uppermost, the poet tends to cancel the misfit between himself and the frame [of authority] by "tragic ambiguity," whereby he both expresses his "criminality" and exorcises it through symbolic punishment." Of course, this "criminality" need not be anything punishable by law, as Burke notes in *Permanence and Change,* but can be a transgression which the author feels he has committed internally. Thus, in "The Lost Son," one has the elements of masturbation and symbolic incest, which would anger the father, and which the protagonist expiates in the symbolic death and rebirth through pit, fire, and ice.

"Authority symbols of the mature adult," says Burke,

> involve such intellectualistic or philosophic concepts as church, state, society, political party, craft. They are largely "forensic." But in treating them with *engrossment* (as the organized selectivity of his work requires) he is induced to integrate them with the deepest responses of his experience. These are found in the "pre-political" period of childhood. They deal with rudiments (tables, chairs, attic, cellar, food, excretion, animals), with peculiarities of sense (different qualities of voice, the sound of rain and wind, the soft thud of wet snow against the window pane, phenomena of heat and cold, etc.), with "formative" events (accidents, illnesses, Christmas, excursions, dreams), and with intimate relationships (parents and other relatives, nurses, teachers,

priests, doctors, policemen, etc., incipient manifestations of the authoritarian relationships).

("Main Components of Ritual")

Here one sees the lost son's engrossment with money as a symbol of "forensic" authority ("Money money money / Water water water") and its association with water, an element with connotations of cleanliness from the "pre-political" childhood period. The forensic, adult authority figure of God, present for the child in the figure of the father, also represents an integration of the adult political world and the "pre-political" childhood world. And what more formative event is there in the life of a child than the premature death of his father?

Hence,

> "symbolic regression" takes place in that the poet, in the thoroughness of his sincerity, necessarily draws upon the pre-forensic pre-political ("autistic") level of informative experience, even when symbolizing his concern with purely forensic matter. A concern with a purely social symbol of authority, when the poet organizes a work with relation to it, will be found to contain vestiges of meanings derived from his family patterns of experiences (for instance, his King or his God or his philosophy may be much like one of his parents, in the "quality" he attaches to the symbol).

The relationship between the lost son's father and God should be obvious by this time, but if one looks at this from the "forensic," adult point of view, what has happened in the son's changing of his father from an angry God to a benevolent one representing order, growth, and protection is that on the adult level he has actually changed his notion of God in the same way, and thus come to some kind of acceptance of death, and not death as punishment or annihilation for sin, but death with the implication of a following rebirth, as figured in the greenhouse as a discovered pattern of experience. Also, included in this pattern would be the possibility of psychic growth.

When rejection of the figure of authority is uppermost, Burke states, there will be elements of symbolic parricide in the poem. But when acceptance is uppermost, there will be symbols of castration and incest-awe. In the ice and fire symbolism of "The Lost Son," we have already noted the elements of castration and incest-awe, and in the various images of decay and rot, slime and the pit, the symbolization of incipient rebirth. As Burke puts it, "Since the ritual of 'transcendence,' whereby he adjusts himself to his adult responsibilities as he sees them, involves a 'dramatic change of identity,' symbolic regression takes place in that he symbolizes rebirth."

A more obvious change of identity occurs in the following stanzas from "The Shape of the Fire":

> Pleasure on ground
> Has no sound,
> Easily maddens
> The uneasy man.
>
> Who, careless, slips
> In coiling ooze
> Is trapped to the lips,
> Leaves more than shoes;
>
> Must pull off clothes
> To jerk like a frog
> On belly and nose
> From the sucking bog.

The masturbatory rhythm found in "The Lost Son" is evident here, as well as the image of Onan, who cast his seed upon the ground and was killed by God. The ooze of the pit, with the lowly frog, a symbol of the young man's evolutionary stage again, are also present. The removal of clothes in this pit also involves a rebirth into a new identity, as Burke notes in *The Philosophy of Literary Form*, where he speaks of

> the importance of the *name* as an important aspect of synecdote (the name as fetishistic representative of the named, as a very revealing part of the same cluster). . . . Such identification by name has a varient in change of clothes, or a change of surroundings in general, a change of "environmental clothes."

And, expanding on this in a note:

> The thought suggests a possible interpretation of nudism as a symbolic divesting (unclothing) of guilt, a symbolic purification arrived at thus: (1) There has been the hiding of the shameful, hence the clothing of the pudenda as the "essence" of guilt; (2) the covering, as synecdochic representative of the covered, has come to participate in the same set of equations, taking on the same quality or essence, literally "by contagion"; (3) hence, by removing the clothes, one may at the same time ritualistically

remove the shame of which the clothes are "representative."
The resultant identity is a *social* one, in that the nudists form
a colony.

In the earlier *Permanence and Change,* Burke had said, "Nudism represents an attempt to return to essentials, to get at the irreducible minimum
of human certainty." Both of these interpretations of divested clothing apply here, the latter when we consider Roethke's statement from "Open
Letter"; "Some of these pieces, then, begin in the mire; as if man is no more
than a shape writhing from the old rock." What is "the old rock" if not "the
irreducible minimum of human certainty," a phrase which points to another
relevant statement of Burke's: "[The artist will] tend to found his art upon
an irreducible minimum of belief. This irreducible minimum is, obviously,
his personal range of experiences, his own exaltations and depressions, his
specific kinds of triumph and difficulty" (*Counter-Statement.*)
    Seager relates that one of Roethke's idiosyncrasies during the writing of
these poems was

> popping out of his clothes, wandering around [Shingle Cottage]
> naked for a while, then dressing slowly, four or five times a day.
> There are some complex "birthday-suit" meanings here, the rit-
> ual of starting clean like a baby, casting one's skin like a snake,
> and then donning the skin again. It was not exhibitionism. No
> one saw. It was all a kind of magic.

One could speculate that the "magic" included the arrival at that "irreducible minimum of human certainty."
    In part 4 of "Praise to the End!", after crawling from the mire, the
protagonist says, "I lost my identity to a pebble." The change here is accompanied by a reintegration with nature: "The minnows love me, and the
humped and spitting creatures," and a new identity is secured: "The dark
showed me a face." And finally, in "O, Thou Opening, O," he says, "Forgive me a minute, nymph. / I'll change the image, and my shoes," a statement which is certainly related to Burke's ideas on change of identity and
the divesting of clothing.
    In "Main Components of Ritual" Burke continues:

> The change of identity (whereby he is at once the same man and
> a new man) gives him a greater complexity of coordinates. He
> "sees around the corner." He is "prophetic," endowed with
> "perspective." We need not here concern ourselves with the ac-
> curacy of his perspectives; we need only note its existence. It

makes him either "wiser" or "more foolish" than he was—in any case, it forms the basis upon which the ramifications of his work is based. Thus, in Mann's novels, Joseph is not equipped to be a "prophet" until he has been reborn in the pit.

After the lost son's rebirth, with his subsequent new perspectives on God, his father, and his past, he too is "wiser" in that he knows the virtue of waiting for the "lively understandable spirit." Changes of perspective, Burke says, "tend to be symbolized by imagery referring to behavior of the eye." Examining the final section of "The Lost Son," "*It was beginning winter*," one finds that the young man has become passive. He is waiting for the moment of illumination. The most active sense here is sight, for he *sees* the light moving slowly over the brown landscape, the weeds swinging over the blue snow. There is little activity of the other senses, as in earlier sections of the poem.

As a process of socialization whereby the poet adjusts himself to the necessities of survival in the adult world, the rebirth process will involve a "womb-heaven," the embryo, and a "first revolution" which takes place when the shelter of that embryo becomes a confinement. "Hence," says Burke, "when you examine this ritual, you find such symbols as the 'pit,' a symbolic return to, and return from the womb." One need only note again in passing that the title of section 2 of "The Lost Son" is "The Pit," and that it corresponds to Burke's notion of what a "pit" is and does, but more important is Roethke's reference in "Open Letter" to the greenhouse as a "womb-heaven," a "symbol for the whole of life, a womb, a heaven-on-earth." Such similarities in phrasing are additional proof of Roethke's familiarity with Burke's critical theories.

The return to and from the womb, Burke goes on to explain, "involves 'incest-awe,'"

> since the adult can return to the mother, not as a sexually inexperienced infant, but as a lover. It involves homosexuality (actual or symbolic) since it involves an affront to the bipolar relationships of mother and father, and since a shift in allegiance to the symbols of authority equals the symbolic slaying of a parent. It involves castration symbolism, connotations of the "neuter," by way of punishment for the symbolic offense.

We have already noted the elements of incest-awe and castration in "The Lost Son," and Burke has said in *Attitudes Toward History* that often redemption by decay, symbolized by green newness arising from filth and rot, as in "The Lost Son," "seems to gravitate towards connotations of the homosexual (as in the novels of André Gide)." We would qualify any such reading of homosexual activity in these poems by noting Burke's later statement in *The Philosophy of Literary Form* that

> symbolic incest is often but a roundabout mode of self-engrossment, *quite likely at the decadent end of individualism,* where the poet is but expressing in sexual imagery a pattern of thought that we might call simply "communion with the self," and is giving this state of mind concrete material body in the imagery of sexual cohabitation with someone "of the same substance" as the self [italics mine].

This helps explain incest-awe in these poems not as incest-awe as such, but as onanistic "self-engrossment," which we have already seen in action. And we might also read in the images of sprouting seed the same kind of activity.

Again, we might see the guilt of the young man, especially in the confrontation with his father, as caused by this transference of allegiance to the mother, hence the feeling that the son is responsible for the father's death. Biographically, the death of Roethke's father at the onset of puberty may have aroused just such guilt.

In any case, "The Lost Son" and other poems of this sequence may be read as rituals of rebirth, private masses whereby the young man accommodates himself to the adult forensic world by returning to the autistic world of childhood and beyond into the subconscious mind, enduring a change of identity (which makes him both a new man and the old man) with a resulting change of perspective which permits him to live his life in a better way. In other words, a situation containing a problem has been presented, and a strategy for overcoming that situation has been carried out. As Burke has said in *The Philosophy of Literary Form:*

> *The difference between the symbolic drama and the drama of living is a difference between imaginary obstacles and real obstacles.* But: the imaginary obstacles of symbolic drama must, to have the relevance necessary for the producing of effects upon audiences, reflect the real obstacles of living drama.

JAMES DICKEY

The Greatest American Poet:
Theodore Roethke

Once there were three men in the living room of an apartment in Seattle. Two of them were present in body, watching each other with the wariness of new acquaintance, and the other was there by telephone. The two in Carolyn Kizer's apartment were Theodore Roethke and I, and the voice was Allan Seager in Michigan. All three had been drinking, I the most, Roethke the next most, and Seager, apparently, the least. After a long-distance joke about people I had never heard of, Roethke said, "Allan, I want you to meet a friend of mine. He's a great admirer of yours, by the way."

I picked up the phone and said, according to conviction and opportunity, "This is Charles Berry."

"This is *who?*"

"Your son, Amos. Charles Berry, the poet."

"The *hell* it is!"

"I thought you might like to know what happened to Charles after the end of the novel. In one way or the other, he became me. My name is James Dickey."

"Well, thanks for telling me. But I had other plans for Charles. Maybe even using him in another novel. I think he did finally become a poet. But not you."

"No, no; it's a joke."

"I had it figured. But it ain't funny."

"Sorry," I said. "I meant it as a kind of tribute, I guess."

"Well, thanks, I guess."

"Joke or not, I think your book *Amos Berry* is a great novel."

From *Sorties.* © 1971 by James Dickey. Doubleday, 1971.

"I do too, but nobody else does. It's out of print, with the rest of my stuff."

"Listen," I said, trying to get into the phone, "I doubt if I'd've tried to be a poet if it weren't for Charles Berry. There was no call for poetry in my background, any more than there was in his. But he wanted to try, and he kept on with it. So I did, too."

"How about Amos? What did you think of him?"

"I like to think he's possible. My God! A middle-aged businessman trying to kick off all of industrial society! Get rid of the whole of Western civilization and go it on his own!"

"Yeah, but he failed."

"He failed, but it was a failure that mattered. And the scenes after the rebellious poet-son meets the rebellious father who's just killed his employer and gotten away with it—well, that's a *meeting!* And Amos turns out to be proud of his boy, who's doing this equally insane thing of writing poetry. Right?"

"Sure. Sure he's proud. Like many another, when the son has guts and does something strange and true to what he is. Say, is Ted Roethke still around there?"

"Yes. He's right here. Want to speak to him?"

"No; but he's another one. He's one of those sons. But his father didn't live long enough to know it."

That was my introduction to Allan Seager, a remarkable man and a writer whose works—*Equinox, The Inheritance, Amos Berry, Hilda Manning, The Old Man of the Mountain, The Death of Anger, A Frieze of Girls*—will, as Henry James said of his own, "kick off their tombstones" time after time, in our time and after. His last book and his only biography, *The Glass House,* is this life of Roethke, who is in my opinion the greatest poet this country has yet produced.

During his life and after his death in 1963, people interested in poetry heard a great many rumors about Roethke. Most of these had to do with his eccentricities, his periodic insanity, his drinking, his outbursts of violence, his unpredictability. He came to be seen as a self-destructive American genius somewhat in the pattern of Dylan Thomas. Roethke had a terrifying half-tragic, half-low-comedy life out of which he lifted, by the strangest and most unlikely means, and by endless labors and innumerable false starts, the poetry that all of us owe it to ourselves to know and cherish. If Beethoven said, "He who truly understands my music can never know unhappiness again," Roethke's best work says with equal authority, "He who truly opens himself to my poems will never again conceive his earthly life as worthless."

The Glass House is the record—no, the story, for Seager's novelistic talents give it that kind of compellingness—of how such poetry as Roethke's came to exist. It was written by a man who battled for his whole adult life against public indifference to novels and stories he knew were good, and fought to his last conscious hour to finish this book. Some time after meeting him by telephone, which was in the spring of 1963, I came to know him better, and two summers ago spent a week with him in Tecumseh, Michigan. Most of that time we talked about the biography and about Roethke, and went over the sections he had completed. From the first few words Seager read me, I could tell that this was no *mere* literary biography; there was too much of a sense of personal identification between author and subject to allow for mereness. Seager said to me, in substance, what he had written to a friend some time before this:

> Beatrice Roethke, the widow of Theodore Roethke, has asked me to write the authorized life of her husband. I was in college with him and knew him fairly intimately the rest of his life. It is a book I'd like to do. Quite aside from trying to evoke the character that made the poetry, there are a good many things to say about the abrasion of the artist in America that he exemplifies. We were both born in Michigan, he in Saginaw, I in Adrian. We both came from the same social stratum. Much of his life I have acted out myself.

Though Seager did not witness the whole process of Roethke's development, not having known the poet in his childhood, he did see a great deal of it, and he told me that he had seen what happened to Roethke happen "in an evolutionary way." More than once he said, "Ted started out as a phony and became genuine, like Yeats." And, "I had no idea that he'd end up as fine a poet as he did. No one knew that in the early days, Ted least of all. We all knew he *wanted* to be a great poet or a great something, but to a lot of us that didn't seem enough. I could have told you, though, that his self-destructiveness would get worse. I could have told you that awful things were going to happen to him. He was headed that way; at times he seemed eager to speed up the process."

I saw Roethke only twice myself. I saw only a sad fat man who talked continually of joy, and although I liked him well enough for such a short acquaintance, came away from him each time with a distinct sense of relief. Like everyone else who knew him even faintly, I was pressed into service in the cause of his ego, which reeled and tottered pathetically at all hours and under all circumstances, and required not only props, but the *right* props.

What did I think of Robert Lowell, Randall Jarrell, and "the Eastern literary gang"? What did I think of the "gutless Limey reviewers" in the *Times Literary Supplement?* I spent an afternoon with him trying to answer such questions, before giving a reading at the University of Washington. Carolyn Kizer, an old friend and former student of Roethke's, had given a party the day before the reading, and I was introduced to Roethke there. Though I had heard various things about him, ranging from the need to be honest with him to the absolute need *not* to be honest, I was hardly prepared for the way in which, as Southerners used to say, he "carried on." I was identified in his mind only as the man who had said (in the *Virginia Quarterly Review,* to be exact) that he was the greatest poet then writing in English. He kept getting another drink and bringing me one and starting the conversation over from that point, leading (more or less naturally for him, I soon discovered) into a detailed and meticulously quoted list of what other poets and critics had said about him. I got the impression that my name was added to those of Auden, Stanley Kunitz, Louise Bogan, and Rolfe Humphries not because I was in any way as distinguished in Roethke's mind as they were, but because I had provided him with a kind of *climactic* comment; something he needed that these others hadn't quite managed to say, at least in print. And later, when he introduced me at the reading, he began with the comment, and talked for eight or ten minutes about himself, occasionally mentioning me as though by afterthought. I did not resent this, though I found it curious, and I bring it up now only to call attention to qualities that must have astonished and confounded others besides myself.

Why should a poet of Roethke's stature conduct himself in this childish and embarrassing way? Why all this insistence on being the best, the acknowledged best, the *written-up* best? Wasn't the poetry itself enough? And why the really appalling pettiness about other writers, like Lowell, who were not poets to him but rivals merely? There was never a moment that I was with Roethke when I was not conscious of something like this going on in his mind; never a moment when he did not have the look of a man fighting for his life in some way known only to him. The strain was in the very air around him; his broad, babyish face had an expression of constant bewilderment and betrayal, a continuing agony of doubt. He seemed to cringe and brace himself at the same time. He would glare from the corners of his eyes and turn wordlessly away. Then he would enter into a long involved story about himself. "I used to spar with Steve Hamas," he would say. I remember trying to remember who Steve Hamas was, and by the time I had faintly conjured up an American heavyweight who was knocked out by Max Schmeling, Roethke was glaring at me anxiously. "What the hell's wrong?" he said. "You think I'm a damned liar?"

I did indeed, but until he asked me, I thought he was just rambling on in the way of a man who did not intend for others to take him seriously. He *seemed* serious enough, for he developed the stories at great length, as though he had told them, to others or to himself, a good many times before. Such a situation puts a stranger in rather a tough spot. If he suspects that the story is a lie, he must either pretend to go along with it, or hopefully enter a tacit conspiracy with the speaker in assuming that the whole thing is a joke, a put-on. Unfortunately I chose the latter, and I could not have done worse for either of us. He sank, or fell, rather, into a steep and bitter silence—we were driving around Seattle at the time—and there was no more said on that or any other subject until we reached his house on John Street. I must have been awfully slow to catch on to what he wanted of me, for in retrospect it seems quite clear that he wished me to help protect him from his sense of inadequacy, his dissatisfaction with what he was as a man.

My own disappointment, however, was not at all in the *fact* that Roethke lied, but in the obviousness and uncreativeness of the manner in which he did it. Lying of an inspired, habitual, inventive kind, given a personality, a form, and a rhythm, is mainly what poetry *is*, I have always believed. All art, as Picasso is reported to have said, is a lie that makes us see the truth. There are innumerable empirical "truths" in the world billions a day, an hour, a minute—but only a few poems that surpass and transfigure them: only a few structures of words which do not so much tell the truth as *make* it. I would have found Roethke's lies a good deal more memorable if they had had some of the qualities of his best poems, and had not been simply the productions of the grown-up baby that he resembled physically. Since that time I have much regretted that Roethke did not write his prize-fighting poems, his gangster poems and tycoon poems, committing his art to these as fully as he committed himself to them in conversation. This might have given his work the range and variety of subject matter that it so badly needed, particularly toward the end of his life, when he was beginning to repeat himself: they might have been the themes to make of him a poet of the stature of Yeats or Rilke.

Yet this is only speculation; his poems are as we have them, and many of them will be read as long as words retain the power to evoke a world and to relate the reader, through that world, to a more intense and meaningful version of his own. There is no poetry anywhere that is so valuably conscious of the human body as Roethke's; no poetry that can place the body in an *environment*—wind, seascape, greenhouse, forest, desert,

mountainside, among animals or insects or stones—so vividly and evoca-
tively, waking unheard of exchanges between the place and human respon-
siveness at its most creative. He more than any other is a poet of pure being.
He is a great poet not because he tells you how it is with *him*—as, for
example, the "confessional" poets endlessly do—but how it can be with
you. When you read him, you realize with a great surge of astonishment and
joy that, truly, you are not yet dead.

Roethke came to possess this ability slowly. *The Glass House* is like a
long letter by a friend, telling how he came to have it. The friend's concern
and occasional bewilderment about the subject are apparent, and also some
of the impatience that Roethke's self-indulgent conduct often aroused even
in those closest to him. But the main thrust of his life, his emergence from
Saginaw, Michigan (of all places), into the heroic role of an artist working
against the terrible odds of himself for a new vision, is always clear; clearer
than it ever was to Roethke, who aspired to self-transcendence but continually despaired of attaining it.

Heroic Roethke certainly was; he struggled against more than most
men are aware is possible. His guilt and panic never left him. No amount of
praise could ever have been enough to reassure him or put down his sense
of chagrin and bafflement over his relationship to his father, the florist Otto
Roethke, who died early in Roethke's life and so placed himself beyond
reconciliation. None of his lies—of being a nationally ranked tennis player,
of having an "in" with the Detroit "Purple Gang," of having all kinds of
high-powered business interests and hundreds of women in love with him—
would ever have shriven him completely, but these lures and ruses and
deceptions did enable him to exist, though painfully, and to write; they were
the paraphernalia of the wounded artist who cannot survive without them.

These things Seager deals with incisively and sympathetically. He is
wonderful on the genesis of the poetry, and his accounts of Roethke's
greatest breakthrough, the achievement of what Kenneth Burke calls his
"greenhouse line," are moving indeed, and show in astonishing detail the
extent to which Roethke lived his poems and identified his bodily existence
with them in one animistic rite after another.

> On days when he was not teaching, he moped around Shingle
> Cottage alone, scribbling lines in his notebooks, sometimes, he
> told me, drinking a lot as a deliberate stimulus (later he came to
> see alcohol as a depressant and used to curb his manic states),
> popping out of his clothes, wandering around the cottage naked
> for a while, then dressing slowly, four or five times a day. There

are some complex "birthday-suit" meanings here, the ritual of starting clean like a baby, casting one's skin like a snake, and then donning the skin again. It was not exhibitionism. No one saw. It was all a kind of magic.

He broke through to what had always been there; he discovered his childhood in a new way, and found the way to tell it, not "like it was" but as it might have been if it included all its own meanings, rhythms, and symbolic extensions. He found, in other words, the form for it: *his* form. Few writers are so obviously rooted (and in Roethke's case the word has special connotations because the poet has so magnificently put them there) in their childhood as Roethke, and Seager shows us in just what ways this was so: the authoritarian Prussian father and his specialized and exotic (especially in frozen, logged-out Saginaw) vocation of florist, the greenhouse, the "far field" behind it, the game park, the strange, irreducible life of stems and worms, the protection of fragile blooms by steam pipes, by eternal vigilance, and by getting "in there" with the plants and working with them as they not only required but seemed to want. Later there are the early efforts to write, the drinking, the first manic states, the terrible depressions, the marriage to Beatrice O'Connell (a former student of his at Bennington), the successive books, the prizes, the recognitions, the travels, the death at fifty-six.

I doubt very much if Roethke will ever have another biography as good as this one. And yet something is wrong here, even so. One senses too much of an effort to mitigate certain traits of Roethke's, particularly in regard to his relations with women. It may be argued that a number of people's feelings and privacy are being spared, and that may be, as has been adjudged in other cases, reason enough to be reticent. And yet a whole—and very important—dimension of the subject has thereby been left out of account, and one cannot help believing that a writer of Seager's ability and fierce honesty would have found a way to deal with it if he had not been constrained. To his credit, however, he does his best to suggest what he cannot overtly say. For it is no good to assert, as some have done, that Roethke was a big lovable clumsy affectionate bear who just incidentally wrote wonderful poems. It is no good to insist that Seager show "the good times as well as the bad" in anything like equal proportions; these are not the proportions of the man's life. The driving force of him was agony, and to know him we must know all the forms it took. The names of people may be concealed, but the incidents we must know. It is far worse to leave these matters to rumor than to entrust them to a man of Seager's integrity.

Mrs. Roethke, in especial, must be blamed for this wavering of purpose, this evasiveness that was so far from Seager's nature as to seem to belong to someone else. It may be that she has come to regard herself as the sole repository of the "truth" of Roethke, which is understandable as a human—particularly a wifely—attitude, but is not pardonable in one who commissions a biography from a serious writer. Allan Seager was not a lesser man than Roethke, someone to be sacrificed to another writer's already overguarded reputation. As a human being he was altogether more admirable than his subject. He was a hard and devoted worker, and he believed deeply in this book; as he said, he had acted out much of it himself. If he hadn't spent the last years of his life on *The Glass House,* he might have been able to finish the big novel he had been working on for years. As it was—thanks again to Mrs. Roethke, who, in addition to other obstacles she placed in Seager's way, even refused him permission to quote her husband's poems—he died without knowing whether all the obstacles had been removed.

Certainly this is a dreadful misplacement of loyalty, for Roethke deserves the monument that this book could have been. He had, almost exclusively by his art, all but won out over his babydom, of which this constant overprotectiveness on the part of other people was the most pernicious part. He deserved to be treated, at last, as a man as well as a great poet. And it should be in the *exact* documentation of this triumph—this heroism—that we ought to see him stand forth with no excuses made, no whitewash needed. Seager had all the gifts: the devotion to his subject, the personal knowledge of it, the talent and the patience and the honesty, and everything but the time and the cooperation, and above all, the recognition of his own stature as an artist with a great personal stake in the enterprise. He died of lung cancer last May.

Since I was close to the book for some time, I am bound to be prejudiced; I am glad to be. Even allowing for prejudice, however, I can still say that this is the best biography of an American poet I have read since Philip Horton's *Hart Crane,* and that it is like no other. God knows what it would have been if Allan Seager had had his way, had been able to do the job he envisioned, even as he lay dying.

J. D. McCLATCHY

Sweating Light from a Stone:
Identifying Theodore Roethke

In a familiar photograph of Theodore Roethke by Imogen Cunningham, the hulking poet sits hunched in weeds at the base of a high, cracked wall on which are painted a huge hand pointing out beyond the frame, and Roethke's initial, the letter R, drawn half the size of the man. His face is puffy, tired, uneasy; the eyes are sharp; the mouth half-open to ask, it seems, a question. The picture was taken near the end of his life, and in many ways its details summarize his career, by portraying the elements of its central dilemma.

In his last significant essay, "On 'Identity,' " Roethke defined that career—and so, to a greater extent than for many poets, his life—as the transition, the transformation, of the self to the soul. Though the terms are not clearly defined—as usual, Roethke's "ideas" are vague and unmanageable—he implies a movement from Nature to God, from the Other to the One, transcending one's guilt and one's past. "Creativity," ultimately the exaltation of the One in the Other and of the soul in both, is a going-out of the self towards the soul, towards others, towards God, towards "the light," towards love. And in this way is "identity" created and confirmed. "It is paradoxical that a very sharp sense of the being, the identity of some other being—and in some instances, even an inanimate thing—brings a corresponding heightening and awareness of one's own self, and, even more mysteriously, in some instances, a feeling of the oneness of the universe."

Ralph Mills [in *On the Poet and His Craft*] has described this as "Roethke's evolutionary theme," the pervasive tone and thrust of the poet's best work, and most critics seem content to follow this lead. Yet what

From *Modern Poetry Studies* 3, no.1 (1972). © 1972 by Jerome Mazzaro.

121

appears here to Roethke and his readers as a definite development, reflected
in the shifting styles and emphases of the successive volumes, seems more
often to have been a dialectic, an unresolved dilemma, which structures the
poetry's themes and images, but which Roethke never really moves beyond.
"Self" and "soul," in other words, remain essentially irreconcilable, perhaps
antagonistic—and these terms open out to others: natural and mystical, the
minimal and the All, mortality and eternity, "the terrible hunger for objects" and "the pure, sensuous form," the Pebble and the Pond, the wren
and the heron, experience and innocence, being and becoming, reduction
and expansion, the depressive and the manic. Roethke's personal and poetic
"identity" seems to have been constantly, agonizingly caught—or lost—
between these poles:

> Beginner,
> Perpetual beginner,
> The soul knows not what to believe,
> In its small folds, stirring sluggishly,
> In the least place of its life,
> A pulse beyond nothingness,
> A fearful ignorance.

When the poetry is read closely, this dialectic and the factors which seem to
have caused it, emerge clearly enough, and though, as a result, Roethke's
achievement may seem to have been slighter, it should appear in a more
honest and helpful perspective.

The title poem of *Open House*, however prophetic, is hardly pertinent
to the poems that follow it:

> My secrets cry aloud.
> I have no need for tongue.
> My heart keeps open house,
> My doors are widely swung.
> An epic of the eyes
> My love, with no disguise.
>
> My truths are all foreknown,
> This anguish self-revealed.
> I'm naked to the bone,
> With nakedness my shield.
> Myself is what I wear:
> I keep the spirit spare.
>
> The anger will endure,
> The deed will speak the truth
> In language strict and pure.

> I stop the lying mouth:
> Rage warps my clearest cry
> To witless agony.

The collection, coldly kissed by contraries, hardly cries aloud his secrets: "Delicate the syllables that release the repression." Though the "anguish" he speaks of in this poem is never specifically explored at length, Roethke's open house does have "an attic of horrors, a closet of fears," which haunt his later work but are only hinted at here:

> All profits disappear: the gain
> Of ease, the hoarded, secret sum;
> And now grim digits of old pain
> Return to litter up our home.
>
> We hunt the cause of ruin, add,
> Subtract, and put ourselves in pawn;
> For all our scratching on the pad,
> We cannot trace the error down.

One of his horrors is "the devouring mother." As he says in an undated notebook entry:

> Did I eat my mother?
> Did my mother eat me?
> Or was the devouring done mutually?

The self-mockery of a poem like "Poetaster" seems only defensive about the devouring:

> Hero of phantasies and catcher of chills,
> Wants singleness of spirit above all else:
> Happy alone in this bedroom counting his pulse.
> O fortunate he whose mama pays the bills!

Likewise there lurks "a father's ghost" in these poems, but it is diffused among references to the "exhausted fathers," the "ancestral eyes" he feels at his back throughout: "The spirit starves / Until the dead have been subdued." There is an important sense of betrayal—a recurrent theme in Roethke's work—in his handling of this theme:

> Exhausted fathers thinned the blood,
> You curse the legacy of pain:
> Darling of an infected brood,
> You feel disaster climb the vein.

> There's a canker at the root, your seed
> Denies the blessing of the sun,
> The light essential to your need.
> Your hopes are murdered and undone.

One aspect of this theme is described by Allan Seager [in *The Glass House*]
in terms of abandonment: "Quite illogically Ted felt that his father, by
dying, had betrayed him, left him far too soon without his love and guidance, and intermittently in those moments when he remembered his father
as flawless, Ted was tormented by guilt for even having entertained the
notion that a great man like his father could have done anything so base as
to betray his son." In "The Premonition" the abandonment is portrayed
through a child's awe ("that face / Was lost in a maze of water"), without
the obsessive guilt and anxiety prominent in the later poetry. Since *Open
House* wears a "toughened skin,"

> What shakes my skull to disrepair
> Shall never touch another ear

and he leaves "The Auction" to its "rubbish of confusion."
   The sense of betrayal is more evident in the awkward poem "Epidermal
Macabre":

> I hate my epidermal dress,
> The savage blood's obscenity,
> The rags of my anatomy,
> And willingly would I dispense
> With false accouterments of sense,
> To sleep immodestly, a most
> Incarnadine and carnal ghost.

Later poems too take up the body's betrayal: its grossness ("I may look like
a beer salesman but I'm a poet," he would say), its illnesses, its sexual needs,
its threats of impotence, eventually its accelerated decay. The flesh is a
"cloak of evil and despair," symbolizing one's isolation from other selves
("our separate skins"), and even from himself:

> So caged and cadged, so close within
> A coat of unessential skin,

> I would put off myself and flee
> My inaccessibility.

The poem "To My Sister" warns her against "the vice of flesh" to "Remain
secure from pain."

And certainly hovering near the body's betrayal is that of the mind. "Against Disaster"—written, said Roethke, "in a period of terror before a 'breakdown' "—tries to "rout the specter of alarm," but the poem "Silence" dramatizes its persistence:

> There is a noise within the brow
> That pulses undiminished now
> In accents measured by the blood.
> It breaks upon my solitude—
> A hammer on the crystal walls
> Of sense at rapid intervals.

All of these concerns return in the next volume, but there they are reimagined within experiences which allow them a resonance this cautious first book restricts. In the next volume, also, they begin to underlie the emerging dilemma. But in *Open House,*

> Necessity starves on the stoop of invention.
> The sleep was not deep, but the waking is slow.

The Lost Son and Other Poems established both the reputation Roethke craved and the world of his imagination—with its greenhouse and its field, bounded by The City and The Abyss. Not only did it inaugurate important technical innovations, but it also exposed the raw center of his dilemma: the consequences of self-consciousness and the inability to construct an identity. But it is important to note first the arrangement of the volume, for the so-called "greenhouse poems" with which it begins ground the series of long poems in one half of Roethke's effort to escape the self-consciousness that torments the four anchor poems—and for that matter, the ten which follow in his next two collections. This initial group of detailed, sensuous poems seeks to recreate the "man-made Avalon, Eden, or paradise" of his father's greenhouse. The last poem of the group, "Frau Bauman, Frau Schmidt, and Frau Schwartze," though added later, sets the retrospective tone of the sequence:

> Now, when I'm alone and cold in my bed,
> They still hover over me,
> These ancient leathery crones,
> With their bandannas stiffened with sweat,
> And their thorn-bitten wrists,
> And their snuff-laden breath blowing lightly over me in my
>   first sleep.

The reimagining not only seeks to evoke the security of childhood, of his "Eden." The poet seeks further to submerge himself in the natural, unconscious process of organic life:

> I can hear, underground, that sucking and sobbing,
> In my veins, in my bones I feel it,—
> The small waters seeping upward,
> The tight grains parting at last.
> When sprouts break out,
> Slippery as fish,
> I quail, lean to beginnings, sheath-wet.

As he says in "The Minimal," the process he identifies himself with is one "Cleansing and caressing, / Creeping and healing." What he seeks to have healed intrudes into the poems as well. Again there is the familiar, unlocalized sense of guilt, as in "Child on Top of a Greenhouse" with "everyone, everyone pointing up and shouting!" More significantly, there is the guilt of violation in "Moss-Gathering":

> And afterwards I always felt mean, jogging back over the
>   logging road,
> As if I had broken the natural order of things in that
>   swampland;
> Disturbed some rhythm, old and of vast importance,
> By pulling off flesh from the living planet;
> As if I had committed, against the whole scheme of life, a
>   desecration.

The longer poems fantasize on this essentially masturbatory guilt, but even here the poet is caught by those shoots which "dangled and drooped, / Lolling obscenely from mildewed crates, / Hung down long yellow evil necks, like tropical snakes." The exorcizing in "Weed Puller" is frantic:

> Under the concrete benches,
> Hacking at black hairy roots,—
> Those lewd monkey-tails hanging from
>   drainholes,—
>
> .   .   .   .
>
> Tugging all day at perverse life.

And posed against his guilt is the order of the adult world and the purity of the natural world:

> The indignity of it!—
> With everything blooming above me,

> Lilies, pale-pink cyclamen, roses,
> Whole fields lovely and inviolate,—
> Me down in that fetor of weeds,
> Crawling on all fours,
> Alive, in a slippery grave.

Or of something inaccessible beyond the natural world:

> A crisp hyacinthine coolness,
> Like that clear autumnal weather of eternity,
> The windless perpetual morning above a September cloud.

The extraordinary sequence of poems beginning with "The Lost Son," much of it still too private and obscure, has received the majority of the critical attention paid to Roethke, and has been consistently interpreted in the terms the poet himself outlined in his "Open Letter": "Each poem—there are now eight in all and there probably will be at least one more—is complete in itself; yet each in a sense is a stage in a kind of struggle out of the slime; part of a slow spiritual progress; an effort to be born, and later, to be something more." Stanley Kunitz [in "News of the Root"] calls it "the record of a psychic adventure, the poet's quest of himself"; Ralph Mills sees it as "a spiritual journey undertaken by a child-protagonist," which, "while it is basically psychic and spiritual, also has similarities with quest myths: the hero's descent into the underworld of the self; a series of ordeals he must pass or an enemy to be vanquished; his victorious return to familiar reality, which is now changed by his efforts. . . . What he is aiming at is a poetic 'history of the psyche' (his phrase) which opens with the earliest stages of life and traces the evolution of the spirit in its ordeal of inner and outer conflicts, its desire for 'unity of being,' to borrow a term from Dante by way of Yeats, that final condition of grace which is a harmony of the self with all things." C. W. Truesdale [in "Theodore Roethke and the Landscape of American Poetry"] says, "The controlling metaphor in all of these poems is organic growth, a progression from the darkness of a maternal earth into sunlight and vision"; Frederick J. Hoffman [in "Theodore Roethke: The Poetic Shape of Death"] maintains that the poems "move chiefly from dark (the 'underness' that exists everywhere) to light: or, from the dark recesses of the almost entirely quiescent self, to a world where the light requires an activity of the mind, what he called 'spirit' or 'soul.' " The most extended treatment of the poems, by Karl Malkoff [in *An Introduction to the Poetry*] goes so far as to see the individual poems representing distinct Freudian stages of the child's psychic development (oral, anal, latent, etc.).

The interpretations could be further duplicated and all clearly originate in Roethke's own reading of his work. But while the poems may indeed resemble the "evolutionary theme," there is reason to doubt that this is the final word—or, indeed, was the first word. For Roethke's own interpretation, written after the fact, may in turn have been dependent on critics' help. There is evidence of this habit in his letters. For instance, on June 13, 1947, he writes to his editor about "The Shape of the Fire": "Auden, for instance, liked this last one best; read it over four or five times, kept saying 'This is extremely good,' etc. The last part,—the euphoric section,—made him think of Traherne, as I remember: no 'influence' but the same kind of heightened tone, I think he meant. I mention this because Aswell is currently on a Dylan Thomas jag: sees that Welshman in everything." And then, in a letter to John Crowe Ransom on July 28, he protests the "influence" of Thomas by casually saying: "But I'm nobody's Dylan: I never went to school to him. If there's an ancestor, it's Traherne (the prose)." Or he would say: "Maybe a possible angle is that 'The Shape of the Fire' represents, with its quick shifts in rhythm and association, a poem that creates a genuine imaginative order out of what comes from the unconscious, as opposed to the merely automatic responses of the surrealists. (I didn't dream this up myself: it's a point made by Bogan and others.)" A telling letter was written to Kenneth Burke on March 16, 1947: "I guess I'll have to make some sort of rationale or explanation for that second piece 'The Long Alley.' If you ever get brooding on it again, and think of a way of giving some leads to the reader, let me see them. Somehow, I seem psychologically unable to 'explain' something that is so close to me." Burke may well have been the source of Roethke's confident interpretation in "Open Letter"; after all, Roethke was exceptionally dependent on him throughout this period of composition.

Roethke's own comments at the time do not suggest the "journey" or "progression" that he may later have imposed on them. Instead, he writes: "Recently while on a Guggenheim fellowship, I wrote a sequence of three longer poems called 'The Lost Son,' 'The Long Alley,' 'The Shape of the Fire,' which dealt with a spiritual crisis. But I have not exhausted the theme: I wish to go beyond these poems. This means going into myself more deeply and objectifying more fully what I find." Certainly "crisis" is a more apt description of the poems. And ironically, it was Kenneth Burke who first—and, apparently, alone—discerned the true dilemma: "The transformations seem like a struggle less to be born than to avoid being undone. . . . The enduring of such discomforts is a 'birth' in the sense that, if the poet survives the ordeal, he is essentially stronger, and has to this extent *forged himself* an identity."

Though Roethke "survives" the poems, it is still without any identity, however much he seeks to "forge" or merely assert one. These poems—indeed, all of his work—can be characterized, with Burke, as "in search of an essential parenthood." It was a search which Allan Seager traces in Roethke's own life as well, with its series of substitute fathers—Pop Crouse and Pa Burke, Rolfe Humphries and Stanley Kunitz and Robert Heilman, editors and psychoanalysts, W. H. Auden and W. B. Yeats—and it dominated all of his significant relationships with women, including his wife. It is undoubtedly related to the source of his "manic-depressive" psychosis, which usually results from a highly disciplined childhood (Seager cites the Roethke family's strong sense of *Tüchtigkeit*) encouraging crippling feelings of dependence, unworthiness, and abandonment. As a result, the self alternates collapsing under the stress of reality, and agressively self-asserting to override the claustrophobic complex of fears and hostility. Part of Roethke's "thug" mask—with its swaggering and drinking and bragging, its obsessive egotism—is this expansive defense. And though the psychosis is more evidently felt in the later poetry, it pulses through the Lost Son-sequence as well.

The mingled awe and fear in the image of his father, arrested by death, inspires both the terrible dependence and longing, and a terrifying sense of guilt in his own autoerotic urges, both of which paralyse the necessary struggle for psychic and sexual identity—the "spiritual crisis" of the poems. The opening section of "The Lost Son," which fishes in "an old wound," deals with this "hard time," associating the death of his father and the discovery of the phallus:

> Voice, come out of the silence.
> Say something.
> Appear in the form of a spider
> Or a moth beating the curtain
>
> . . . .
> The shape of a rat?
>   It's bigger than that.
>   It's less than a leg
>   And more than a nose,
>   Just under the water
>   It usually goes . . .
>
> . . . .
> Take the skin of a cat
> And the back of an eel,
> Then roll them in grease,—
> That's the way it would feel.

And the cycle of need and guilt, of discovery and repression, informs the rest
of the poem:

> Dogs of the groin
> Barked and howled,
> The sun was against me,
> The moon would not have me.
>
> The weeds whined,
> The snakes cried,
> The cows and briars
> Said to me: Die . . .
>
> . . . .
>
> What gliding shape
> Beckoning through halls,
> Stood poised on the stair,
> Fell dreamily down?
>
> From the mouths of jugs
> Perched on many shelves,
> I saw substance flowing
> That cold morning.

The guilt at his hands' "perpetual agitation," the childhood fears of castration and the adult fears of impotence, alternate with defiant gestures to
taunt or exorcize the guilt—usually expressed in terms of exposing his
nakedness:

> How cool the grass is.
> Has the bird left? . . .
> These sweeps of light undo me.
> Look, look, the ditch is running white!
> I've more veins than a tree!

As he says in a later poem, "I shed my clothes to slow my daemon down."
And Seager relates how Roethke, while working on these poems, would be
"popping out of his clothes, wandering around the cottage naked for a
while, then dressing slowly, four or five times a day."

   The ending of the poem ("It will come again. / Be still. / Wait.") is an
uncertain truce, certainly not an affirmation or emergence or what M. L.
Rosenthal [in *The Modern Poets*] calls a "victory over the frenzy through a
Freudian rebirth of the Self." For, as Roethke says in "The Long Alley,"

"My gates are all caves," dark dead-ends. "There's no joy in soft bones,"
but his "gristle" is unmerciful:

> Tricksy comes and tricksy goes
> Bold in fear therefore;
>
> . . . .
>
> So up and away and what do we do
> But barley-break and squeeze
>
> . . . .
>
> Gilliflower ha,
> Gilliflower ho,
> My love's locked in
> The old silo.

The orgasmic ecstasy of the fourth section ("Sweet Jesus, make me sweat
. . . A pierce of angels!") gives way in the end to despair:

> Call off the dogs, my paws are gone.
> This wind brings many fish;
> The lakes will be happy:
> Give me my hands:
> I'll take the fire.

The only way beyond the self, now, is to collapse back into it. "A Field of
Light" attempts the unconscious submersion into natural life, and with it
"The dirt left my hand," but, in "The Shape of the Fire," "Water recedes to
the crying of spiders":

> Mother me out of here. What more will the bones allow?
>
> . . . .
>
> Must pull off clothes
> To jerk like a frog
> On belly and nose
> From the sucking bog.
>
> My meat eats me. Who waits at the gate?
> Mother of quartz, your words writhe into my ear.
> Renew the light, lewd whisper.

And he ends by invoking "that minnowy world of weeds and ditches" and
"The light, the full sun"—wisdom and ecstasy—in order to escape the
self-consciousness of guilt.

Though critics, again following Roethke, persist in treating *Praise to
the End!* merely as a continuation of *The Lost Son,* there are important

differences in tone, technique and emphasis. On the whole, it is a less
successful book, if only because the dilemma of the earlier book repetitively
persists. Roethke is still tied down by his "knot of gristle," and forced to
listen to "the ghost of some great howl / Dead in the wall." "The mouth
asks. The hand takes." The best poem in the volume, "Praise to the End!,"
only returns to the guilt and the inability:

> It's dark in this wood, soft mocker.
> For whom have I swelled like a seed?
> What a bone-ache I have.
> Father of tensions, I'm down to my skin at last.

Though they lack the greater intensity, Roethke's lines resemble those of
Whitman:

> The sentries desert every other part of me,
> They have left me helpless to a red marauder,
> They all come to the headland to witness and assist against me.
> I am given up by traitors,
> I talk wildly, I have lost my wits, I and nobody else am the
>   greatest traitor,
> I went myself first to the headland, my own hands carried me
>   there.
>
> You villain touch! what are you doing? my breath is tight in
>   its throat,
> Unclench your floodgates, you are too much for me.
>
>   ("Song of Myself")

Roethke's struggle is also less intense: "My palm-sweat flashes gold." His
constant surrender—as though to death ("onanism equals death," he says)—
parallels his surrender to water and to light: "I ache for another choice."
These are clearly the central, restricting images in Roethke's poetry. Though
they may modualte and shift, reverse and reject any rigid values assigned
them, they remain the poles of his vision, the extremes within which and
towards which his narrow range of other images cluster. The world of *The
Lost Son* and *Praise to the End!* is essentially a fluid one—washed with
ooze, streams, bogs, rivers, steam, semen, amniotic fluid—and this is appropriate to the fluid nature of memories, reconstructions, and guilt. It is
also the world of the "greenhouse poems" in which the series was grounded.
The poet finds, however, that "The eye perishes in the small vision. . . . Go
where light is." It is the light that blinds *The Far Field*. But the light is

blocked by the third most prominent of Roethke's images—the stone, or the wall: the gut-stone of isolation and impotence, the wall of guilt between father and son, between self and soul. The last poem of the Lost Son-series, "O, Thou Opening, O" from *The Waking,* seems mostly a pastiche, and summarizes the forced relationships:

> The dark has its own light.
> A son has many fathers.
> Stand by a slow stream:
> Hear the sigh of what is.
> Be a pleased rock
> On a plain day.

A poem rejected from the series and from the collected edition, "The Changeling," reiterates the arrangement, one that is forever disintegrating:

> I'm taught
> As water teaches stone. Believe me, extremest oriole,
> I can hear light on a dry day.

There is an interlude, however, before the major confrontation with this finally elaborated dialectic. The "Love Poems" in *Words for the Wind,* in their shift from adhesiveness to amativeness, represent again the effort both to resolve the self and to secure an identity, which while it results in several beautiful poems is finally unsuccessful. There is a tremulous balance at the start of the sequence (" 'O love me while I am, / You green thing in my way!' ") which at last gives way to older and stronger sexual guilt and father-fear, and to the abiding, self-conscious realization of the inevitability of the stone's isolation and impenetrability: "How terrible the need for solitude."

The woman seems, at first, the harmonization of Roethke's two instinctive drives:

> She knows the speech of light, and makes it plain
> A lively thing can come to life again
>
> . . . .
>
> She moves as water moves, and comes to me,
> Stayed by what was, and pulled by what would be.

And she is able to transform his world into an ecstatic illusion:

> She turned the field into a glittering sea;
> I played in flame and water like a boy

> And I swayed out beyond the white seafoam;
> Like a wet log, I sang within a flame.
> In that last while, eternity's confine,
> I came to love, I came into my own.

"I start to leave myself," he says in the next poem, as he seeks an identity in the Other:

> And I dance round and round,
> A fond and foolish man,
> And see and suffer myself
> In another being, at last.
>
> Is she what I become?
> Is this my final Face?

Or, as Martin Buber (whom Roethke was reading at the time) says: "I become through my relation to the *Thou*; as I become *I*, I say *Thou*. . . . Through the *Thou* a man becomes *I*. That which confronts him comes and disappears, relational events condense, then are scattered, and in the change consciousness of the unchanging partner, of the *I*, grows clear, and each time stronger." But in the swirling movements of love in "Words for the Wind," one senses an undercurrent of concern and doubt. "Motion can keep me still: / she kissed me out of thought," and "Those who embrace, believe." But the sense of self-delusion is strong:

> I stayed, and light fell
> Across her pulsing throat;
> I stared, and a garden stone
> Slowly became the moon.

That moon, bright with false light, is still the cold, dead stone, "the loveless stone," incapable of prolonged commitment and forced back on its own incapacity: "And so I stood appart, / Hidden in my own heart." "The Renewal" confronts these dreads:

> Sudden renewal of the self—from where?
> A raw ghost drinks the fluid in my spine;
> I know I love, yet know not where I am;
> I paw the dark, the shifting midnight air.
> Will the self, lost, be found again? In form?
> I walk the night to keep my five wits warm.

Guilt drains the possibility of renewal, obscures all but "the dogs of the groin." There is no way to survive the experience of love except by an ecstatic expansion of the self:

> Dry bones! Dry bones! I find my loving heart,
> Illumination brought to such a pitch
> I see the rubblestones begin to stretch
> As if reality had split apart
> And the whole motion of the soul lay bare:
> I find that love, and I am everywhere.

The conclusion is forced and false; the result is annihilation, tapped from a self-destructive violence within that is more than merely sexual:

> Love me, my violence,
> Light of my spirit, light
> Beyond the look of love
>
> . . . .
>
> Father, I'm far from home,
> And I have gone nowhere.
>
> The close dark hugs me hard,
> And all the birds are stone.
> I fear for my own joy;
> I fear myself in the field,
> For I would drown in fire.

It is violence—physical, psychic, sexual—he has courted throughout his career. Among the resolutions he enters in his notebook in 1944 is this one: "To wish for an illness—for something to come to grips with, a break from reality."

"Memory," the last poem of the sequence, following Roethke's pattern of retrospective, focusing final poems, closes with a tender, powerful image of despair. The love he has sought, he realizes, is only a security against the terrors and confusions of the self—this is the "desire" that "hides from desire." But the love he has haunted vanishes in and with this poem:

> A doe drinks by a stream,
> A doe and its fawn.
> When I follow after them,
> The grass changes to stone.

The remaining poems in *Words for the Wind* extend these insights by exploring the inner emptiness:

> I turned upon my spine,
> I turned and turned again,
> A cold God-furious man
> Writhing until the last
> Forms of his secret life
> Lay with the dross of death.
>
> I was myself, alone.

Increasingly there looms the feeling of this notebook entry: "I'm sick of women. I want God." But before he moves on to what he calls "a hunt, a drive towards God: an effort to break through the barriers of rational experience," he circles back to make his peace with the past. His memorial tribute to Yeats, "The Dying Man," seeks out all of his fathers: "I must love the wall." He tries hard—the strain tells—to push past his anxiety into acceptance and celebration: "I bare a wound, and dare myself to bleed. . . . All exultation is a dangerous thing." It overwhelms him here; if he is still standing at the end, it is only because of the metrical brace. The inability to discover the final source of dread, to *name* the "first principles" of identity, leaves him where he began:

> The vision moves, and yet remains the same.
> In heaven's praise, I dread the thing I am.
>
> The edges of the summit still appall
> When we brood on the dead or the beloved;
> Nor can imagination do it all
> In this last place of light.

The "Meditations of an Old Woman" is both a summing-up and a departure. Certainly Roethke is describing his own career in these lines:

> A prince of small beginnings, enduring the slow stretches of
>   change,
> Who spoke first in the coarse short-hand of the subliminal
>   depths,
> Made from his terror and dismay a grave philosophical
>   language.

But the contemplative is an uncomfortable mode for Roethke. He becomes diffuse and repetitive. There are still strong sections here, however, as in this ideal projection of the balance:

> My shadow steadies in a shifting stream;
> I live in air; the long light is my home;

> I dare caress the stones, the field my friend;
> A light wind rises: I become the wind.

But the peace is asserted rather than achieved in these poems. The clear tendency of the sequence is toward the wrenching exaltation of his power in *The Far Field:*

> The sun! The sun! And all we can become!
> And the time ripe for running to the moon!
> In the long fields, I leave my father's eye;
> And shake the secrets from my deepest bones;
> . . . .
> I'm wet with another life.

The dilemma—"I love the world; I want more than the world"—is reaching towards its fullest statement.

Roethke's sudden death made the posthumous publication of *The Far Field* seem evidence that its author had escaped a common fate of the American poet—to have survived his own last vision. But although the dualism of that vision is given its most detailed and intense embodiment here, it remains unresolved, absorbing Roethke's imaginative range and, essentially, keeping "the long journey out of self" circling, stalking the impulse to escape the self without that self ever having been authenticated. "Meditation at Oyster River" offers a pure version of the situation. Like the classic meditation, it opens with a *compositio loci:* from a high rock—isolation's bleak stone—the poet watches a riverbank, twilit with Keatsian stillness and fulness. The second section contrasts the poet's fearful self-consciousness:

> The self persists like a dying star,
> In sleep, afraid. Death's face rises afresh,
> Among the shy beasts.

and his longing (like that in the "Ode to a Nightingale," which it so recalls) to merge with nature, to be washed into a sea of forgetfulness:

> With these I would be.
> And with water: the waves coming forward, without cessation,
> The waves, altered by sand-bars, beds of kelp, miscellaneous
>   driftwood,
> Topped by cross-winds, tugged at by sinuous undercurrents
> The tide rustling in, sliding between the ridges of stone,
> The tongues of water, creeping in, quietly.

In the third section, however, the reductionist longings have unsettled the poet ("I shift on my rock, and I think"), and the "wrist-thick cascade" changes into a huge, ice-bound river, "cracking and heaving from the pressure" of a spring thaw—of the expansionist spirit:

> And I long for the blast of dynamite,
> The sudden sucking roar as the culvert loosens its debris of
>   branches and sticks,
> Welter of tin cans, pails, old bird nests, a child's shoe riding a
>   log,
> As the piled ice breaks away from the battered spiles,
> And the whole river begins to move forward, its bridges
>   shaking.

The last section, then, quietly returns—in hesitation, retreat, and, one senses, frustration—to the first "in this waning of light," the faded vision of the alternative obliterations between which he oscillates.

The poems in this "North American Sequence," for the most part, explore the middle-state: "The soul at a still-stand, / At ease after rocking the flesh to sleep." But it is, he realizes, "the dead middle way,"

> Where impulse no longer dictates, nor the darkening shadow,
> A vulnerable place,
> Surrounded by sand, broken shells, the wreckage of water.

"I have come to a still, but not a deep center," he says in "The Far Field," and death drives him towards his two extremes:

> —Or to lie naked in sand,
> In the silted shallows of a slow river,
> Fingering a shell,
> Thinking:
> Once I was something like this, mindless,
> Or perhaps with another mind, less peculiar;
> Or to sink down
>
> . . . .
> A man faced with his own immensity
> Wakes all the waves, all their loose wandering fire.
> The murmur of the absolute, the why
> Of being born fails on his naked ears.
> His spirit moves like monumental wind
> That gentles on a sunny blue plateau.
> He is the end of things, the final man.

That last phrase recalls Stevens, and we might borrow lines from him also to define the state towards which Roethke inclines in the central "Sequence, Sometimes Metaphysical":

> No doubt we live beyond ourselves in air,
> In an element that does not do for us,
> So well, that which we do for ourselves, too big,
> A thing not planned for imagery and belief.
> ("Looking across the Fields and
> Watching the Birds Fly")

Roethke has found that "Too much reality can be a dazzle, a surfeit; / Too close immediacy an exhaustion," and there is an important sense, often overlooked by his critics, in which this notebook entry speaks for Roethke: "I hate the external world. Don't you understand that?" What he longs for now is an "absolute" element, a final solipsism:

> a pure extreme of light
> Breaks on me as my meager flesh breaks down—
> The soul delights in that extremity.

But it "does not do." "In a Dark Time" is probably the most penetrating of these poems, and has been sufficiently explicated, by Roethke and others. "I take the central experience," says the poet, "to be fairly common: to break from the bondage of the self, from the barriers of the 'real' world, to come as close to God as possible." Death and guilt, the Other and the self are all extorted, the natural is transformed into the mystical, as he ascends towards what he calls "God":

> A fallen man, I climb out of my fear.
> The mind enters itself, and God the mind,
> And one is One, free in the tearing wind.

Imagery and belief *are* impossible. The absolutism of these lines Roethke realizes himself in an important gloss: "In the Platonic sense, the one becomes the many, in this moment. But also—and this is what terrified me—the one not merely makes his peace with God (Mr. Ransom's phrase) he—if we read One as the Godhead theologically placed above God— transcends God: he becomes the Godhead itself, not only the veritable creator of the universe but the creator of the revealed God." It is, in other words, a leap beyond revelation, beyond resolution. It is as far beyond his experience as the next poem's prayer:

> Make me, O Lord, a last, a simple thing
> Time cannot overwhelm.

The impossibility of both is explicit, and the poet is forced desperately back where he began, beginning again. "This last pure stretch of joy, / The dire dimension of a final thing" leaves us a terrible, helpless image. We return with the poet to the central fact: "Self, self, the stinking self offends my eyes." What he searched for to avoid it only led him back around to it again and again, though it spun off poems that have become as necessary for us as they were for him. If Roethke's work never develops far beyond its initial impulses and needs, nor ever achieves the desired syncretism or an integration sufficient to allow it the depth and dimension which the greatest poets reveal, at least it *survives*. And that is not the least we can ask of modern poetry—or of a man.

ROSEMARY SULLIVAN

Wet with Another Life: "Meditations of an Old Woman"

I recover my tenderness by long looking.
By midnight I love everything alive.
Who took the darkness from the air?
I'm wet with another life.
    —"What Can I Tell My Bones"

It is always the case with the true poet that after the opening miscellany of a first book, his work seems, even if in retrospect, programmatic and consecutive. There is a continuity to his thought through all its transformations as he moves toward a unification of his vision. Many critics would like to deny Roethke this order, insisting that after the sequence of love poems, he fell into self-repetition, and that his poetry achieved no new insights. If it is true that he had one central preoccupation, few could have been larger and more encompassing. This was his desire to trace the evolution of spirit—as he said, "to see the self so completely that it might become the soul." He wrote: "To know what is happening within us, this is the most difficult awareness. To be loyal to what happens to me." He pursued this awareness systematically so that his poetry took on the consecutive order of his life, a finding and piecing together of his knowledge of an inner self.

He began his interior excavations with the "Lost Son" sequence, attempting to penetrate the terrors and vicissitudes of his own mind. Like Rimbaud, he at least partly induced his first experience of mental disorder, deliberately seeking out preternatural experience in an effort to break down the domination of the conscious ego. The process was disintegrative, a

---

From *Theodore Roethke: The Garden Master*. © 1975 by the University of Washington Press.

breaking up of the established modes of consciousness in order to break back into intuitive vision. In those early poems, the poet was a kind of nocturnal fisher, penetrating to the racial unconscious in an attempt to relive his selfhood back to its mindless source. But the process brings with it the threat of madness. Roethke insisted on this. He wrote in his notebook begun November 1955:

> I can't go flying apart just for those who want the benefit of a few verbal kicks. My God, do you know what poems like that cost? They're not written vicariously: they come out of actual suffering; real madness."
>
> "I've got to go beyond. That's all there is to it."
>
> "Beyond what?"
>
> "The human, you fool. Don't you see what I've done: I've come this far and I can't stop. It's too late."

If, through the experience of psychological disorder, Roethke came to fear madness, he nevertheless discovered what he felt to be a natural propensity for mystical insight. The discovery was inherent in the experience itself. Periodic bouts of manic depressive psychosis subjected him to violent oscillations between extreme psychic states of expansion and contraction; poles which can be artificially reproduced, as in Rimbaud's famous experiments with drugs. In certain cases, the affective intensity of the experience of mania has been compared to natural mystical experience, defined as an intense "enthusiasm" stimulating a sense of numinous energy, as though the self had penetrated to a center of feeling little in keeping with the conscious mind. This "natural" experience is examined by William James in *The Varieties of Religious Experience.* In John Custance's *Adventure into the Unconscious* and *The Diary of Vaslav Nijinski,* both of which Roethke read, the experience of expansion and release is a direct consequence of mental aberration. Roethke's private psychic experiences were thus the source of his interest in mysticism. As was apparent from the *Praise to the End!* sequence, he subjected these to rigorous analysis, rejecting the delusions of elation as well as the temptations of depression. But he remained convinced of the mind's inherent capacity to extend beyond the self, as have all who have had such experiences. After his experiments with drugs, William James wrote: "I feel that the experience must mean something, if only one could lay hold of it. I cannot escape from its authority."

It must be said that Roethke's interest in mysticism was not orthodox. He never submitted to the discipline of the senses which has as its end the apprehension of Absolute Being. In the last year of his life he admitted: "I can't claim that the soul, my soul, was absorbed in God. No, God for me still remains someone to be confronted, to be dueled with." Yet his interest in mysticism was not a literary affectation. He turned to it as a means to unify and order a life disordered and deracinated to the extreme. Allan Seager indicates [in *The Glass House*] that, at this period of his life, a profound impulse toward wholeness and unity was movingly apparent, perhaps as a reaction to the fatuity of extreme responses characterizing his earlier experience. Seager diagnoses this new equanimity and search for harmony as the consequence of a final, total acceptance of his periodic disorders, hitherto dismissed as unpleasant incidents. Acceptance was an initial step toward resolution. Seager insists that Roethke's tremendous dignity as a human being, which everyone felt who met him, came from his heroic determination to resolve the discords of private life into an affirmative poetic order.

Mysticism was a subject which always interested him. He had been reading Saint Theresa, John of the Cross, and Meister Eckhart as early as 1942, but only in "Meditations of an Old Woman" are the fruits of this reading strongly apparent in his poetry. Two books, in particular, helped him to formulate his attitude toward mysticism, and are therefore seminal to an understanding of this new sequence: Paul Tillich's *The Courage to Be*, a study of the existential anxiety he was trying to identify and transcend; and Evelyn Underhill's *Mysticism,* an exploration of the inward transmutation of consciousness in mystical experience. But until as late as the "Sequence, Sometimes Metaphysical," he was apprehensive of the exclusive other-worldliness of orthodox mysticism, defined as the encounter with Absolute Being. He wanted, instead, a "rampant, triumphant, fleshly mysticism, the full spasm of the human, not simply beauty and darkness." One is reminded of Yeats, who insisted that his mystical concept "unity of being," far from being "distant and therefore intellectually understandable [would be] immanent . . . , taking upon itself pain and ugliness, 'eye of newt, and toe of frog.' " This notion of a secular mysticism, that is, a mystical apprehension of a spiritual reality which is immanent and not transcendent, embracing the vicissitudes of natural experience, is important in assessing Roethke's understanding of the works of both Tillich and Underhill.

In the case of the former, he was deeply affected by Paul Tillich's analysis of existential anxiety as the desperate awareness of the threat of nonbeing which is inherent in existence itself. He borrowed this definition of anxiety for his own poem "The Pure Fury," and also mentions the idea in his commentary on the poem "In a Dark Time." In *The Courage to Be* Tillich formulates an ontology of anxiety, dividing the concept into three categories: the anxiety of fate and death, of guilt and condemnation, of emptiness and meaninglessness; and traces the historical predominance of each. His essential point is that contemporary consciousness is threatened by spiritual nonbeing: the anxiety, potentially present in every individual, which has become a general conviction—that the spiritual center is lost, that the determining causes of existence have no ultimate necessity. Roethke took this problem of self-affirmation as the subject of "Meditations of an Old Woman." He identified the emotional poles of the poem in a phrase in his notebooks: "Horror, which is unbelief, is the opposite of ecstasy." The poem moves from horror, the threat of spiritual nonbeing, to joy, "the entirely unique experience of the courage to say yes to one's own being." After Tillich, this courage is an existential act—the affirmation of one's essential being in a courageous leap of faith which incorporates the anxiety of nonbeing into itself.

Critics have complained that the specific causes of anxiety in Roethke's later poetry are often difficult to locate. The implication is that he failed to define the source of what are presumed to be his neurotic preoccupations. But his darker poems are rarely concerned with private neurosis; their theme is Tillich's existential anxiety—the vague, yet overpowering presentiment that the self can be totally, utterly annihilated. It is this presentiment which lies behind the brooding fear and undirected exasperation of so many of the poems. Transcendence could only be achieved by a deeper penetration into the numinous experiences of expansion and release which have played such a large part in his poetry. Consequently, he turned to Underhill's *Mysticism*, a book which, as his notebooks indicate, he considered seminal to his work.

In *Mysticism* Evelyn Underhill defines mystical experience as a psychological process, an alchemical transmutation of consciousness from the egoistic center to a deeper center of meaning. She traces this spiritual metamorphosis through various stages: from the moment of initiation when the mystic sense is awakened and suprasensible reality breaks in upon the soul, through a purgative cleansing of vision, to illumination, the indwelling conviction of a divine presence—all preliminary stages to the more drastic spiritual encounter, union with the Absolute. Through Underhill, Roethke found both a descriptive order and imagery which made sense out of what were obviously personal experiences of inward transmutation, charged with the highest and deepest numinous significance. So many of his poems, especially "Meditations of an Old Woman" and "The Abyss," follow the psychological progression as she describes it. They begin with the painful apprehension of personal insufficiency, aggravated by the awareness of the possibility of a deeper reality. This is followed by a desire for purification through self-castigation and mortification, which Underhill calls the painful descent into the "cell of self-knowledge." This leads to illumination, a sudden breakthrough to a heightened visionary joy in the awakening of transcendental consciousness. These are only the first three, as it were, secular stages of mystical insight; he never laid claim to the last stages which lead to union with Absolute Being.

Roethke accepted Underhill's analysis of mystical vision while rejecting the doctrines of Christianity itself; for he was never interested in formal religion and only toward the end of his life did he use the term God freely and with conviction. He wrote, "In crawling out of the swamp, I don't need a system." Instead, he acknowledged her basic premise—that nihilism, which is a despair of meaning to existence, can only be countered by trust in man's "innate but strictly irrational instinct for the Real" and by a belief in that ground of personality, inarticulate but inextinguishable, by which one is aware of a greater energy transcending the self. From this perspective, mystical experience is essentially a psychological process, a reintegration with the numinous substratum of being achieved through a purgative cleansing of vision, a stripping away and casting off of the old self until a new core is reached where, as Eliot would say, humility is endless.

Roethke once wrote that the subject of his poetry was the quest for identity. In his terms, this meant a "hunger for a reality more than the immediate: a desire not only for a finality, for a consciousness beyond the mundane, but a desire for quietude, a desire for joy." He called the state he was seeking (taking the phrase from Stephen Spender), "a final innocence." He insisted that contemplation instills a method of being, and defined meditation as one simple state, the contemplative merged like a bird in air, in fullness, clearness. Obviously he thought of contemplation as a process of integration, an act of self-perception. The self, he insisted, once perceived, becomes the soul. "I am not speaking of the empirical self, the flesh-bound ego; it's a single word: *myself,* the aggregate of the several selves, if you will." He came to believe in the individual soul as other than the ego, something of which this "other self" is the imperishable center, and to which death has no meaning. As in all notions of mystical apprehension, he saw the ego as the limitation that opposes itself to the infinite. The state of consciousness, freed from the ego, lost in a vaster consciousness, can initiate the deeper self into modes of infinite being. He was seeking the inexhaustible power of simple things, the purity of elemental being; and he wanted to reestablish an original relation to the universe. In this he aligned himself with the American transcendentalists, particularly with Emerson. The way back into divine nature was through the innocent eye. The old woman in his

sequence can say: "I recover my tenderness by long looking / By midnight
I love everything alive." The innocent child becomes her perfect image of the
buried soul; the child as a symbol of the primitive state of being, relieved of
the active will and conscious thought and reabsorbed into the flowing con-
tinuum of unselfconscious nature. Consciousness is the curse—fractured,
rational consciousness, straining after metaphysical assurances and alienat-
ing the self from the source of its sustenance in nature. To consciousness,
Roethke opposes the order of "not-knowing, bearing being itself." It is clear
from his notebooks that he came to this notion through his readings of
mystical literature, particularly the fourteenth-century anonymous tract,
The Cloud of Unknowing. The underlying idea of this treatise is that Reality
can never be apprehended through intelligence. Roethke wrote in his notebook: "In the very real sense, don't know anything." In this assertion he
aligns himself with the mystical tradition of antirationalism. As Henri
Bergson put it most succinctly: "Intelligence enables us to conceive possibilities, it does not attain any Reality."

Many critics, the most eloquent among them W. D. Snodgrass, have
seen in Roethke's antirationalism and his consequent idealization of primitive life an impulse toward regression for its own sake and a retreat from
the complexities of human relationships. His interest in mysticism appears
to them as a desire to lose all awareness of otherness in an ecstasy of
withdrawal into the illusion of eternity. Such complaints have been raised
against mysticism in general. Jung, for example, in the early stages of his
career, identified the mystic impulse with the drive to recover the undif-
ferentiated bliss of the ouroboros. Later he came to repudiate this entirely,
seeing in mysticism an attempt to explore the transcendental instinct as an
elemental part of the human personality. The difference in attitudes seems
to be one of temperament as well as one of emphasis. One attitude sees in
mysticism only the withdrawal from reasoned order and moral discrimination. The other sees it as an attempt to trace the evolution of spiritual
consciousness. From the perspective of the poet, the most serious accusa-
tions against mysticism are those of exclusive other-worldliness and of rejection of this life for the illusion of eternity. Most apologists of mysticism,
Evelyn Underhill, R. C. Zaehner, Henri Bergson, insist that, on the contrary,
mysticism which ends in the solipsism of Buddhism is an aberration. True
mysticism leads to action; the mystic is the exploratory consciousness of his
race. Whether this is generally acceptable is not important here. What is
important is that Roethke always saw the allurements of withdrawal into
ecstasy as entirely negative and life-denying. In the "North American Sequence" he wrote: "And I acknowledge my foolishness with God, / My

desire for the peaks, the black ravines, the rolling mists . . . / The unsinging fields where no lungs breathe," and many of his poems record his struggle against this impulse. As has been said, he wanted a rampant, triumphant, fleshly mysticism, the full spasm of the human. One might complain, as many critics have done, that in Eliot's particular brand of Catholic mysticism this destructive process is at work. Man is plagued by hints and guesses of an ideal which can neither be reached nor brought into the twittering world of peripheral reality, except by the saint. But like Yeats, Roethke tried to find the realm of the spiritual within life itself. The pure moments he speaks of continually are moments of unity of being, a primitive variant on Yeats' theme; moments of calm beyond doubt during which he seems to discern the deepest rhythms of nature not described but felt passionately, ubiquitously; moments transcending death because accepting it as an inevitable process of life. Roethke's most determined conviction was the belief that "Eternity is now." Once the doors of perception are cleansed, the world will appear as it is, infinite. Like Blake or Yeats in his later life, he sought not withdrawal, but a transfiguration of present life and the present self.

Roethke began "Meditations of an Old Woman" in 1955 shortly after the death of his mother, who is the model for its central figure. Her death seems to have goaded him to a systematic exploration of his basic beliefs. In *Words for the Wind* he had turned to love as a sustaining principle of order; but, in the retrospective glance of old age, there comes a time when love is no longer possible. He sees his mother in this situation: an old woman forced to meditate on death and to will transcendence of it. In the sequence he tries to reproduce her final meditations, her sense of isolation and estrangement, her anxiety over death and meaninglessness, her desperate gropings for an answer, however symbolic and indirect, to the question of meaning to existence. In effect, she tries to piece together, from the minor moments of spiritual ecstasy of her lifetime, a coherent impression of the soul.

In writing his poem Roethke confronted a problem central to the poet who would make spiritual consciousness the subject of his poetry. Because the modern poet has at hand no universally held conscious formulation of belief, he can take nothing for granted. He has not only to find his own language for experiences which Donne, Herbert, Vaughan, or Traherne could convey through traditional metaphors, but he must also identify those intuitive experiences within an order that genuinely interprets, makes sense of spiritual experience. If, like Eliot, he believes in Anglo-Catholicism, he must still make his belief emotionally understandable to the sensibility unprepared to accept that tradition. Or if, like Yeats, he erects his own elaborate scaffolding to accommodate his spiritual vision, he must begin with experiences like unity of being which the reader can identify as his own. In other words his position is defensive; he must begin at the beginning, tracing the evolution of his own spiritual consciousness starting with vague suggestions which are explored until the mind reaches an intuition. The modern poem attempting to relate spiritual experience to contemporary consciousness must be a private exploration of religious instinct, eschewing all conventional pieties which might be acceptable in a less heterogeneous age.

Without the systematic imagination of a Yeats, Roethke was forced to withdraw into the interior world of psychological experience to examine the phenomenon of consciousness itself. He discovered assurances of spiritual reality in the pure moment of intuitive being—those minor moments of spiritual blessedness which come to the self as a kind of reprieve. It is for this reason that the old woman begins her anatomy of the spirit by examining her own alternate modes of consciousness: moments of ecstasy, reverie, dream, memory, hallucination, tracing those powers in the self that are inconsistent with its limitation to quotidian reality and may form the basis of a new conception of the self.

The withdrawal into the world of inner experience brings with it its own kind of imagery: an imagery deriving from dreams, not from observation, and retaining the inconsequence, the half-understood but deeply felt significance of dreams, their symbolic truth. The development of the poem is not the development of narrative but is rather a deeper and deeper exploration of an original theme. There is less a progression of thought than a circling round a state of mind, a final innocence, which is aspired to, yet continually despaired of. The overall movement of the sequence is successfully climaxed in the experience of rebirth, the movement from the stasis of the entirely quiescent self to the freedom of new life.

The first poem opens with the old woman's description of the landscape, but in Roethke's traditional manner, all natural objects are assimilated until they become symbols of the mind's emotional tone: trees tilt, stones loosen, the wind "eats at the weak plateau." The spirit's journey is objectified in metaphors of frenzied aimless mobility: a cross-country bus ride, dreams of abortive journeys, and marine images, of the lobster's backward motion, of the salmon's movement against the current; all images of constricted, partial vision as the spirit searches for "another life, / Another way and place in which to continue." What the old woman seeks and cannot find in her searches among the "waste lonely places / Behind the eye" is the moment of revelation. Inevitably she is disappointed; there can be "no riven tree, or lamb dropped by an eagle." There are only moments of heightened consciousness in nature, in which we recognize what Eliot has called the "hints and guesses," moments impossible to define except as a kind of stillness in which there is expectancy:

> A fume reminds me, drifting across wet gravel;
> A cold wind comes over stones;
> A flame, intense, visible,
> Plays over the dry pods,
> Runs fitfully along the stubble,
> Moves over the field,
> Without burning.

This image of light playing over dry stubble in winter which appeared for the first time in "The Lost Son" holds for Roethke the persistent fascination that "light on a broken column," the image associated with the rose garden, held for Eliot. The word "reminds" is implied in both experiences. It seems that the moment wakens in the mind a sense of loss, a memory half guessed or hint half understood. If only the memory can be awakened and probed for its meaning, a spiritual equilibrium might finally be achieved. It is as though Roethke were insisting that the psychic disposition for mystical experience is there potentially, awaiting only a signal to express itself in action.

In the second meditation, the intimations of the autonomy of the spirit begin to be explored. "Why," Eliot has asked in *The Use of Poetry and the Use of Criticism,* "for all of us, out of all that we have heard, seen, felt, in a lifetime, do certain images recur, charged with emotion, rather than others? The song of one bird, the leap of one fish, at a particular place and time, the scent of one flower . . . such memories may have symbolic value, but of what we cannot tell, for they come to represent the depths of feeling into which we cannot peer." In section 3 of the meditation the old woman reverts to such moments: the overwhelming memory of perfume from half-opened buds when a dress caught on a rosebrier; fleeting images on the sill of the eye in the slow coming out of sleep; palpable hallucinations of tree-shrews from a remembered illness. Such moments forbid a premature closing of accounts with reality because they bring a conviction of definite types of mentality inconsistent with ordinary consciousness. In such moments consciousness seems to come in contact with the deeper unnamed feelings which form the substratum of our being and to which we rarely penetrate. These moments, charged with numinous energy, bring the joyful sensation of release: "The body, delighting in thresholds, / Rocks in and out of itself." The conviction comes of the mobility of consciousness which has been arbitrarily limited to the rational. The problem becomes one of vision: "The eye altering, alters all." The limitations placed on reality are subjective, and inward transmutation is the clue to preternatural experience.

Louis Martz [in *The Poetry of Meditation*] has called the subject of the meditative poem "the creation of the self." In her third meditation, the old woman touches, if only momentarily, this deep-buried self, the ghost within her own breast:

> A voice keeps rising in my early sleep,
> A muffled voice, a low sweet watery noise.
> Dare I embrace a ghost from my own breast?
> A spirit plays before me like a child,
> A child at play, a wind-excited bird.

Roethke describes the interior revelation as a "low sweet watery noise," a voice from the unconscious. Explained in psychological terms, the long process of inward contemplation has activated one of the traditional archetypes from the unconscious—that of the divine child, always a symbol of nascent spiritual life and of immanent rebirth. In mystical terms the self has experienced the initiatory moment of spiritual awakening. From his notebooks, it is clear that Roethke was familiar with the Jungian concept of individuation through the activation of the archetypal symbol—a process of transmutation of personality from a state of dissociation to a higher unity through integration with the unconscious mind. Yet it hardly seems necessary to invoke elaborate psychological justification for what is an ordinary conception—the soul perceived as innocent child, unless the inference of M. L. Rosenthal [in *The New Poets*] is accepted as general: that Roethke has resuscitated the rustic memorial of a belief in the soul. The perception is so delicate and evanescent that no strong claims are made as to its authenticity. The experience brings nothing that can be known in the sense of a sustaining dogma, but simply a sense of union with a presence, momentarily exhilarating, but for that very reason dangerously tenuous. In fact, the old woman comes to dismiss it herself as a possible illusion.

In search of assurances she turns in section 3 to a sustaining memory from youth when, for one mystical moment, "reality" came closer and the mind exceeded its finite bounds. The one conviction Roethke held to tenaciously was that there is a wholeness of what we are that can rarely be known, a wholeness which for some inexplicable reason we have been denied. As has been said, mystical experience was for him not so much a search for God as an evanescent intuition of this wholeness when momentarily the confusion of the separate divided selves is transcended. Roethke is very precise in his delineation of the stages of the experience. It begins as a familiar moment of stasis: what he referred to as moments "fixed under the eye of eternity." As in the later poem "In a Dark Time," it is a moment when the correspondences, analogies reminding the self of the invisible world, become apparent. The images of "Islamic moon" and "daemon" seem to be borrowed from Yeats's *A Vision* to define the experience as one of integration, a movement from the pure subjectivity of the empirical self to the higher objectivity that is the ideal of eastern mysticism. This at least would appear to be the only explanation for the curious line: "Out, out you secret beasts, / You birds, you western birds." In Yeats's symbology, the bird is the natural emblem for the spiritual introspection that is lacking to western sensibility. The daimon, again in Yeats's system, is man's antithetical image, or ultimate self; sometimes it would seem a separate spiritual entity which imposes its remembered life on its mortal counterpart, thus creating the human being's body of fate. Roethke seems to temper Yeats's concept with the more familiar daemon of neo-Platonism, so that the line: "I shed my clothes to slow my daemon down" implies simply a quest for union with the higher spiritual self. It might be felt that Roethke is here too dependent on extraneous symbolism. His terminology is familiar: "Islamic moon," "daemon," "holy line," "western birds," "fire," but it intrudes into the atmosphere of the poem. One minds this invasion from the East because it has not been assimilated to the general emotional tone. Yet it is a momentary invasion, since the frenzied appeal to the primitive realm carries the reader back to a familiar world: "I said farewell to sighs, / Once to the toad, / Once to the frog, / And once to my flowing thighs." The traditional hierarchical progression from animal through man to spirit is never forthcoming in Roethke's work. Instead his spiritual quest is always in some sense a return, a regression to the subliminal world of toad and frog. He sought a primitive kind of innocence, an escape from self to the condition of the bird: "A rapt thing with a name." There is always something fragile and delicate in the purity of being he advocated. Even the purgatorial fire, the cleansing ecstasy of the mystical moment, is to be found in "a small place." The ideal, as the old woman says in the fourth meditation, is to "flame into being!" "to blaze like a tree." Only primitive life can know this concentration continuously. In Roethke's evolutionary scheme of things, man never looms very large. Little is accorded to the achievements of human intelligence. For him there is no significant difference between what he calls the "coarse short-hand of the subliminal depths" and the "grave philosophical language"—both are enunciations of the same terror and dismay. Like D. H. Lawrence, he values the natural self.

The sequence ends with the last poem, "What Can I Tell My Bones?" It is a moving elegy to the spirit's hunger and desolation. In it, Roethke achieves exactly what he is after: a personal, intuitive exploration of the meaning of preternatural experience based on the traditional principles of the mystic quest, which are yet so deeply buried as in no way to obtrude upon the delicate surface of the poem.

In the first part of the poem, Roethke identifies the old woman's state of mind in terms borrowed from the traditional mystical description of the purgative state, a state of pain and effort in which the self is only aware of its finitude and isolation while longing "for absolutes that never come." Such desolation is not an obsolescent state. It is part of the contemporary problem of spiritual anxiety, the terror of immanent nonbeing: "The self says, I am; / The heart says, I am less; / The spirit says, you are nothing." Nothing could be more explicit than the old woman's cry: "The cause of God in me—has it gone?" To speak of the fear of death is to oversimplify; it is more precisely the fear of meaninglessness, of a lack of ultimate purpose to existence. The essential predicate of the religious personality is the desire for a principle of Love to which the belief and power of the individual life may be united. Lacking this principle, the self is without center. The old woman says: "My desire's a wind trapped in a cave. . . . / Love is my wound." She thinks of the essential tenet of mysticism—that God seeks union with the living soul. To her, longing for rebirth, this has a precise and desperate irony: "I rock in my own dark, / Thinking, God has need of me. / The dead love the unborn."

It is difficult to determine exactly what Roethke means when he speaks of God. No doubt it seems easier to accept Yeats's Thirteenth Circle, or Eliot's Word intersecting time, because each is so well accommodated within a system. The closest one can come to Roethke's meaning is to speak of an energetic principle of love directing all of life. Perhaps it is almost impossible to be a lyric poet without some such notion of a deistic principle. Roethke often quoted Meister Eckhart with approbation: "God must be brought to birth in the soul again, and again." The implication is that God's existence is predicated upon the self's bringing God to birth in the soul. This would seem to be confirmed in his commentary on the poem "In a Dark Time" where he writes that the self in the mystical moment "becomes the Godhead itself, not only the veritable creator of the universe but the creator of the revealed God." He adds that God "in his most supreme manifestation, risks being maimed, if not destroyed." It is clear that his conception of God is far from orthodox. He confessed that his vision was very incomplete. Yet he continually professed a hope that "some other form or aspect of God will endure with man again, will save him from himself." His attitude, . . . his refusal to accept preconceived notions of divinity, implying as it does a rejection of dogmatism and an abhorrence of self-delusion—"that pelludious Jesus-shimmer"—is eminently appealing to modern sensibility.

In section 3 the movement of the entire sequence toward rebirth finally reaches its climax. If one is not familiar with Roethke's severe economy, the climax will appear abrupt and terse, for it is conveyed entirely through impressionistic images. The central image, familiar from "The Lost Son," is of weeds which "turn toward the wind weed-skeletons." The verb is active. In the moment of extremity the dead life submits to the natural forces assimilating it to cyclic processes. It is an image of abasement and acceptance. Such is the condition of the self in the moment of reversal which Roethke insisted must come quickly or not at all: "Simply by the leap of the heart do we begin again." "We cry and we are heard." In the moment of extremity the will, with its fear of death which militates against existence, must give way; a new innocence is discovered in submission:

> To what more vast permission have I come?
> . . . .
> I no longer cry for green in the midst of cinders,
> Or dream of the dead, and their holes.
> Mercy has many arms.

This new permission hardly involves the notion of God. It is something simpler, more personal; a primitive variant of the purgative cleansing of vision:

> My spirit rises with the rising wind;
> I'm thick with leaves and tender as a dove,
> I take the liberties a short life permits—
> I seek my own meekness;
> I recover my tenderness by long looking.
> By midnight I love everything alive.
> Who took the darkness from the air?
> I'm wet with another life.
> Yes, I have gone and stayed.

Long-looking, the act of meditation by which the self recovers its meekness: "Be still! Be still and know." In submission, the old woman achieves an almost mystical calm of rapport with elemental nature. M. L. Rosenthal compared the stillness of such moments to the light-spirited seriousness which we are told the early Christians possessed, a sweetness of nature derived from the literal rendering of the minutiae of nature, and from accepting their meaning without quarreling about ultimates. It is this reverent attitude to nature's particulars that frees the self. "Renunciation does not take away," Roethke wrote. "It gives. It gives the inexhaustible power of simple things." Humility, a capacity for reverence, a new unthought-of nonchalance with the best of nature, is the core of Roethke's aesthetic. John Crowe Ransom wrote that Roethke's old woman makes the best kind of saint it is advisable to try for.

It would be a mistake to seek a rigid intellectual formulation for this "permission" which the old woman achieves. As John Crowe Ransom [in "On Theodore Roethke's 'In a Dark Time' "] added: "She has not had to pray for this revelation, and does not bother as to where it came from, being scarcely conscious of her metaphysics." But it can be taken a step further if appeal is made to Paul Tillich, whose influence on Roethke has already been mentioned. The old woman has broken through to that state of absolute faith which Tillich has called "the courage to be." Able finally to abandon the need for certainties, she can say "Yes" to being. No concrete assurances have been discovered that might stem the realities of fate and death; as she knows, Providence and immortality remain fictions. But they no longer concern her because her faith is declared in being itself, and in the transpersonal presence of divinity which is its source. This is what Tillich means by the courage to be which can incorporate nonbeing into itself. It is the leap of faith made without final assurances because faith is all. Roethke's character achieves her personal variant of this courage, although her "permission" is at once more delicate and more energetic than its philosophical counterpart:

> What came to me vaguely is now clear,
> As if released by a spirit,
> Or agency outside me.
> Unprayed-for,
> And final.

In the original *Words for the Wind* published in 1958, "Meditations of an Old Woman" concluded the volume. After the strict formality of the love poems, it seemed a radical stylistic experiment, signaling a new departure in Roethke's work. Obviously he had turned to the powerful influence of T. S. Eliot's *Four Quartets* to liberate himself from the formality of his earlier writing. He explained the reason for this in an interview reported by Cleanth Brooks and Robert Penn Warren in *Conversations on the Craft of Poetry:*

There are areas of experience in modern life that simply cannot be rendered by either the formal lyric or straight prose. We need the catalogue in our time. We need the eye close to the object, the poem about the single incident—the animal, the child. We must permit poetry to extend consciousness as far, as deeply, as particularly as it can, to recapture, in Stanley Kunitz's phrase, what it has lost to some extent to prose.

To appreciate this statement it is necessary to remember the atmosphere of the time. The general ambition of poetry of the fifties, stimulated no doubt by the publication of William Carlos Williams's *Paterson* I and II in 1947 and 1948, was to discover larger comprehensive forms of expression to accommodate the intractable nature of contemporary experience. This central stimulus led to the creation of projective verse. Speaking on behalf of the poets of his generation, Charles Olson had written in 1950:

> I would hazard the guess that, if projective verse is practiced long enough . . . verse again can carry much larger material than it has carried in our language since the Elizabethans . . . if I think that the *Cantos* make more "dramatic" sense . . . it is not because I think they have solved the problem but because the methodology of the verse in them points a way by which, one day, the problem of larger content and of larger forms may be solved.

The proliferation of the sequence or series of poems was the obvious result: Allen Ginsberg's *Howl,* Robert Lowell's *Life Studies,* and Olson's own *Maximus Poems.* Yet to some poets, this kind of comprehensiveness was at best ambiguous, the order of a sequence being based, more often than not, on the simple assertion that all of a poet's activities constitute a unity. Eliot's *Four Quartets* seemed, at least to Roethke, to offer a more fruitful example of how the sequence could be made to satisfy demands for larger, comprehensive forms without sacrificing exacting standards of unity and coherence.

It must be admitted that he could hardly have chosen a more difficult poet to emulate. In the *Four Quartets* Eliot found an idiom and a metric that were entirely idiosyncratic, making imitation admittedly dangerous. However, Roethke learned three valuable lessons of poetic technique. First, he learned how to adapt meter to mood, and to incorporate radical shifts of metrical style within the contemplative poem. This was something he had already discovered in the frenetic, rhythmic juxtapositions of the *Praise to the End!* sequence, so that Eliot's example served mainly to reinforce a personal technique. He also learned how to manipulate symbolism as a means to unify the long sentence. It is clear that the thematic material of the *Quartets* is less an idea or myth than certain common symbols, in particular, the four elements: earth, air, fire, water, each a thematic center of images in the separate quartets. Roethke uses symbolism in a similar fashion, if less dogmatically, so that the symbols of wind, fire, water, light, recur within his sequence with constant modification.

Finally Roethke learned from metrical and syntactical innovations in the *Quartets*. In his essay "Vers Libre," Eliot insisted that any good verse he had read either took a simple form like iambic pentameter and constantly withdrew from it, or took no form at all, and constantly approximated a simple one. Helen Gardener seems to have correctly identified the metrical pattern to which *The Quartets* approximate as a four stress line with a strong medial pause. Eliot's syntactical patterns are equally simple. Allen Tate has called his style a form of deliberate peregrination, of statement followed by constant modification, supported by an intentionally fractured syntax. The common pattern is of noun followed by adjectives: "the River / Is a strong brown god—sullen, untamed and intractable." This very resistance to a fluid vocabulary joined to a deliberate metrical uncertainty defines his personal voice.

In parts of his sequence, Roethke comes close to Eliot's metric and syntax. Eliot writes:

> Now the light falls
> Across the open field, leaving the deep lane
> Shuttered with branches, dark in the afternoon,
> Where you lean against a bank while a van passes,
> And the deep lane insists on the direction
> Into the village.

Roethke writes:

> Often I think of myself as riding—
> Alone, on a bus through western country,
> I sit above the back wheels, where the jolts are hardest
> . . . .
> And we ride, we ride, taking the curves
> Somewhat closer, the trucks coming
> Down from behind the last ranges,
> Their black shapes breaking past.

Roethke has borrowed not only the four stress line with strong medial pause, but more importantly, Eliot's prosaic mannerisms: the proliferation of adverbs, prepositional and adverbial phrases, and the fractured syntax of the declarative sentence with its string of clausal modifiers. These echoes jar against the integrity of his own voice. Though not numerous in terms of the whole sequence, they do disturb:

> And we bounce and sway along toward midnight,
> The lights tilting up, skyward, as we come over a little rise,
> Then down, as we roll like a boat from a wave-crest.

> All journeys, I think, are the same:
> The movement is forward, after a few wavers,
> And for a while we are all alone,
> Busy, obvious with ourselves,
> The drunken soldier, the old lady with her peppermints.

Eliot writes:

> When the train starts, and the passengers are settled
> To fruit, periodicals and business letters
>
> . . . .
>
> Their faces relax from grief into relief,
> To the sleepy rhythm of a hundred hours

Or

> Or as, when an underground train, in the tube, stops
>   too long between stations
> And the conversation rises and slowly fades into silence

The effectiveness of Eliot's journey images as metaphors for interior journeys are an obvious temptation to any poet, but Roethke's syntax and rhythm are again so similar to Eliot's that the echoes can seem detrimental. Yet it must be added that the imagination of Roethke's persona, at once more sensuous and affectionate than Eliot's, lays claim to a very different emotional response.

Sometimes it is the echo of a single line obviously alien to Roethke's own endemic manner that drives the reader back to the Eliot source: "It is difficult to say all things are well, / When the worst is about to arrive" or "We start from the dark. Pain teaches us little." The easy philosophical gravity of the lines is a tone Eliot has worked too well. As he himself said, a great poet can exhaust a particular pose for all those who come after him.

Even so, the delicate line between allusion and imitation is frustratingly ambiguous. We can allow Roethke the line "Do these bones live? Can I live with these bones?" though the memory of Eliot's "Shall these bones live? Shall these / Bones live?" is clearly in mind, because the echo is functional. In both cases, the image sums up a tradition and depends on that tradition for its full implications. Furthermore, the phrase is assimilated to Roethke's characteristic style by its context. The line which follows, "Mother, mother of us all, tell me where I am!" reproduces the desperate, agonized plea that is so much a part of his tone.

One must question the pressures that lead to poetic flaws like unintentional echoes and extraneous or esoteric symbolism. Any poet obviously works under the current pressures of contemporary poetic modes. Roethke was acutely sensitive to the criticism that his poetry was exclusive, self-involved, as opposed to socially relevant, and was aware that the current trend was toward inclusiveness, toward a more philosophical poetry. He wished to extend the capacit· ·f his poetry to explore meditative themes. Inevitably, he felt that an assault on the Eliot cult was in order. But to dismiss "Meditations of an Old Woman" as mere pastiche is narrow and destructive. The poem contains some of the finest passages Roethke wrote, and some of his deepest insights into the introspective workings of sensibility. The pressure of his own imagination, the effortless and inescapable presence of his own individuality, is so palpably pervasive throughout the sequence that such a gesture is patently ridiculous.

When *Words for the Wind* was published in New York in the fall of 1958 it was widely reviewed as the work of a major poet. F. Cudworth Flint in the *Virginia Quarterly Review* wrote that, "of his chosen terrain, Mr. Roethke is master." Richard Eberhart, in the *New York Times,* called the book a major achievement in the romantic tradition of American poetry. Delmore Schwartz in *Poetry* remarked that "It is sufficiently clear by now that Roethke is a very important poet"; and W. D. Snodgrass, in the *Hudson Review,* insisted that the new work was an accomplishment in language and form about which many of Roethke's contemporaries had only been dreaming. The book received many of the prominent literary awards of that year, among them the Bollingen Award and the National Book Award, firmly establishing Roethke's reputation and prestige as a poet. It probably convinced him as well that he was ready to begin the poem he had long contemplated, the "North American Sequence."

JAY PARINI

Blake and Roethke:
When Everything Comes to One

> *Not all the dead are used: we must take*
> *what we can from them.*
> —Theodore Roethke, *Notebooks*

In an essay entitled "How to Write Like Somebody Else" Theodore Roethke said that in a time when "the romantic notion of the inspired poet still has considerable credence, true 'imitation' takes a certain courage. One dares to stand up to a great style, to compete with papa." Implicit in this statement is a distinction between false imitation, which comes down to mimicry of certain stylistic effects, and true imitation, which involves a confrontation, an appropriation and *re*-creation of the precursor's visionary stance. This latter kind of imitation occurs in the case of Blake and Roethke. For Blake remains the single most important poet for Roethke, not so much on the level of style (though I shall point to similarities at this level) but at the deeper level of mythopoetic action. Both poets were intent upon making a system or a personal *mythos* (in Northrop Frye's sense of the term as a shaping principle of literary form), and this mythos moves beyond allegory to anagogy, so that the characters in the system do not simply represent another stage or level of reality but move toward embodiment. This is the stage often called "mystical," when (as Roethke said) "The mind enters itself, and God the mind, / And one is One, free in the tearing wind." Here Roethke seems close to the heart of Blake's visionary stance; as Frye has said

---

From *William Blake and the Moderns,* edited by Robert J. Bertholf and Annette S. Levitt. © 1982 by the State University of New York. State University of New York Press, 1982.

[in *Fearful Symmetry*] "the true God for such visionaries is not the orthodox Creator . . . but an unattached creative Word. . . . Unity with this God could be attained only by an effort of vision which not only rejects the duality of subject and object but attacks the far more difficult antithesis of being and nonbeing as well."

It is mostly in his last volume, *The Far Field,* that Roethke comes to express his visionary sense of wonder, particularly in the "Sequence, Sometimes Metaphysical" and the "North American Sequence." Here Roethke approaches the apocalyptic identification of the kingdom with his own body that was Blake's culmination in *Jerusalem.* When one is one, free in the tearing wind, Blake's vision has been accomplished, although his imagery is drawn from the New Testament and Roethke's is taken from the Old Testament. It was Blake's method, especially in the later phase, to outleap the world, to claim the transcendental vision directly; whereas Roethke, fascinated by the spirit *as manifest* in nature, ascends the ladder of creation by gradual—indeed loving—steps. But the influence of Blake on Roethke can be detected much earlier, in the "Lost Son" sequences. In these poems Roethke set out to create his mythos, the struggle of the lost son in his quest for identity and his efforts to overcome Papa. Blake proposed the same process in his "Orc cycle," which occupies a central position in his work as a whole. Orc represents the natural man, and his struggle to resolve the contraries of Los and to overcome the opposing spectres of Urizen and Urthona becomes the equivalent mythos in Blake. Orc, like the lost son, moves through various stages of maturation; he opposes the old man, Urizen, until he naturally becomes an old man himself (at which point regeneration occurs and the cycle begins again). "Implicit in the myth of Orc and Urizen," Frye comments, "is the allegory of the young striking down the old, the most obvious symbol of which is the son's revolt against a father." The Oedipal myth resides at the base of Blake's cycle, and it is this same myth that links Roethke's sequences to Blake.

Orc, says Martin Price [in "The Standard of Energy], "embodies the rebellious principle of renewed and independent life." He is the son of Los, the redeeming power of imagination, and Enitharmon, the "first female now separate." But Orc is fallen man as well. Los and Enitharmon chain their son to a rock, and the matter of Blake's cycle involves Orc's struggle for freedom, especially against Urizen (who is a negative aspect of Los). Urizen represents pure rationality and lifeless order, a version of Roethke's Papa, who represents *ordnung* in *The Lost Son.* Blake does not oppose intellect in its complete form, where it combines with freshness of perception and feeling, but in this fallen (Urizenic) aspect he condemns it. "Like Milton,"

Price says, "Blake sees all human existence as shot through with moments of fall and moments of redemption, and one fall provides an archetype for all others." Blake's myth, ultimately, like Roethke's, looks forward to a redemptive vision, to the restoration of that primal unity lost in the fall. But Blake's protagonist, Orc, must first release himself from the treadmill of desire; as Frye puts it, "The natural tendency of desire (Orc) in itself is to find its object. Hence the effect of the creative impulse on desire is bound to be restrictive unless the release of desire becomes the inevitable by-product of creation."

The body of Roethke's work focuses on the single mythos that begins in *The Lost Son,* Roethke's second book (1948). This volume provides the key to the rest of his work, for all the essential symbols of his system are present here in one form or another. Papa, the Urizenic father, is Otto Roethke, the greenhouse owner. Otto is at times seen as God; he is terrifying and powerful. Roethke's mother, Helen, is present but in the background. Like Enitharmon, she is passive, sometimes conflated with nature itself in its passive aspect. The greenhouse is a cultured Beulah-world apart from the harsher nature outside, Roethke's "symbol for the whole of life, a womb, a heaven-on-earth." In his notebooks of the forties Roethke tried to understand this luminous symbol occupying the center of his work: "what was this greenhouse? It was a jungle, and it was paradise, it was order and disorder. Was it an escape? No, for it was a reality harder than the various suspensions of terror." There is also the open field, a place of illumination and, sometimes, mystical experience. "The Lost Son" itself, the title poem, contains the primary symbols; it is the text which informs the rest of his work, reiterating the elementary hero-myth with its classic pattern of flight (separation from the tribe), testing in the wilderness, descent into the underworld, and return (atonement, transfiguration). This cycle, like the Orc cycle in Blake, recurs in successive volumes—though it finds fullest expression in *The Lost Son, Praise to the End!* (1951), and *The Waking* (1953), of which the initial poem, "O, Thou Opening, O" completes the *Lost Son* sequence per se.

In "The Lost Son" Roethke invokes the Blakean dialectic of innocence and experience. Scattered through his working notebooks of the period (1943-53) is the famous proverb from *The Marriage of Heaven and Hell:* "Without Contraries is no progresion," which could serve as an epigraph to Roethke's *Collected Poems.* In Blake's system, the mind pulls into its own orbit those forces which might exist outside of its control; the dialectic absorbs all resistances; necessities become internal. Hence the lost son journeys toward identity, self-affirmation and, later, self-transcendence; but his path remains tortuous, marked by detours and culs-de-sac as in section 3 (of five sections), which begins:

> Where do the roots go?
>   Look down under the leaves.
> Who put the moss there?
>   These stones have been here too long.
> Who stunned the dirt into noise?
>   Ask the mole, he knows.

In the last line above Roethke alludes directly to *The Book of Thel* and Blake's epigraph: "Does the Eagle know what is in the pit? / Or wilt thou go ask the Mole?" The lost son is instructed to look downward, to dig into nether regions of psychic history for answers to his questions.

The Book of Thel concerns the failure of a heroine, Thel. She fails to progress from innocence, from Beulah (an earthly paradise, associated with unfallen sexuality) to Generation (fallen sexuality, but a necessary condition, the phase at which Orc begins his struggle). By failing to make this "fall," Thel refuses to exercise one of the vital powers of the soul, the *will*. She is timid, afraid of incarnation and the terrors of sense experience. By staying a virgin for too long, she forfeits the opportunity of progress and final redemption. As a result, she cannot remain static—Blake does not admit of this possibility—rather, she is destined to fall back into the solipsistic state of Ulro, the lowest condition in Blake's scheme. Her fear recalls the moment in section 4 of "The Lost Son" where the boy says "Fear was my father, Father Fear." But unlike Thel, the lost son passes from the world of the greenhouse and his family cloister into the dangerous zone of Generation, here represented as a swampy bogland:

> Hunting along the river,
> Down among the rubbish, the bug-riddled foliage,
> By the muddy pond-edge, by the bog-holes,
> By the shrunken lake, hunting, in the heat of summer.

At this stage of his journey the boy-hero enters into the cyclical *process* of nature; the summer (which Blake associates with Generation) gives way to late autumn or early winter in the last section of the poem, a time when

> It was beginning winter,
> An in-between time,
> The landscape still partly brown:
> The bones of weeds kept swinging in the wind,
> Above the blue snow.

"The Lost Son" cannot be said to conclude; conclusion goes against the cyclical grain. Instead, the hero reaches an "irresolute resolution," an ending which is as well as beginning. This parallels the movement of Blake's cycle, where each poem achieves a partial conclusion, as in *The Book of Urizen:*

> 8. So Fuzon call'd all together
> The remaining children of Urizen:
> and they left the pendulous earth:
> They called it Egypt, & left it.
>
> 9. And the salt ocean rolled englob'd.

This ending prepares for the opening of *The Book of Ahania,* where the Orc cycle is resumed: "Fuzon, on a chariot iron-wing'd / On spiked flames rose." The last section of "The Lost Son" seems a long way from the seasonless paradise of Eden, the uppermost estate in Blake's overall scheme; but a partial cleansing of the senses certainly occurs: "The mind moved, not along, / Through the clear air, in the silence." *The Book of Thel,* on the other hand, ends with an unredemptive thud as Thel is shown "the secret of the land unknown" but has not the courage to make an adequate response; indeed, "The Virgin started from her seat, & with a shriek, / Fled back unhindered till she came into the vales of Har." She will doubtless lapse into the condition of nonparticipation characteristic of Ulro, where desires go perpetually unsatisfied; having failed to make the journey *through* desire which can lead to freedom from desire. Her destiny is the "single vision" Blake reviled, a dreadful retreat from the "threefold vision" of Beulah or the ideal "fourfold vision" enjoyed by those in Eden. Roethke's "lost son," and this again has parallels in the Orc cycle, lacks none of the required courage; just as Orc has the dual aspect of Adonis, the dying and reviving god, and Prometheus, the thief of fire, the protagonist of the "Lost Son" sequence is dismembered, psychologically, in the wilderness, buried (section 2 of "The Lost Son"), and revived; like Prometheus, he accepts the responsibility of fire: "I'll take the fire." The fire, in this case, is sexual desire; the lost son sees that he must face up to his passion if he will control it.

The contraries of innocence and experience, so crucial to Blake's system, operate in the whole of Roethke's work, but they have a special place in *The Lost Son,* which concerns the hero at the point of maturation where sexuality must be repressed (Thel's choice) or accepted (the option taken by Blake's later heroine, Oothoon). The "married land" of Beulah from which Roethke's hero is "lost" appears once again in the lyric "The Waking,"

which precedes the "Lost Son" sequence in the 1948 volume. The poem
recalls the opening of Blake's lyric from *Poetical Sketches*, "How sweet I
roam'd from field to field, / And tasted all the summer's pride"—although
Roethke avoids the harsh ironies into which Blake falls:

> I strolled across
> An open field;
> The sun was out;
> Heat was happy.
>
> This way! This way!
> The wren's throat shimmered,
> Either to other,
> The blossoms sang.
>
> The stones sang,
> The little ones did,
> And flowers jumped
> Like small goats.
>
> A ragged fringe
> Of daisies waved;
> I wasn't alone
> In a grove of apples.

Roethke's lyric invokes the world of *Songs of Innocence,* a place where the
glowworm gives counsel ("A Dream"), the sun "make[s] happy the skies"
("The Ecchoing Green"), and "the green woods laugh, with the voice of joy
/ And the dimpling stream runs laughing by" ("Laughing Song"). The last
lines of Roethke's poem recreate the bliss of "Infant Joy," where Blake
writes:

> Pretty joy!
> Sweet joy but two days old.
> Sweet joy I call thee:
> Thou dost smile.
> I sing the while
> Sweet joy befall thee.

In much the same way does Roethke conclude:

> My ears knew
> An early joy.

> And all the waters
> Of all the streams
> Sang in my veins
> That summer day.

But neither poet has yet dramatized the separation of subject and object which follows inevitably as the realm of innocence gives way to experience. In Roethke as in Blake, the fall of man is coincident with the creation; both poets posit a condition of unity, a golden age, prior to the fall. And both look ahead to restoration of that unity, a state raised above "the hateful siege of contraries" (in Milton's phrase). "Blake gives us," says Price, "a world conceived as the manifestation of imaginative energy, hardened into opacity as energy fails, raised through intense and confident assertion to the image of One Man, containing all powers within himself and exercising them in the creation of works of art." Likewise Roethke, in "The Far Field," envisions "the end of things, the final man" whose "spirit moves like monumental wind / That gentles on a sunny blue plateau." But this is to look well beyond Orc and the lost son.

The poems of Roethke's sequence, individually and as a whole, recapitulate the journey from disorganized innocence through Generation, the crucible of summer, to organized innocence. As Bloom [in *The Visionary Company*] observes, "the only road to creativity and apocalypse lies through the realm of summer, the hard world of experience." Roethke's dialectic exacts a share of pain for each portion of joy in this summery woodland where

> Small winds made
> A chilly nose;
> The softest cove
> Cried for sound.

Or where the hero

> Reached for a grape
> And the leaves changed;
> A stone's shape
> Became a clam.

Not until the end of summer, "Along the low ground dry only in August," does the hero catch a glimpse of Eden, and that only after an intimation of mortality ("Was it dust I was kissing?"):

> I could watch! I could watch!
> I saw the separateness of all things!
> My heart lifted up with the great grasses;
> The weeds believed me, and the nesting birds.
> There were clouds making a rout of shapes crossing a
>   windbreak of cedars,
> And a bee shaking drops from a rain-soaked honeysuckle.
> The worms were delighted as wrens.
> And I walked, I walked through the light air;
> I moved with the morning.

The intensity of the lost son in his moment of ecstasy contrasts sharply with the infantile joy of "The Waking," although the sense of oneness with the natural world remains constant. Having come through the harsh world of experience, where the division of subject and object is underscored, the boy-hero enters this momentary flash of vision. It is the dramatic context which provides the intensity.

One self-contained sequence of brief lyrics within *The Lost Son* has come to be known as the Greenhouse Poems; it contains some of Roethke's most widely anthologized pieces. These tough, sensual, and concrete poems recreate the texture of experience in the manner of *The Songs of Experience* and serve as a prelude to the "Lost Son" sequence in the way Blake's *Songs* adumbrate the Orc cycle. Roethke's lyrics establish the mythopoetic context necessary for the "Lost Son" sequence to work and prepare the ground for the symbolist methods characteristic of the later poems. In short, he invents a sequence of natural fables; his poems exploit various mythic structures and allude to such standard hermetic symbols as the rose and the worm. "Cuttings" is the first fable:

> Sticks-in-a-drowse over sugary loam,
> Their intricate stem-fur dries;
> But still the delicate slips keep coaxing up water;
> The small cells bulge;
>
> One nub of growth
> Nudges a sand-crumb loose,
> Pokes through a musty sheath
> Its pale tendrilous horn.

The human parallels (the metaphor) are submerged; the sticks are "in-a-drowse," and the slips "coax" up water: both figures suggest a form of consciousness above the level commonly associated with the plant world. Roethke's cuttings are primordial nerve ends, low on the phylogenetic scale, but they prefigure something higher. The poem calls up a state of beginnings, a condition where the life-force is reduced to an urge, an importunate breathing. Again, the poem derives its force from the tacit myth of awakening.

Still, it is in the "Lost Son" sequence as it stretches over three books that Roethke accrues his largest debts to Blake. The lost son gropes toward self-awareness and separate identity in the manner of Blake's "fierce child," Orc, born in *The Book of Urizen* and struggling through many of the major poems against his various opposing spectres. The apocalyptic imagery and associational logic of both poets operate within a consistent, albeit difficult, symbol system. These systems are closed, and full of internal references. The lost son engages in the cycles of nature, advancing slowly toward his goal of identity and self-transcendence; his way out of nature is *through* it. Blake, by contrast, does not himself identify with Orc or suggest that his involvement with the natural cycles is a good thing. For him, the cycles of nature were a kind of death, a grinding down. As Frye explains, "the vision of life as an Orc cycle is the pessimistic view of life." In Blake's system, Orc is equivalent to the giant Albion in his fallen aspect. At the end of the cycle, Orc comes face-to-face with Urizen and the spectre of Urthona, who represents clock time (an aspect of the grinding down effected by the natural cycles). Orc's destiny is, of course, to become Urizen himself; then the cycle must begin again. Roethke's "lost son"—on the other hand—goes beyond these cycles, transcending the self-consciousness which leads into Ulro and the fate of Orc. Nonetheless both Roethke and Blake were aiming toward a myth of creation and destruction, a poetics of redemption.

The "Lost Son" sequence resumes in *Praise to the End!* with the hero-as-infant; the language of these poems suggests the process of disintegration which accompanies the fall into creation, akin to the breakup of the giant Albion into the four Zoas in Blake's system. Both poets reformulated the myth of disintegration at several stages in their careers. La Belle [in *The Echoing Wood of Theodore Roethke*] finds this myth in Blake emerging in the *Songs of Innocence* and compares the "Little Boy Lost" to Roethke's "lost son": "For both poets, the physical condition of the little boy lost in the Stygian darkness and trapped in the mire is an emblem for a state of psychological disorientation and for a loss of the true vision of innocence." In Blake's companion piece, "The Little Boy Found," the child is restored to innocence by God, who is "ever nigh," and who "Appeared like his father in white." In a similar way the lost son encounters Papa, who represents *ordnung* or authority (in its negative Urizenic aspect, however), upon his return from "The Pit" and the terrifying journey into experience. Throughout the "Lost Son" sequence Papa reappears at crucial moments as a "beard in a cloud" to provide (or force) order.

Praise to the End! opens with a birth poem, "Where Knock Is Open Wide," in which the poet reconstitutes the dreamworld of infancy. The poem opens with the infant-hero in some confusion over what is happening to him; he cannot distinguish cause from effect: "I know it's an owl. He's making it darker." He still thinks he is in Beulah-land, the state of primal unity, where God answers to every need within the instant: "God, give me a near. I hear flowers." This world is absolutely self-centered, and all sexual pleasure is onanistic: "Hello happy hands." But the truth of his new condition, which is postlapsarian, occurs to him rather suddenly: "I fell! I fell!" he cries, "The worm has moved away. / My tears are tired." He complains, "God's somewhere else," and darkness seems to have come for "a long long time."

"I Need, I Need" follows immediately and reviews the condition of loss. The title derives from the ninth design of Blake's series *For Children: The Gates of Paradise* (1793) with its inscription, "I want! I want!" The poem chronicles the infant's first encounters with unsatisfied desire, the terror of Blake's Orc as well. "I can't taste my mother," Roethke's infant cries. For the first time, the hero feels cut off from his source, separate. His consciousness has been divided, which leads him to wish for a prior state. And so unsatisfied desire leads necessarily to the habit of wishing:

> I wish I was a pifflebob
> I wish I was a funny
> I wish I had ten thousand hats,
> And made a lot of money.

Through this section Roethke uses the language of schoolchildren without being condescending; he enters into the child's consciousness by imitating verbal patterns that are thought to be childlike, a technique used by Blake in his *Songs of Innocence*. As S. Foster Damon has written [in *William Blake*]: "Blake does not contemplate children, in the manner of Wordsworth, Hugo, and Longfellow; he actually enters into their souls and speaks through their own mouths." So Roethke, in the above passage, uses the most basic of childhood tropes, a series of wishes. In Blake's engraving there are three figures, one of whom is a naked child, poised for climbing a moonbeam and, clearly, destined to failure. The child here has yet to move from innocence to experience, although the picture itself contains within its perimeter both contrary states. As La Belle says, "The viewpoint and the final significance of many of Blake's and Roethke's poems about childhood become very complex because the two contrary states of innocence and experience are not mutually exclusive and can exist in the same child or the same poem at once."

In Roethke's sequence, the states of innocence and experience alternate, and nature is by turns sympathetic and antagonistic. In "I Need, I Need," a poem about the fall into experience, nature appears unresponsive:

> Went down cellar,
> Talked to a faucet;
> The drippy water
> Had nothing to say.

But nature responds with robust sympathy in the next poem, "Bring the Day," which begins with a nursery rhyme-like chant:

> Bees and lilies there were,
> Bees and lilies there were,
> Either to other,—
> Which would you rather?
> Bees and lilies were there.
>
> The green grasses,—would they?
> The green grasses?—
> She asked her skin
> To let me in:
> The far leaves were for it.

Similar rhythms occur in many of Blake's *Songs*, such as "The Ecchoing Green"—though Roethke remains more tentative than Blake throughout:

> The Sun does arise,
> And make happy the skies.
> The merry bells ring
> To welcome the Spring.
> The skylark and thrush,
> The birds of the bush,
> Sing louder around,
> To the bells cheerful sound.
> While our sports shall be seen
> On the Ecchoing green.

Both poets use what Hopkins called "sprung rhythm," a meter familiar to readers of Mother Goose; other devices common to the nursery rhyme are used, such as repetition, short lines, internal rhyming, and alliteration. Roethke, in his essay "Some Remarks on Rhythm," comments on Blake's "A Poison Tree": "The whole poem is a masterly example of variation in rhythm, of playing against meter. It's what Blake called 'the bounding line,' the nervousness, the tension, the energy in the whole poem. And this is a clue to everything. Rhythm gives us the very psychic energy of the speaker, in one emotional situation at least." True enough; but more than meter is involved. The underlying pattern of gradually sharpened antitheses which force the hero of Roethke's sequence into a moral choice works as a principle of organization in much the same way as it does in Blake's Orc cycles and the later prophetic books.

The progress of Roethke's infant-hero in *Praise to the End!* is steady but not linear. "By snails, by leaps of frog, I came here," he says. The hero treks a landscape of few comforts, a *paysage moralisé* where "Eternity howls in the last crags. / The field is no longer simple." As he says, "It's a soul's crossing time." This setting resembles the familiar testing ground of most quest literature; Roethke's woodlands, far from being the enchanted forests one associates with childhood, come closer to Dante's *selva oscura*: "It's a dark wood, soft mocker." These dark woodlands resemble in character the Urizenic "dens / Mountain, moor, & wilderness" that trap Orc in the *Book of Urizen*. The path through these dark woods which leads to transcendental vision is beset with crossroads and detours. Sometimes the hero makes a wrong turn and finds himself in a place of total disaffection:

> Touch and arouse. Suck and sob. Curse and mourn.
> It's a cold scrape in a low place.
> The dead crow dries on a pole.
> Shapes in the shade
> Watch.

Yet later the hero can say with pride: "I've crawled from the mire, alert as a saint or a dog; / I know the back-stream's joy, and the stone's eternal pulseless longing." In general, the speaker arrives at some temporary conclusion near the end of each poem, slipping back again at the start of the next one, but never back quite so far. "I go back because I want to go forward," Roethke says in his notebooks. The lost son accepts his difficult quest with a certain equanimity: "What grace I have is enough."

What Roethke's "lost son" and Blake's hero, Orc, have in common is a belief in the powers of intuition. "Knowledge," Blake writes, "is not by deduction but Immediate by Perception or Sense at once." Conceptual discourse bears no interest. In *Jerusalem,* Blake's last prophetic book, the contraries of rational and emotional discourse find mythic equivalents:

> Rational Philosophy and Mathematic Demonstration
> Is divided in the intoxications of pleasure & affection
> Two Contraries War against each other in fury & blood,
> And Los fixes them on his Anvil, incessant his blows:
> He fixes them with strong blows. placing the stones &
>   timbers.
> To Create a World of Generation from the World of Death:
> Dividing the Masculine & Feminine: for the comingling
> Of Albions Luvahs Spectres was Hermaphroditic

Los, the terrifying artificer, creates out of these contraries a better world; however, the act of submitting to these contraries, to the sublunary world of Generation, requires genuine courage. Those without this courage, like Thel, must slip back inexorably into the sleep of Ulro.

The naïve romantic sides with "feeling" against "reason" in a simpleminded way. Blake does not do this; for his ultimate goal, Jerusalem, is a vision of the giant Albion restored. Head (Urizen), body (Tharmas), loins (Orc), and legs (Urthona) come together in the end. The imagination subsumes both "feeling" and "thought." "The act of creation," says Frye, "is not producing something out of nothing, but the act of setting free what we already possess." Nevertheless Blake, with some justice, attacks the "single vision" of Locke, Newton, and other rationalist thinkers of his time:

> I turn my eyes to the Schools & Universities of Europe
> And there behold the Loom of Locke whose Woof rages dire
> Washd by the Water-wheels of Newton. black the cloth
> In heavy wreathes folds over every Nation; cruel Works
> Of many Wheels I view, wheel without wheel, with cogs
>   tyrannic
> Moving by compulsion each other: not as those in Eden:
>   which
> Wheel within Wheel in freedom revolve in harmony & peace.

Roethke says, in a much less complex way, the same thing in the last poem of *Praise to the End!* entitled "I Cry, Love! Love!" (itself a quotation from Blake):

Reason? That dreary shed, that hutch for grubby schoolboys!
The hedgewren's song says something else.
I care for a cat's cry and the hugs, live as water.

The lost son is learning to begin, as Blake suggests, with perception and sense.

The title of this poem comes from the *Visions of the Daughters of Albion* (1793) in which the character of Oothoon answers to the feckless virgin, Thel. Oothoon attempts to move beyond innocence into experience, from Beulah into Generation; she is "a virgin fill'd with virgin fancies / Open to joy and to delight where ever beauty appears." Her failure to do as she wishes comes as no fault of her own; rather, the object of her desire, Theotormon, is utterly self-enthralled, sitting "Upon the margind ocean conversing with shadows dire." The central passage in *Visions* gave Roethke his theme:

I cry, Love! Love! Love! happy happy Love! free as the mountain
    wind!
Can that be Love, that drinks another as a sponge drinks water?
That clouds with jealousy his nights, with weepings all the day:
To spin a web of age around him, grey and hoary! dark!
Till his eyes sicken at the fruit that hangs before his sight.
Such is self-love that envies all! a creeping skeleton
With lamplike eyes watching around the frozen marriage bed.

Oothoon makes the crucial distinction between narcissism and "that generous love" which attaches itself to another person; the first is nugatory, even destructive, denying the reality of anything beyond the self. It brings on the dread sleep of Ulro. But this "happy happy love" does not drink another "as a sponge drinks water," merely feeding on the other person's energies. It exults in the other, celebrating itself in the process; it knows how "everything that lives is holy"—a phrase which Roethke liked to quote.

The hero in "I Cry Love! Love!" says, "Delight me otherly, white spirit," playing on "utterly" to gain a double sense. The maturing speaker now sees that he can discover his own identity only through another. "Bless me and the maze I'm in!" he says, accepting the siege of contraries and the world of objects: "Hello, thingy spirit." He has now fully accepted the fall into creation and will try to use this misfortune to his best advantage. He accepts Blake's sacramental view of nature, that everything alive is holy:

"Behold, in the lout's eye, / Love." The last stanza of the poem brings this realization to its conclusion:

> Who untied the tree? I remember now.
> We met in a nest. Before I lived.
> The dark hair sighed.
> We never enter
> Alone.

The question "Who untied the tree?" shows how mature the boy has become; it is equivalent to "Who made me and turned me loose in this fallen world?" He recollects a spirit who was present with him in the womb, the nest. And he takes great comfort merely in the fact that someone other than himself exists. The narrow self-consciousness of Ulro is denied, and the possibility of self-transcendence through love seems within the hero's reach.

But such optimism proves short-lived. As Roethke later notes: "From me to Thee's a long and terrible way." His last three books, from *The Waking* (which brings the "Lost Son" cycle to a close) to *Words for the Wind* (1958) and the posthumous *The Far Field* (1964), record the steady movement toward self-transcendence on "the long journey out of the self." The myth of the lost son, with its attendant symbols, remains at the center of his work, but the myth widens. A similar pattern occurs in Blake as he recapitulates his personal myth in *Milton* and *Jerusalem* (both written and etched between 1804 and 1820). As Frye says, "*Milton* describes the attainment by the poet of the vision that *Jerusalem* expounds in terms of all humanity." It is the same myth, the story of the fall of man, his struggle through the cycles of nature, and his redemption, which occupies him almost from the beginning. Similarly, *Words for the Wind* describes the transcendence of the self through love of another, the major theme of Roethke in his middle years (1953–59). *The Far Field* represents his *Jerusalem* or *Paradiso;* it recounts his hero's attainment of "the imperishable quiet at the heart of form."

"North American Sequence," in particular, moves toward a fullness of vision characteristic of *Jerusalem.* Blake's identification of the New Golgotha with the body and his daring to look directly into the fierce light of the godhead find an analog in Roethke's last meditations. In "The Longing," for instance, he writes:

> I would be a stream, winding between great striated
>   rocks in late summer;
> A leaf, I would love the leaves, delighting in the
>   redolent disorder of this mortal life.

The meditations all contain passages where the poet wishes to identify with the world outside himself, to enter the body of nature and move with his "body thinking," thereby extending human consciousness, perhaps indefinitely. The mortal self, as in *Jerusalem,* is destined for extinction: "Annihilate the Selfhood in me." Nothing will come of retaining the old self but the dreaded sleep of Ulro. Los, the heroic figure in Blake's epic, confronts the spectres which threaten him, saying:

> I know that Albion hath divided me, and that thou O my
>   Spectre,
> Hast just cause to be irritated: but look stedfastly upon me:
> Comfort thyself in my strength the time will arrive
> When all Albions injuries shall cease, and when we shall
> Embrace him tenfold bright, rising from his tomb in
>   immortality.

The great themes of *Jerusalem*—the restoration of the God in man and the triumph of imagination and fourfold vision—occupy Roethke as well in his last poems. In a moment of summary vision he declares:

> My eyes extend beyond the farthest bloom of the waves;
> I lose and find myself in the long water;
> I am gathered together once more;
> I embrace the world.

Roethke, unlike Blake in method, embraces the world to find redemptive vision; yet both poets discover themselves transfigured, sloughing off the old self for the new one, the Self, to be born.

But the quest, even in this last book, remains antithetical. The hero often lapses into self-doubt as he proceeds. He reenters the jungle world of "The Lost Son" in "The Long Waters," which begins the "North American Sequence."

> I return where fire has been,
> To the charred edge of the sea
> Where the yellowish prongs of grass poke through the
>   blackened ash,
> And the bunched logs peel in the afternoon sunlight.

In these "unsinging fields where no lungs breathe," the old fear returns, and the poet cries out for help to Blake's nurse, Mnetha, the guardian of Beulah: "Mnetha, Mother of Har, protect me / From the worm's advance. . . ." As in *Jerusalem,* the poet in *The Far Field* sharpens the antitheses, moving gradually toward illumination, restoration. In these last poems Roethke is working out an *analogia visionis* not unlike Blake's; he reads the world as "A steady storm of correspondences!" and approaches that apocalypse where "one is One, free in the tearing wind." This comes very close to Blake's "mysticism," which "is to be conceived neither as a human attempt to reach God nor a divine attempt to reach man, but as the realization in total experience of the identity of God and Man in which both the human creature and the superhuman Creator disappear." Roethke puts it this way in "A Walk in Late Summer":

> It lies upon us to undo the lie
> Of living merely in the realm of time.
> Existence moves toward a certain end—
> A thing all earthly lovers understand.

This end toward which all existence moves is the restoration of that primal unity of perception sought after by Blake; it also involves a resolution of contraries and a rejection of temporal or clock time (the spectre of Urthona) in favor of an eternal present. For Blake, this condition is represented, finally, by Golgonooza, the city of art. For Roethke, in his final mystical sequences, the rose becomes his symbol of eternity (as it had for Dante, Rilke, Eliot, and Yeats before him): "this rose, this rose in the sea-wind, / Rooted in stone, keeping the whole of light."

The Far Field gives final evidence of Roethke's continuing dialogue with Blake; the "North American Sequence" with its search for "imperishable quiet at the heart of form" parallels Blake's "fearful symmetry." For it is in the city of art that fallen man is restored in the New Golgotha (Golgonooza). As God and man come together in the figure of the visionary poet, the apocalypse occurs, and the mythopoetic action moves from allegory to anagogy: the level where spiritual truth is embodied. It is, at last, at the level of mythic structure that Blake affected Roethke most significantly. This structure, according to Frye, has its fittest analogy in music: "The beauty of *Jerusalem* is the beauty of intense concentration, the beauty of the Sutra, of the aphorisms which are the form of so much of the greatest vision, of a figured bass indicating the harmonic progression of ideas too tremendous to be expressed by a single melody." It is this same "harmonic progression of ideas" which underlies Roethke's mystical sequence, too. Commenting on "The Longing," which opens the "North American Sequence," Hugh B. Staples writes:

In a manner that suggests counterpoint in music, the principle of alternation controls the elaborate pattern of contrasting elements in the poem: body and soul, the sense of self and the release from subjectivity, earth and water, past and present, motion and stasis. . . . The sequence, then, can be regarded as a tone poem consisting of an overture ("The Longing"), in which the major themes appear, followed by four movements in which the tensions and oppositions of the whole sequence are summarized and move toward a resolution.

Roethke's sequence, then, moves in the manner of *Jerusalem*—via a series of gradually heightened antitheses—toward its resolution, the resurrection of Roethke's "final man" or Albion restored.

The last poem in Roethke's last book is "Once More, the Round," and here the poet provides more than could be wished for, a final summary of his complex relationship to Blake couched in Blakean terms, a poem in celebration of the cosmic dance and visionary mode:

> What's greater, Pebble or Pond?
> What can be known? The Unknown.
> My true self runs toward a Hill
> More! O More! visible.
>
> Now I adore my life
> With the Bird, the abiding Leaf,
> With the Fish, the questing Snail,
> And the Eye altering all;
> And I dance with William Blake
> For love, for Love's sake;
>
> And everything comes to One,
> As we dance on, dance on, dance on.

THOMAS GARDNER

"North American Sequence": Theodore Roethke and the Contemporary American Long Poem

Theodore Roethke's "North American Sequence," like a number of other important long poems written by Americans in the last twenty years, is a self-portrait. It is an attempt, in Roethke's words, to create "A body with the motion of a soul" and stands as an early example of such contemporary self-portraits as Robert Duncan's *Passages,* John Berryman's *Dreams Songs,* Galway Kinnell's *Book of Nightmares,* John Ashbery's "Self-Portrait in a Convex Mirror," Robert Lowell's *History,* and James Merrill's *Changing Light at Sandover.* Each of these poems, to use Roethke's terms again, seeks to represent—give an external "body" or shape to—the poet's fluid inner world of thoughts and feelings—his moving "soul." Each of these poets asks, in one form or another, a question raised by Roethke in 1963: "The human problem is to find out what one really *is*: whether one exists, whether existence is possible. But how?" By looking at how Roethke gives shape to his inner world in "North American Sequence"—how he "creates his self in publicly accessible linguistic shapes," as one theorist [Frank Lentricchia] has put it—I hope to suggest an approach to the problem of self-portraiture that can be applied not just to Roethke's work but to the range of contemporary poems I have named above.

The single most important model for contemporary long poems is still Whitman's "Song of Myself." In section 50 of that poem, Whitman provides an account of the process of self-creation that has been quite useful for recent poets in thinking about how one gives body to the unformulated self:

From *Essays in Literature* 11, no. 2 (Fall 1984). © 1984 by Western Illinois University.

> There is that in me—I do not know what it is—but I know
>   it is in me.
>
> Wrench'd and sweaty—calm and cool then my body becomes,
> I sleep—I sleep long.
>
> I do not know it—it is without name—it is a word unsaid,
> It is not in any dictionary, utterance, symbol.
>
> Something it swings on more than the earth I swing on.
> To it the creation is the friend whose embracing awakes me.

Whitman attempts to realize a self by discovering what is unknown ("I do not know what it is"), asleep ("I sleep long"), or "unsaid" in his inner nature that yet gives it form. The culmination of the process is finally beyond the reach of writing, a fact that Whitman acknowledges when he says that this fully realized identity "swings on more than the earth I swing on." Distant, almost alien, it seems to inhabit a different planet. But when he continues and points to "the creation" as the friend "whose embracing awakes me" to it, he indicates a mechanism by which that identity might be gradually awakened.

Whitman's embrace of the surrounding creation is central to most contemporary long poems. In an address delivered the year he died on "the way, the means, of establishing a personal identity," Roethke acknowledges the role of the world outside the self in developing awareness of "what one really is." "It is paradoxical," he writes, "that a very sharp sense of the being, the identity of some other being—and in some instances, even an inanimate thing—brings a corresponding heightening and awareness of one's own self. . . . Yet how, exactly, might Roethke's embrace of the other work? Roethke describes how the other awakens the self in this account of his response to the work of Louise Bogan:

> I loved her so much, her poetry, that I just *had* to become, for
> a brief moment, a part of her world. For it *is* her world, and I
> had filled myself with it, and I *had* to create something that
> would honor her in her own terms. That, I think, expresses as
> best I can what really goes on with the hero- or heroine-
> worshiping young. . . . That poem is a true release in its way. I
> was too clumsy and stupid to articulate my own emotions: she
> helped me to say something about the external world.

Unable to articulate his own emotions, Roethke "filled" himself with the images and rhythms of Bogan's world, then, making his own poem out of that new material and of what was released in him ("something that would honor her in her own terms"), became a part of her world. The result of that union was an emotional "release"—what he describes in "North American Sequence" as a moving forward of the spirit.

Two things need to be stressed in this procedure: the role of the other in providing new material for the poet to work with and against, and the role of the poet in making something new out of that material. I intend to show in the following reading of "North American Sequence" how Roethke's self-portrait evolves by this process. David Kalstone notes that one of the aims of "contemporary attempts to find a notation that adequately represents the facets of the self" is "to elaborate, to keep fluid the written image of the self." Roethke's poem provides a clear example of how the constant infusion of new material and the equally constant activity of the poet combine to create what Roethke has called "a shape of change"—a fluid, developing representation of self.

"The Longing," the first poem of the sequence, presents a blasted landscape that functions as an obvious correlative for the condition of Roethke's consciousness. All is asleep or decaying, slowed to a decidedly uneasy rest with no "balm" or promise anywhere apparent:

> A kingdom of stinks and sighs,
> Fetor of cockroaches, dead fish, petroleum,
>
> . . . .
>
> The slag heaps fume at the edge of the raw cities:
> The gulls wheel over their singular garbage.

The longing of the poem's title is touched on by suggestions that an earlier state has exhausted itself, leaving only memories of a once-vibrant world: "The greatest trees no longer shimmer; / Not even the soot dances." In parallel fashion, Roethke notes that his own spirit—fatigued by lust, drained by unfulfilled dreams—is also unable to actively engage the world: "Less and less the illuminated lips, / Hands active, eyes cherished; / Happiness left to dogs and children—." Without contact, his spirit cannot develop and takes on the shape of a slug—a creature Roethke has described in another poem as "the cold slime come into being":

> The spirit fails to move forward,
> But shrinks into a half-life, less than itself,
> Falls back, a slug, a loose worm
> Ready for any crevice,
> An eyeless starer.

As Richard Blessing notes [in *Theodore Roethke's Dynamic Vision*], Roethke's pun on eyeless is quite important, for without the eyes actively responding to the world, the poet's internal "I" must always be less than itself. Unable to touch another and so represent its inner world, the spirit is simply asleep, deep within a crevice.

The memory of a shimmering landscape in the poem's first section and the prediction of that state regained in the second section ("The light cries out, and I am there to hear—" indicate that exhaustion and waking of the spirit are joined cyclically. In fact, the shock of finding oneself inarticulate and being forced to gain speech again seems to be a necessary condition for an increase in consciousness. Roethke writes in an essay:

> Are not some experiences so powerful and so profound (I am not speaking here of the merely compulsive) that they repeat themselves, thrust themselves upon us, again and again, with variation and change, each time bringing us closer to our own most particular (and thus most universal) reality? We go, as Yeats said, from exhaustion to exhaustion. To begin from the depths and come out—that is difficult; for few know where the depths are or can recognize them; or, if they do, are afraid.

Continually lifting himself from the depths and giving body to what was shapeless gives Roethke the opportunity, through the "variation and change" of each new act of formation, to unfold more and more of this own "most particular . . . reality." In this opening poem, Roethke finds himself stalled and exhausted; as the sequence continues, he will continually drop back to this state, often by raising new questions and fears, in order to give himself an opportunity to work himself out of the mire once again. Repeatedly made shapeless, he will define a self by slowly flowering, petal after petal: "To this extent I'm a stalk. / —How free; how all alone. / Out of these nothings / —All beginnings come."

The first beginning that comes is an expression of longing and an anticipation of the sequence's method of development:

> I would with the fish, the blackening salmon, and the mad
>   lemmings,
> The children dancing, the flowers widening.
> Who sighs from faraway?
> I would unlearn the lingo of exasperation, all the distortions
>   of malice and hatred;

> I would believe my pain: and the eye quiet on the growing
>   rose;
> I would delight in my hands, the branch singing, altering the
>   excessive bird;
> I long for the imperishable quiet at the heart of form;
> I would be a stream, winding between great striated rocks
>   in late summer;
> A leaf, I would love the leaves, delighting in the redolent
>   disorder of this mortal life.

The "imperishable quiet" that Roethke longs for here seems to be a core of identity—an imperishable core known only as it manifests itself in perishable ("mortal") form. By moving with the fish, dancing with the children, or widening with the flowers; or by becoming a stream or a drifting leaf, part of the "disorder of this mortal life," the unformulated heart will be made to take on shape. The image of the "eye quiet on the growing rose," with another pun on "I," is a statement of the wish to share movement with the growing rose in order to become aware of the self's own quiet places. That longing is given an object in the next five poems, each of which is set "where the sea and fresh water meet." In the last poem of the sequence, Roethke describes this setting as "the place of my desire"—the landscape where his fears and desires are brought to consciousness and his sleeping spirit is awakened.

"Meditation at Oyster River" begins with Roethke sitting on a rock at the edge of a bay, the mouth of a river at his back. Though the world around him steadily increases in activity, he seems as weary and tentative as he had been in "The Longing." The "first tide-ripples" slowly move toward where he waits, protected by "a barrier of small stones" and a "sunken log." When he is surrounded and "one long undulant ripple" has broken through, he responds: "I dabble my toes in the brackish foam sliding forward, / Then retire to a rock higher up on the cliff-side." In short, he refuses the embrace and refuses in such a manner as to call attention to his refusal. Cary Nelson [in *Our Last First Poets*] observes that, "The decision is a partial rejection. He resists the natural world even while reaffirming his need for it." This twin rejection and reaffirmation calls attention to a problem that must be dealt with before there can be any movement of the spirit. The problem is made clear again a few lines later when the world outside comes back to life—"The dew revives on the beach-grass; / The salt-soaked wood of a fire crackles"—while the poet remains unmoving. Eventually, in a pattern that will be repeated throughout the sequence, the problem of the failed embrace triggers an unstated question—why am I refusing contact?—that the second

section of the poem begins to investigate. That is, now that he is conscious
of the problem, Roethke can work with it, and in doing so, bring some of
his inner world to the surface. He writes:

> The self persists like a dying star,
> In sleep, afraid. Death's face rises afresh,
> Among the shy beasts, the deer at the salt-lick,
> The doe with its sloped shoulders loping across the highway,
> The young snake, poised in green leaves, waiting for its fly,
> The hummingbird, whirring from quince-blossom to
>   morning-glory—
> With these I would be.

The problem expressed here is fundamental to the poem: though he would
be part of the "loping," "whirring" world surrounding him, he is unable to
break away from a persistent awareness of himself. To relax his attention on
his own boundaries and become absorbed in something other than himself
is, he fears, to give up what makes him unique. Thus, "death face" insistently includes itself in the catalogue of animals Roethke would be with. As
James McMichael writes [in "Roethke's North America"], "What he desires
is outside him, outside the self. But this desire is blunted by the unavoidable
awareness and fear that to be lured out of the confines of the self is to court
death, the absolute loss of self."

    How to move beyond this fear? Rather than addressing the problem of
his persistent, fearful self directly, Roethke muses, almost playfully, about
what would happen if he were released from self-absorption into movement. He thinks, first, of a "trembling . . . Michigan brook in April, / Over
a lip of stone, the tiny rivulet," then of a "wrist-thick cascade tumbling from
a cleft rock" and finally of the Tittebawasee River, poised,

>   between winter and spring,
> When the ice melts along the edges in early afternoon.
> And the midchannel begins cracking and heaving from the
>   pressure beneath,
> The ice piling high against the iron-bound spiles,
> Gleaming, freezing hard again, creaking at midnight.

Though they don't demonstrate actual movement on the poet's part, these
accelerating, increasingly powerful metaphors for how his spirit *might* move
do verbalize a desire. Avoiding his fear of dissolving the self by looking past
it for a moment, the three metaphors and these following lines act out and
give form to his need to move:

And I long for the blast of dynamite,
The sudden sucking roar as the culvert loosens its debris
        of branches and sticks,
Welter of tin cans, pails, old bird nests, a child's shoe riding
        a log,
As the piled ice breaks away from the battered spiles,
And the whole river begins to move forward, its bridges
        shaking.

By becoming aware of the problem raised by the failed embrace and creating a series of metaphors in response to it, Roethke has also enabled himself to become more a part of the seaside setting. As will be seen throughout the sequence, each increase in consciousness is paralleled by an increasing ability to join with ocean. Here, he records a steady rocking of the spirit ("I rock with the motion of morning") as he leans to move forward then pulls himself back, finally "lull[ing]" himself into a "half-sleep." He is in between, no longer sealed off by his barrier of rocks; but because the fear of dissolving his self has not been addressed fully, he is still unable to completely embrace his surroundings:

And the spirit runs, intermittently,
In and out of the small waves,
Runs with the intrepid shorebirds—
How graceful the small before danger!

The next poem in the sequence, "Journey to the Interior," uses the word rehearse—"I rehearse myself for this: / The stand at the stretch in the face of death"—to describe the structure of memory and speculation that Roethke constructs to prepare himself to confront directly his fear of dissolving the boundaries of self. Again, the structure is a response to the problem raised by the failed embrace; it is a made object, demonstrating an unfolding of awareness. The poem begins by comparing the movement out of the self and toward the world to a journey:

In the long journey out of the self,
There are many detours, washed-out interrupted raw places
Where the shade slides dangerously
And the back wheels hang almost over the edge
At the sudden veering, the moment of turning.

Thinking about the dangerous, unpredictable "detours" on this journey encourages Roethke to go one step further and spell out two possible dead ends where the veering spirit might destroy itself. The first is the risk of

violent, surging expansion: "The arroyo cracking the road, the wind-bitten
buttes, the canyons, / Creeks swollen in midsummer from the flash-flood
roaring into the narrow valley." The second is the risk of reduction and
annihilation:

> —Or the path narrowing,
> Winding upward toward the stream with its sharp stones,
> The upland of alder and birchtrees,
> Through the swamp alive with quicksand,
> The way blocked at last by a fallen fir-tree,
> The thickets darkening,
> The ravines ugly.

The two dangers parallel the swings of Roethke's manic-depressive tenden-
cies outlined by his biographer Allan Seager. In this context, where the
dangers of reaching out toward new levels of identity are being evaluated,
Seager's suggestion that the first episode of Roethke's illness may have been
deliberately self-induced—and thus may have been thought through—seems
to find some support.

Demonstrating to himself that the movement might also be a positive
one, Roethke counterbalances the fear of annihilation by recounting a long,
circuitous journey that, he remembers, gently led him out of himself. The
journey itself—taking Roethke from self-absorption to union with the external—is another rehearsal for the present decision to make or refuse contact with the sea. Emphasis is given to the dangers of the road ("dangerous
downhill places, where the wheels whined beyond eighty—"), then to the
boy's sense of pride at his mastery of the terrain:

> The trick was to throw the car sideways and charge over the
>   hill, full of the throttle.
> Grinding up and over the narrow road, spitting and roaring.
> A chance? Perhaps. But the road was part of me, and its ditches,
> And the dust lay thick on my eyelids,—Who ever wore
>   goggles?

Gradually, the speaker disappears and the landscape, a blur of small towns
and discarded objects, takes over: "An old bridge below with a buckled iron
railing, broken by some idiot plunger; / Underneath, the sluggish water running between weeds, broken wheels, tires, stones." This is the sort of exhausted landscape Roethke had turned away from in "The Longing." Now,
however, transfixed by the rhythm of the speeding car, he begins to lose
himself to the flashing scenery. He seems to be still, with the world flowing
by ("The floating hawks, the jackrabbits, the grazing cattle— / I am not

moving but they are") until, finally forgetting himself, he becomes a part of his surroundings, both still and moving:

> I rise and fall in the slow sea of a grassy plain,
> The wind veering the car slightly to the right,
> Whipping the line of white laundry, bending the cottonwoods
>   apart.

With the same wind moving the car and the cottonwoods, inside and outside are joined. Though the memory itself is quite powerful, the reference to the "slow sea" reminds the reader that this journey is being recounted as a contrast to Roethke's current failure to embrace the waves around him.

The memory concludes with what Roethke has called "the first stage in mystical illumination:"

> I rise and fall, and time folds
> Into a long moment;
> And I hear the lichen speak,
> And the ivy advance with its white lizard feet—
> On the shimmering road,
> On the dusty detour.

Although this passage has been cited by several commentators as a mystical culmination to the sequence, the word "detour" is a reminder that this moment of union in which "all is one and one is all" is only one of several possible results of the journey out of the self. Roethke is investigating whether one can move out of the self and not be destroyed, not simply the possibility of illumination. This memory serves as an assurance that the journey might be made safely. In fact, as the tense change indicates—from past ("the road was part of me") to present ("And all flows past")—recounting the memory has led the poet to experience a similar feeling beside the ocean: "I see the flower of all water, above and below me, the never receding, / Moving, unmoving in a parched land, white in the moonlight." By rehearsing these detours, both negative and positive, Roethke has increased his awareness and brought himself to a point where he can make a decision about moving beyond the soul's "still-stand." What is the result? Claiming only a blind man's intuition, Roethke changes position, moving away from his fear of death and, with his "body thinking," out toward the world:

> As a blind man, lifting a curtain, knows it is morning,
> I know this change:
> One one side of silence there is no smile;
> But when I breathe with the birds,

> The spirit of wrath becomes the spirit of blessing,
> And the dead begin from their dark to sing in my sleep.

From a position of silence, Roethke has gazed at the disastrous, unsmiling face of the journey out of the self ("the spirit of wrath"), then at the breathing, singing aspect of the journey, and has chosen to risk contact. His rehearsal has indeed "made something" out of his first contact with the sea, thus making possible a greater embrace.

What we have been observing is the way Roethke, by continually raising new questions and problems, repeatedly gives himself opportunities to struggle out of the mire. The problem raised in "The Long Waters," implicit in the previous poems, is how to make contact with the external world. He begins by acknowledging that the senses, as demonstrated by innumerable small creatures, seem to provide both that contact and a means of making and expressing newly-discovered distinctions:

> Whether the bees have thoughts, we cannot say,
> But the hind part of the worm wiggles the most,
> Minnows can hear, and butterflies, yellow and blue,
> Rejoice in the language of smells and dancing.

It seems to Roethke that the languages (wiggling, dancing) employed by these creatures illustrate a kind of thinking that he might use himself. Roethke has pursued this idea further in an essay in which he speculates that for the poet who "thinks with his body . . . an idea . . . can be as real as the smell of a flower or a blow to the head. And those so lucky as to bring their whole sensory equipment to bear on the process of thought grow faster, jump more frequently from one plateau to another." The senses then, he proposes, might provide an entrance into the external world and a language to give his ideas shape—make them "real." To choose this manner of thinking is to choose not to rely on those extraordinary insights into our world or those intuitions of some other world that are beyond the range of the senses:

> Therefore I reject the world of the dog
> Though he hear a note higher than C
> And the thrush stopped in the middle of his song.
> And I acknowledge my foolishness with God,
> My desire for the peaks, the black ravines, the rollings mists
> Changing with every twist of the wind,
> The unsinging fields where no lungs breathe,
> Where light is stone.

Instead, he situates himself at that place of his desire, a world full of potential where the sense might be fully engaged:

> I return where fire has been,
> To the charred edge of the sea
> Where the yellowish prongs of grass poke through the
>   blackened ash,
> And the bunched logs peel in the afternoon sunlight,
> Where the fresh and salt waters meet,
> And the sea-winds move through the pine trees,
> A country of bays and inlets, and small streams flowing
>   seaward.

This is a complete world where the four elements—fire, water, earth, wind—all meet and interpenetrate. Grass pokes "through" the fire's ash, winds "move through" the pines, fire touches the sea, fresh waters meet salt. In short, this is a universe no longer threatening, as in "Oyster River," but open to the penetration of the senses.

Characteristically, Roethke immediately retreats from his decision to immerse himself in the sea-edge world. Discovering a new set of problems implicit in his description of the charred, reviving landscape, he thrusts himself back into the depths and gives himself another opportunity to climb out. Addressing Mnetha, Blake's guardian of two "perpetual infants" who are kept forever innocent, he acknowledges his fear of the flurry of change and new birth that the natural world offers him. He reaches back, in fact, to the language-bearing worm and butterfly of the opening lines of the poem and sees them again, now as examples of disorder and retreat:

> Mnetha, Mother of Har, protect me
> From the worm's advance and retreat, from the butterfly's
>   havoc,
> From the slow sinking of the island peninsula, the coral
>   efflorescence,
> The dubious sea-change, the heaving sands, and my tentacled
>   sea-cousins.

Once articulated, however, these fears of the flowering ("coral efflorescence"), changing, and dissolving world can be countered. Roethke does so by calling attention to another, unnamed figure who might intensify that about-to-dissolve world rather than simply free him from it:

> But what of her?—
> Who magnifies the morning with her eyes,

> The star winking beyond itself,
> The cricket-voice deep in the midnight field,
> The blue jay rasping from the stunted pine.

Who "magnifies" the retreating stars or morning, the solitary and threatened voices of the cricket and blue jay? "She" seems to me to be a stand-in for the poet, or for those faculties of imagination and memory that intersect the changing world and magnify its potential. A remembered "pleasure," he argues in the next stanza, dies slowly; it lasts like a "dry bloom" still holding its battered shape under the coming "first snow of the year," and in doing so gives depth and richness to his present contact with the world: "Feeling, I still delight in my last fall." This expression of doubt, then, forcing Roethke to acknowledge the havoc of the sensual world, has also led him to discover the role of human memory and imagination in deepening the order of that world—a significant advance in his thought.

The final three sections of "The Long Waters" further investigate the role of memory and the senses in contacting the world, and do so with a similar pattern of statement, challenge, and a deepened restatement. Roethke begins by repeating his commitment to enter the "rich desolation of wind and water" stretching before him. To move toward that world, he reminds himself, is to enter the advancing and retreating world of time:

> *In time* when the trout and young salmon leap for the
>   low-flying insects,
> And the ivy-branch, cast to the ground, puts down roots into
>   the sawdust,
> And the pine, whole with its roots, sinks into the estuary,
> Where it leans, tilted east, a perch for the osprey,
> And a fisherman dawdles over a wooden bridge,
> These waves, in the sun, remind me of the flowers. (my italics)

In the world of time, advance is cyclically linked to decline: trout leap as insects fly low; a newly cast down branch roots itself while established roots are pried out whole; as a pine tree sinks, an osprey uses its perch to lift itself. Previously, this "dubious" movement would have inspired retreat; now the presence of the poet's memory, "magnifying" the sea's waves into the familiar shapes of lilies and morning-glories helps him to engage his senses and, "Blessed by the lips of a low wind," come forward "To a rich desolation of wind and water." Once again, however, this insight must be tested. The blessing is followed by a quivering moment of doubt where, as another "long swell, burnished, almost oily" washes toward him, he instinctively erects a barrier and uses memory not to deepen his response to water but to find an emblem for his feelings of vulnerability at loosening his boundaries:

> I remember a stone breaking the eddying current,
> Neither white nor red, in the dead middle way,
> Where impulse no longer dictates, nor the darkening shadow,
> A vulnerable place,
> Surrounded by sand, broken shells, the wreckage of water.

Immediately though, as if acknowledging his momentary tendency to remain inert and stone-like "in the dead middle way" has released him, he finds himself awakened again:

> As a fire, seemingly long dead, flares up from a downdraft
>   of air in a chimney,
> Or a breeze moves over the knees from a low hill,
> So the sea wind wakes desire.
> My body shimmers with a light flame.

Now that his senses are in full contact with the world, his spirit is able to awake, move, and (reaching back to "The Longing" for the term) shimmer. The awakening of desire—the way Roethke has become conscious of and found words and a shape for his inner desire—has been a slow process with many stages, arriving at a union that has been doubted, lost, and won several times over.

Interestingly, Roethke chooses to end "The Long Waters" not with these striking lines but with a passage that Cary Nelson rightly characterizes as "mere posturing." Roethke concludes by claiming that, set loose from his fear of dissolution, he is able to "Become another thing," disperse himself to the gathering waters, and "embrace the world." This progression neatly completes the sequence's major themes, but the strikingly pat presentation contrasts noticeably with the painstaking advance and retreat we have just followed. This manner of presentation seems to be a deliberate signal of another problem, one supported by an additional claim that although he senses in the sea's waves a "shape" that corresponds to an aspect of his sleeping spirit, he is unable to label it clearly. That is, Roethke signals his inability, at this stage, to make more than a striking pose of his union with the waves. He writes:

> I see in the advancing and retreating waters
> The shape that came from my sleep, weeping:
> The eternal one, the child, the swaying vine branch,

> The numinous ring around the opening flower,
> The friend that runs before me on the windy headlands,
> Neither voice nor vision.

The last line is particularly telling. To see the shape as a montage of traditional images—alternately the "one," a child, a branch, a numinous ring, a friend running—is to suggest that though a union has been established, there has not yet been a clearly articulated gain. To achieve "Neither voice nor vision" is to put nothing into form and to indicate both a temporary end to one poem and the need for further meditation.

"The Far Field" attempts to articulate what has been gained in embracing "the advancing and retreating waters" by linking the sea to the far field of eternity in order to bring to awareness the problem of "immensity." Is it too much to claim that a single individual might comprehend such an expanse? The poem begins, as has become customary, by answering that unspoken question with an expression of fear that temporarily negates the previous union and provides the poet with another opportunity to remake himself. Roethke imagines driving out a "long peninsula," alone, in a frightening thrust away from the mainland and out toward the sea: "Ending at last in a hopeless sand-rut, / Where the car stalls, / Churning in a snowdrift / Until the headlights darken." Roethke responds to the fear of being overwhelmed and diminished by remembering a series of equivalent "ends" he experienced as a child: a culvert at the end of a field, a pile of discarded cans and tires, the decayed face of a dead rat, the entrails of a cat, blasted by a night watchman. The images parallel the stalled car, but by placing them in a larger context of constantly changing shapes, Roethke remembers that his "grief was not excessive." The field's end was also the "nesting-place of the field-mouse"; the cat's entrails were "strewn over the half-grown flowers"; and both the flower dump and the "twittering restless cloud" of an elm were seen as "ever-changing." In addition to these observations, he also "learned of the eternal" through placing his own body in that larger context: lying "naked in the sand," "fingering a shell," sinking "down to the hips in the mossy quagmire," or sitting with bare knees "astride a wet log" were all ways of "thinking" himself into contact with an older world and reliving earlier shapes: "Once I was something like this, mindless, / Or perhaps with another mind, less peculiar." As a child, then, he reminds himself, he "learned not to fear infinity," by developing a means of thinking about and thereby participating in the constant movement of time and shapes.

This reminder frees him from his opening fear of being overwhelmed; now able to entertain the "thought of my death" and subsequent connection with "earth and air," he is "renewed by death" and experiences a forward movement of the spirit:

> I feel a weightless change, a moving forward
> As of water quivering before a narrowing channel
> When banks converge, and the wide river whitens.

This forward movement, I would suggest, is made possible by the poet teaching himself again how to think about the broad, surrounding expanses. He returns to the combination of stillness and movement first introduced in "The Longing" in order to explain this manner of participating without being dissolved:

> I have come to a still, but not a deep center,
> A point outside the glittering current;
> My eyes stare at the bottom of a river,
> At the irregular stones, iridescent sandgrains,
> My mind moves in more than one place,
> In a country half-land, half-water.

Though still and self-contained, holding himself out of the main current, Roethke is able to join it by learning how to look at it ("my eyes stare") and, most importantly, think about it ("my mind moves").

The quiet tone of these lines is convincing and prepares the reader for a second attempt to define the shape discovered in the union between the individual and the long waters: "The lost self changes, / Turning toward the sea, / A sea-shape turning around." The lost self, the self that has let go of its hold on its original ego, turns toward the sea and, identifying with the waves it faces but also remaining a thinking creature, becomes both a man and a "sea shape turning around." To realize that one has the potential to merge with such an expanse, that one has in fact emerged from that expanse, is to awaken to one's own immensity without being overwhelmed by it: "A man faced with his own immensity / Wakes all the waves, all their loose wandering fire." He wakes these waves within himself, understanding that "finite things reveal [their] infinitude" to the eye that sees their participation in the changing expanse of the world. Indeed, Roethke claims to have done just that: a single man, he is, through such a merger, an "old man" in the sea's "robes of green" or, more abstractly, "the end of things, the final man." Potentially, he might stay within himself and yet, through the movement of mind, imagination, and memory, move far beyond himself: "A ripple widening from a single stone / Winding around the waters of the world."

The final poem of the sequence, "The Rose," is both a summary of the sequence's overall movement and a demonstration, using the North American continent as object, of what Roethke has learned about embracing the other. Its central image is a wild rose blowing in the sea wind, a figure, as Nelson remarks, "for a self exceeding the limits of time and space yet supremely flowering in its place." Indeed, the rose which "Stays in its true place," "Rooted in stone," yet also unfolds its petals and moves with the breeze off the waves—"Flowering out of the dark, / Widening at high noon," "struggling out of the white embrace of the morning-glory," "Moving with the waves, the undulating driftwood"—is a completed version of the spirit which has been given struggling form in the sequence. The rose functions as an ideal image (unlike the poet, it embraces "the whole of light," all of "sound and silence") that Roethke may compare himself to and thus judge where his poem has arrived. In a sense, the ideal rose and *his* apparent distance from its realized potential are the problems that spur his meditation in this poem.

The poem begins with a long description of "this place, where sea and fresh water meet." Everything is in movement: hawks sway in the wind, eagles sail, gulls cry, the tide rises, birds flash and sing. In time, the poet's intense watching and listening open up contact with the world. Building on earlier developed abilities, Roethke writes:

> I sway outside myself
> Into the darkening currents,
> Into the small spillage of driftwood,
> The waters swirling past the tiny headlands.

This embrace, which has been the subject of much of the sequence, is described in quite modest terms. Both the small scale of the movement—"small spillage," "tiny headlands"—and the contrast, in the next lines, to a grander union in memory complete with the a "crown of birds," place this embrace in careful perspective, much like the perspective developed by the many discussions of such a connection throughout the sequence. Through "change and variation," that is, the portrait has been refined. A similar sense of precision informs the second section of the poem where Roethke first compares the spirit's continual movement and development to a ship—"rolling slightly sideways, / The stern high, dipping like a child's boat in a pond— / Our motion continues"—then contrasts that constant motion to the ideal figure of the rose, which "Stays, / Stays in its true place."

This comparison and qualification bring the poet to the point, in the third section, that he must demonstrate in just what way he has learned to embrace the world, to move and stay. Accordingly, in the "silence" of evening with the waves lessening, Roethke deliberately sways outside of himself:

> I think of American sounds in this silence:
> On the banks of the Tombstone, the windharps having their
>   say,
> The thrush singing alone, that easy bird,
> The killdeer whistling away from me.

A long, Whitmanesque catalogue follows in which Roethke consciously fills his silence with sound, seasons, and occupations. He moves outward, as he has learned to do in the course of this poem, through use of his full mental powers: thinking ("I think of American sounds"), memory ("the catbird / Down in the corner of the garden"), and careful discrimination of the various sounds. That is how a poet, in contrast to a rose, moves. Next, he deliberately draws his expanding world back to his perch beside the water, for after showing how far his imagination can move, he must also show it rooted:

> I return to the twittering of swallows above water,
> And that sound, that single sound,
> When the mind remembers all,
> And gently the light enters the sleeping soul,
> A sound so thin it could not woo a bird.

After moving out, then returning, the blind, sluggish "sleeping soul" of "The Longing" finds itself lifted from exhaustion and awakened to the entering world. The thinness of the mind's sound emphasizes both the delicacy of its work and its carefully poised relationship to the shrieking, roaring world external to it.

This delicacy is referred to again in the conclusion of the sequence where Roethke celebrates "the place of my desire," the place where his desire has been drawn out and given form:

> I live with the rocks, their weeds,
> Their filmy fringes of green, their harsh
> Edges, their holes,
> Cut by the sea-slime, far from the crash
> Of the long swell,
> The oily, tar-laden walls
> Of the toppling waves.

By living "with the rocks," Roethke points to the way he has become absorbed by this particular setting in the course of the sequence, but he also insists, in using that phrase, that his proper place is at the edge of the sea, rather than in the middle of crashing swells. He has been out in those waves, of course, but in a way that needs to be carefully set forth:

> Near this rose, in this grove of sun-parched, wind-warped
> madronas,
> Among the half-dead trees, I came upon the true ease of
> myself,
> As if another man appeared out of the depths of my being,
> And I stood outside myself,
> Beyond becoming and perishing,
> A something wholly other,
> As if I swayed out on the wildest wave alive,
> And yet was still.

The "as if" pattern of these lines insists on the connection-making role of the imagination in awakening the spirit. In this place—near the rose, at the edge of the sea—"the depths of his being" have been given shape and body. As we have seen, the process of shaping and questioning and doubting that has allowed the inner world to become apparent has been a long, gradual one. Though the particular manner of making and shaping a form out of the material brought to consciousness by the external world differs for each contemporary poet, a similar awakening of the self can be observed in many other American long poems. By staring at and responding to the world in such a way that "something wholly other" is made conscious, each of these poets creates a self-portrait in which he can stand outside of himself and study that emerging self.

JAMES APPLEWHITE

Death and Rebirth
in a Modern Landscape

In approaching romantic landscape poetry in terms of a typical tension between conscious structure or figure and wild or unconscious moorland or sea, we are participating in a psychological interpretation that has already been made, in effect, by intellectual and artistic developments in our own century. Our time, after all, is that of the discovery of the unconscious. Henri Ellenberger, in the book from whose title this phrase comes, has traced the psychoanalytic movement from its origins in romanticism. Awareness of the doctrines of Freud, Jung, and their followers has permeated modern life and marked modern art and criticism. Maud Bodkin's *Archetypal Patterns in Poetry* represents a pioneering attempt to apply the concepts of C. G. Jung to the interpretation of poetry—an attempt that appears to have influenced the thinking of the modern American poet Theodore Roethke. Our artistic inheritance is Dada, surrealism, and abstract expressionism, movements wherein artists have sought deliberately to introduce change, illogic, and emotional association into their work, to free it from the dominance of the conscious will so that more primal powers may be manifest. The presence of African masks and various totemic deities in our galleries and as influences in the work of painters, sculptors, and other artists attests to our time's fascination with the primitive, the irrational, the unconscious.

The theme of psychological death and rebirth in the context of a landscape imagery symbolizing access to the unconscious comes to an especially clear formulation in the work of Roethke. As a poet who imbibed the

From *Seas and Inland Journeys.* © 1985 by the University of Georgia Press.

central modernist influence (his work is clearly marked by both Yeats and Eliot) and who also returned sympathetically to romantic predecessors, Roethke is representative of the romantic and postromantic themes we have traced as they arise in a new but recognizable form in the period following World War II—a time that saw a reaction to, and reformulation of, the modernist version of the poetic act. We will find in Roethke an explicit interest in the unconscious, as well as a pattern resembling the romantic resuscitation ritual, and the house and ship imagery symbolizing consciousness in its interaction with the unconscious.

In an "Open Letter," published in 1950 with a selection of poems from *The Lost Son and Other Poems,* Roethke acknowledges the poet as "conscious instrument," as opposed to "some kind of over-size aeolian harp upon which strange winds play uncouth tunes," yet sees the poet's task is to "fish, patiently, in that dark pond, the unconscious, or dive in, with or without pants on." The rather playful tone of this beginning does not disguise the essential seriousness of what Roethke is saying, for as he speaks of "The Lost Son" sequence, something of the agony behind these poems of psychic breakdown and regeneration becomes apparent: "Each in a sense is a stage in a kind of struggle out of the slime; part of a slow spiritual progress; an effort to be born, and later, to become something more." The psychic birth to which Roethke refers is a form of that separation of individual consciousness from the unconsciousness of nature that we have identified as central romantic motif.

Roethke sees the movement of these poems as cyclic, as hard-won progressions founded upon a reimmersion of the adult psyche in the primal, chaotic, unconscious world symbolized by memories of his Michigan childhood and its landscape with marshes, rivers, and ponds. "I believe that to go forward as a spiritual man it is necessary first to go back." Thus, as the poems dramatize, there is a regression amounting to breakdown, to a dissolution of the old restrictive consciousness, then an almost deathly absorption in unconsciousness (symbolized by landscape) followed by a painful, difficult journey back into the conscious personality, as if the stages of evolution were being retraced in the life of a single man: "Some of these pieces . . . begin in the mire, as if man is no more than a shape writhing from the old rock." The antiquity he feels in this psychic landscape suggests C. G. Jung's concept of a collective unconscious: "Sometimes one gets the feeling that not even the animals have been there before; but the marsh, the mire, the void, is always there, immediate and terrifying."

This muddy marsh before human history corresponds both to Wordsworth's oceanic reservoir and begetter of individual souls in the Intimations Ode and to W. B. Yeats's "frog-spawn of a blind man's ditch" in "A Dialogue of Self and Soul." Roethke's source, like Yeats's, is presented so as to acknowledge the terror and misery associated with this primordial symbolic water, as well as its fertility. Thus, Roethke's image of the origin of consciousness resembles that of his much-admired W. B. Yeats more than that of Wordsworth. Roethke did, however, name the book of his following *The Lost Son* with a phrase from Wordsworth. "Praise to the end!" occurs in *The Prelude,* book 1, in a passage dealing with exactly this process of cyclical separation/return of a developing consciousness in respect to nature/unconsciousness, which Roethke treats in more explicitly psychological terms.

Karl Malkoff points out that Maud Bodkin's *Archetypal Patterns in Poetry* (with its long exegesis of "The Ancient Mariner" in terms of the "rebirth archetype") was the "application of Jung's ideas to poetry with which Roethke was unquestionably familiar." In his analysis of two other short poems from *The Lost Son,* "Night Crow" and "River Incident," Malkoff establishes the connection between those "unconscious forces" within the mind, the psychic residue of ancestral experience (which Bodkin deals with as "archetypes") and the poetic method of Roethke. Like "Night Crow," he argues, the "atavistic imagery of 'River Incident' probes still further into the nature of the collective unconscious. The protagonist, with sea water in his veins, is taken back to his origins, to man's origins":

> I knew I had been there before,
> In that cold, granitic slime,
> In the dark, in the rolling water.

The return to this "slime" and "water" is seen as the necessary regressive journey for the man who has encountered an obstacle "with which he cannot cope."

Both his own experiences and intuitive inclinations and Maud Bodkin's Jungian analysis of "The Ancient Mariner" appear to have prepared Roethke to deal in poetry with "a state of introversion and regression, preceding a kind of rebirth." And Bodkin had made explicit for Roethke a connection between Jung's "unconscious contents . . . disfigured by the slime of the deep" and Coleridge's "slimy things" that lived within the shadow of the Ancient Mariner's becalmed vessel. Having adduced some of the many references to slimy yet glowing seas that J. L. Lowes found as sources for the poem in Coleridge's reading, Bodkin suggests the paradox that meaning and beauty were to be found in things initially repulsive and alien. "We begin to see what kind of symbolic value the imagination of Coleridge, ever seeking a language for something within, would feel in those shapes, slimy and miscreate in the stagnant water, that yet glowed with gemlike colour and strange fire." In psychological terms, the value of the slime of the unconscious is made clear when the more conscious self, forced by crisis, comes back to this primal origin and is fertilized, reborn through its contact. But such a return, such a "night journey," associated by Bodkin with Jonah's trip into the whale's belly, is dangerous and repugnant to the conscious personality. Returns to the unconscious and its primal sea, therefore, are seen as episodes of death and rebirth.

In the beginning of "The Lost Son," Roethke makes explicit what has to be fished for with some ingenuity in "The Ancient Mariner": that the journey away from the world of the expected, into a different order, is psychic. There is an initial indication of death, a death that pulls the poet downward, into contact with underground spaces of the landscape.

> At Woodlawn I heard the dead cry:
> I was lulled by the slamming of iron,
> A slow drip over stones,
> Toads brooding wells.

The death was perhaps that of the poet's father, although we cannot know it at this point. Here we feel primarily the sense of absorption into another level of being: somnolent, identified with subterranean "drip," close to the perspective of toads. "All the leaves stuck out their tongues" makes us sense that nature is vital yet taunting. Feeling himself incorporated into decay, the poet invites creatures of this minimal, unconscious level to aid him.

> I shook the softening chalk of my bones,
> Saying,
> Snail, snail, glister me forward,
> Bird, soft-sigh me home,
> Worm, be with me.
> This is my hard time.

The conscious self feels soiled, humiliated, useless, and has to call on elements of nature's unselfconscious process for models of how to adapt to the world of dissolution, of loss of the former identity.

The poet is becalmed, like the Ancient Mariner—in a fertile place but in a sterile condition.

> Fished in an old wound,
> The soft pond of repose;

> Nothing nibbled my line,
> Not even the minnows come.

The self-absorption is isolation.

> Sat in an empty house
> Watching shadows crawl,
> Scratching.
> There was one fly.

The house of consciousness is emptied of the old contents. Yet nothing else has taken the place of adult interaction. The protagonist must continue to question, to ask for direction. Finally "Dark hollows" and "The moon" reply, cryptically. Then "The salt said, look by the sea." He must abandon the world of conversation, of external events, for the regressive quest: "You will find no comfort here, / In the kingdom of bang and blab."

At this point the sequence of images seems to shift suddenly into childhood memory—a specific time and place as in the recollections of Wordsworth.

> Running lightly over spongy ground,
> Past the pasture of flat stones,
> The three elms,
> The sheep strewn on a field,
> Over a rickety bridge
> Toward the quick-water, wrinkling and rippling.

Here is motion rather than brooding stasis, and lightness rather than the downward, bone-softening heaviness of the beginning. Childhood offers an opening to the way back, then, a "bridge" from this sterile present to the "quick-water"—where *quick* suggests "alive" as well as "fast-moving." The search into the unconscious wears a healthier aspect as the poet becomes again his childhood self,

> Hunting along the river,
> Down among the rubbish, the bug-riddled foliage,
> By the muddy pond-edge, by the bog-holes,
> By the shrunken lake, hunting, in the heat of summer.

His instinctive boyhood activities provide a model for this return to primal origins now forced upon him by a crisis in adult life. Like Wordsworth in *The Prelude,* book 1, he finds in the native self, before the sophistications of conscious intellect, a pattern for a unified being that incorporates conscious and unconscious dimensions of personality without a disastrous conflict.

Though the model of a more unified psyche is available, however, certain earlier traumas have now to be relived before healing can occur. The phallic, underwater principle of sexuality and its connection with the unconscious is evoked through a kind of altered nursery rhyme.

> The shape of a rat?
>   It's bigger than that.
>   It's less than a leg
>   And more than a nose,
>   Just under the water
>   It usually goes.

Freudians may have their field day with the rat, leg, nose (and later eel and otter) images. But clearly this poet is aware of the symbolism and is dramatizing, through a half-playful, almost child-like voice, the uncomfortable attraction-repulsion surrounding that part of the boy's physical being whose roots are most obviously in the unconscious.

Sexual conflict continues into the present in part 3 of "The Lost Son," as "Dogs of the groin / Barked and howled." The poet feels an alienation so strong that weeds, snakes, cows, even briars "Said to me: Die." The central wounds, his father's early death and his own unresolved feelings about that matter, have now to be faced. "Rub me in father and mother," he asks, cold and alone, needing comfort like a child. But he feared his father. "Fear was my father, Father Fear." The following appears to be a dream version of his father's death from cancer during the poet's adolescence:

> What gliding shape
> Beckoning through halls,
> Stood poised on the stair,
> Fell dreamily down?

The primordial fall seems to unglue the very structure of matter.

> From the mouths of jugs
> Perched on many shelves,
> I saw substance flowing
> That cold morning.

This scene is set, no doubt, in the house of childhood, but it is also the house of consciousness, and that structure is dissolving as the dream ends—"As my own tongue kissed / My lips awake."

"The Lost Son" sequence was continued in *Praise to the End!* (Roethke's next volume), and a section from the poem entitled "Where Knock Is Open Wide" helps clarify the scene of fall and dissolution looked at above. Section 4 presents a memory of the father, beginning with a fishing trip.

> We went by the river.
> Water birds went ching. Went ching.
> Stepped in wet. Over stones.
> One, his nose had a frog,
> But he slipped out.

The language here is more obviously representative of a child's point of view. A crane, perhaps, has speared a frog with its beak ("One, his nose had a frog"). Memories of the father are no longer fearful. He throws back a fish when the child is "sad" for it.

Then there is the lovely image of the florist-father as virtually God-like sustainer of the garden-greenhouse.

> He watered the roses.
> His thumb had a rainbow.
> The stems said, Thank you.
> Dark came early.

His premature death, suggested in the last line above, leads to the following mournful cry:

> That was before. I fell! I fell!
> The worm has moved away.
> My tears are tired.

The fall of the father, then, leads to the fall of the son, and to a mythic sense of fall so apocalyptic that the very structure of consciousness was partially dissolved.

According to our paradigm, individuation itself, the separation of consciousness from its source, as of the child from the womb, is perceived as a fall. But in the case of Roethke (as well as of Sylvia Plath), this archetypal sense of exile, on the child's part, from the "watery cradle" of childhood was reinforced by the untimely death of a father. "The Lost Son" and those related poems represent Roethke's attempt to modify the finality of that fall by a modern, psychological version of Wordsworth's return to the "immortal sea" of origin. For Roethke, a commitment to psychic turmoil, to the breaking down of the old self, was required.

In "The Lost Son," following the dream-vision of the falling figure, ordinary psychic coherence (as well as the normal structure of the land-scape) appears to break down.

> Is this the storm's heart? The ground is unstilling itself.
> My veins are running nowhere. Do the bones cast out their fire?
> . . . .
> All the windows are burning! What's left of my life?

The narration of psychic process moves through an associative, often ob-scure progression from image to image, phrase to phrase, as fragments of nursery rhyme and nonsense are conjoined with suggestions of boggy land-scape and phallic animal life to suggest with maximum directness the less structured perceptual flow of a personality in turmoil, regressing toward childhood. But as "the time-order is going," under "the lash of primordial milk," the protagonist begins to find a way back, through childhood and again toward the present. He revisits the greenhouse of his florist-father, remembering the coming of light and heat after the night. The structure of consciousness is reaffirmed in this house of cypress and glass, with the dirt and slime underfoot. Creation is reaffirmed, reiterated, as the father and order come after the night.

> Once I stayed all night.
> The light in the morning came slowly over the white
> Snow.
> There were many kinds of cool
> Air.
> Then came steam.
>
> Pipe-knock.

> Scurry of warm over small plants.
> Ordnung! ordnung!
> Papa is coming!

> A fine haze moved off the leaves;
> Frost melted on far panes;
> The rose, the chrysanthemum turned toward the light.
> Even the hushed forms, the bent yellowy weeds
> Moved in a slow up-sway.

The poet is inviting us to view this scene through the child's eyes but also in mythic terms. As Roethke said of this passage, "With the coming of steam and 'papa'—the papa on earth and heaven are blended—there is the sense of motion in the greenhouse, my symbol for the whole of life, a womb, a heaven-on-earth." But it is a heaven approached through a kind of hell, a structure of consciousness made fertile again by reunion with the primal ooze of "that dark pond, the unconscious."

Through images suggestive of the original act of creation and thus, by extension, of the conscious psyche's birth from the unconsciousness of nature, the artist revisits or relives the process of his own individuation at a quite early stage. Courage is needed to face the world before creation has finished, for chaos represents an unconscious and threatening condition. Yet here the rank vegetation and slime of the earlier sections are successfully incorporated within a more stable house of glass. Even the lowest "hushed forms" respond to the benign illumination, with an "up-sway" as if moving in water.

The symbolic separation of the conscious from the unconscious, seen by Jung in the creation story in Genesis, is to be found in the landscape structures of both Wordsworth and Roethke. For Roethke it is the celebration of sunrise illuminating the greenhouse, assimilating the dark materials of ooze and slime into a single, unitary round, "A Womb, a heaven-on-earth." For Wordsworth, most centrally, it is the moon-illuminated sky above Mount Snowdon in *The Prelude*, book 14, into which lighted space, from

> A fixed, abysmal, gloomy, breathing-place—
> Mounted the roar of waters, torrents, streams
> Innumerable, roaring with one voice
> Heard over earth and sea, and in that hour,
> For so it seems, felt by the starry heavens.

These are triumphant reconciliations of the dualities of consciousness and unconsciousness, of human psyche and the objective landscape. These are assertions of a vital correspondence between an inner structure and an outer world of experience into which we are able to project the ordering and unifying ability of imagination. Such moments transcend alienation and say, in effect, that the poet is immersed in a collective origin where nature and the deep psyche are continuous and now claims the right to interact with the landscape on a level of reidentification yet creative freedom. The resuscitation ritual, in bringing the poet's psyche back to life, makes nature live again for the senses, as fertile source of those symbols that allow artistic expression.

Thus, the regressive journey back into the minimal, the inarticulate, has ended in a return to the greenhouse-consciousness by a poet now possessed of a new body of imagery, a new language. Those minimal, unconscious things—stems rooting, shoots "Lolling obscenely from mildewed crates" ("Root Cellar"), even "bacterial creepers" in wounds ("The Minimal"), have been incorporated into a more unified consciousness and given names and meanings in the total drama of the psyche, which now claims nature as a part of itself, as its source. A very similar claim for nature as origin of the psyche's vitality, and of symbolic language, is urged by Wordsworth in the Snowdon scene we have looked at above. Those "higher minds" who are properly attuned to nature "build up greatest things / From least suggestions." They inhabit "a world of life," and, while not "enthralled" (or enslaved) by "sensible impressions," are nevertheless "by their quickening impulse made more prompt / To hold fit converse with the spiritual world."

Robert Pinsky [in *The Situation of Poetry*] argues that the romantic impulse toward loss of self in the landscape, as seen in Keats's "Ode to a Nightingale," continued into the twentieth century, has made the poem pursue "the condition of a thing." Roethke is singled out as the contemporary poet who has carried furthest this "attempt to get back to the plainest roots of the situation." Certainly Roethke's vocabulary of lowly particulars seems to assemble things into poems, yet the poems would not affect us as they do had these particulars no symbolic power. Pinsky wishes to reemphasize the necessarily abstract quality of language, to point out the illusion involved in words as objects. Yet words do evoke objects, and the discovery or dramatization of an intelligible correspondence between objects and psychic states creates a fresh artistic excitement. Eliot has said that the "only way of expressing emotion in the form of art is by finding an 'objective correlative'; in other words, a set of objects, a situation, a chain of events which shall be the formula of that *particular* emotion." His own life-measuring "coffee spoons" in "Prufrock," the butterfly upon the pin, as well as the "white hair of the waves," are all objective correlatives.

The question, of course, is how the object comes to be correlated with the emotion. A name such as Lazarus, traditionally associated with resurrection, is one sort of symbol—a symbol, we might say, out of civilization's collective consciousness. Eliot, and to a lesser (but still important) extent, Sylvia Plath, depend upon these symbols. Another category of symbols was first brought into importance by the romantics: images drawn from direct observation of nature, from personal experience and the immediate environment. Such symbols depend upon interrelationships in the developing context of the poem—that is to say, upon the total structure of landscape imagery and upon the reactions of the observer. As we have seen, a typical division or tension separates images of the observing self from that which the self observes, and which it more and more closely approaches as the poetic action progresses. As Coleridge said, "In looking at objects of Nature . . . I seem to be seeking, as it were *asking* for, a symbolical language for something within me that already and for ever exists, than observing anything new." The drama of the romantic self's approach to the not-self of nature depends upon just this obscure intuition that the self and the not-self, at some deep enough level, are coextensive and correspond.

The drama in one sense is that of the creation of language—thus the fascination of Adam's naming of the animals in Genesis, and, more generally, of the creation story as a whole. The drama is also that of escape from isolation, transcendence of the psyche/ world, mind/matter separation made threatening by the development of science and philosophy. Roethke, like the romantics, attempts to get back to "the plainest roots of the situation" precisely because he feels those roots in danger. Sterile consciousness threatens to enclose him, along with the many other "duplicate gray standard faces" ("Dolor"). But the experience of return to the minimal, the memory of response from mere things remains, perhaps as memory from childhood. So the drama unfolds again, the civilized man shucking off his inhibiting garments of convention and learned mind/world separation.

> Must pull off clothes
> To jerk like a frog
> On belly and nose
> From the sucking bog.
> ("The Shape of the Fire")

When light comes to the greenhouse in "The Lost Son," we feel the freshness of creation having begun over again, of consciousness having risen into the light directly from its sources, and still in contact with them.

The question of archetypes is central, of course, and not finally answerable. Yet we can assert that certain situations, divisions, tensions, and contrasting types of structures are traceable from romanticism. This scenario of individuation, this coming into light from the dark, this identification of the separateness of the self beside the all-embracing sea, or in relation to the "muddy pond-edge," is inevitable in landscape poetry deriving from Wordsworth and Coleridge. The self realizes its separateness and expressive autonomy in relation to the environment with which it formerly identified, and which it still carries within itself in the unconscious, just as we carry a residuum of ancient sea water in the salt of our blood. The language with which the new self is born is partly that of the biological facts of its condition of life and history, and partly that of the innate patterns of its development. Thus, for Roethke, objects such as stems, roots, and bacteria are caught up into a "situation, a chain of events"—which is consciousness' dissolution or loss of identity, followed by reindividuation—and thus correlated with emotion. There is nostalgia/disgust for the slime of this biological origin, and exhilaration/elegiac regret at the reseparation into freedom, autonomy, and limitation. Part of eternal, mindless nature falls into the freedom to realize itself, to act and to die. The garden of Genesis is the scene of the oldest drama.

Pinsky's evaluation of the romantic impulse toward unconsciousness, as seen also in Roethke, is not quite fair because it fails to comprehend just how closely the mind of the poet is related to this landscape that calls him to itself. Keats feels not merely aesthetic charm and the hope of escape from personal cares in the bird's timeless song, he also feels the nostalgia of having formerly belonged to this "warm South," this Provençal landscape of collective song and underground wine. But he is committed, as we all are, to the "alien corn" of our individual adult lives. In *A Study in the Process of Individuation,* Jung describes a "fantasy-image" of one of his patients, who imagined herself "with the lower half of her body in the earth, stuck fast in a block of rock." Just as for Wordsworth, the scene of this psychic birth is beside the ocean: "The region round about was a beach strewn with boulders. In the background was the sea." With the help of the good doctor himself, in his guise as sorcerer, the stone is burst open and she is able to step free. Keats has had to be both sorcerer and figure released, and his return at the end of "Ode to a Nightingale" leaves him partly undecided between vision and dream, waking and sleep. From the perspective of the collective sea, ordinary reality may be the illusion from which we awake in vision and in death.

What disturbs Pinsky in Roethke's poetry is probably the relative absence of that more rational, abstracting consciousness that he feels should be acknowledged as a legitimate and inevitable part of the poetic act. Roethke's triumph as poet of the primal does tend to leave him perhaps too continuously in the realm of sense perception and visceral intuition, with too little of the specifically human wisdom we find in the Eliot of *Four Quartets* or in Auden or in Yeats. But we must also remember that intellectual self-consciousness has become, in our time, a potential imprisonment, a bell jar or bottle enclosing the ship of the psyche. Roethke exercised his particular genius in escaping this trap by presiding over the destruction of something in himself. Having fled from abstraction to childhood and the particular, he must assert his ultimate values through symbols rather than concepts. It is therefore particularly interesting to see how, in Wordsworth's terms, he uses the "least suggestions," the "sensible impressions" of lowly organic life, "to hold fit converse with the spiritual world."

The cyclic struggle "out of the slime," the "effort to be born, and later, to become something more," of "The Lost Son," is repeated over and over in the poems that continued that sequence into Roethke's next book, *Praise to the End!* We need not follow this movement in its repetitive detail and variation. Yet the poem that ends *The Lost Son* and so served as the original conclusion to development presents images that deserve our attention. The boat, a vehicle for psychic voyaging upon the "enchafèd flood" of the romantics that became Roethke's own greenhouse-ship of "Big Wind," appears in the second stanza of "The Shape of the Fire."

> Water recedes to the crying of spiders.
> An old scow bumps over black rocks.
> A cracked pod calls.

The recession of water suggests psychic sterility, the "crying of spiders" psychological torment and perhaps personal neurosis. The psychic ship is aground, an "old scow." The sounds convey effort, heaviness, drought. The association of a "cracked pod" with this vessel more becalmed than the Ancient Mariner's implies that out of its wreck may come the kernel of a rebirth, just as a pod must crack open to release its seed.

But the immediate context of rebirth is the suffering of dissolution. "What more will the bones allow?" the poet cries out. "These flowers are all fangs"—his central image of the spirituality in physical things has become venomously threatening. The agony is partly that of chaos. A few stanzas on we meet "Him with the platitudes and rubber doughnuts, / Melting at the knees, a varicose horror." This figure may be recalled from the mental institution where Roethke underwent treatment during his psychic collapse, but it is also, we suspect, a potential image of the self for this poet who stands appalled by the "melting" he must undergo. And the agony is also the threat that the human dimension, the sense of spirituality and sacredness, may be wholly lost in this descent into the primordial slime of the unconscious. "Where's the eye?" he asks, questioning a more conscious sensory function. "The eye's in the sty," he replies. The human identity may be lost entirely.

> Who, careless, slips
> In coiling ooze
> Is trapped to the lips,
> Leaves more than shoes;

> Must pull off clothes
> To jerk like a frog
> On belly and nose
> From the sucking bog.

Yet in the triumphant sections 4 and 5, Roethke transmutes the base metal of sensuality and unconsciousness into a kind of spiritual gold. Water is the central image, as it unobtrusively pervades memory from childhood—in particular, the shoreline world of herons and "little crabs" in "silvery craters." The climactic image in section 5 is of a Wordsworthian moment of transcendance (like the boat-rowing episode in *The Prelude*) wherein the physical, unconscious water shines with a numinous presence.

> To stare into the after-light, the glitter left on the lake's surface,
> When the sun has fallen behind a wooded island;
> To follow the drips sliding from a lifted oar,
> Held up, while the rower breathes, and the small boat drifts
>   quietly shoreward;
> To know that light falls and fills, often without our knowing,
> As an opaque vase fills to the brim from a quick pouring,
> Fills and trembles at the edge yet does not flow over,
> Still holding and feeding the stem of the contained flower.

Here the water is purified, and spiritualized by light. The psyche as "old scow" in the beginning has been transformed into a "small boat" that moves now without conscious effort, supported by the light-filled lake, just as a rose is sustained in its vase by water filled even above the brim. A beautiful balance is suggested by the boat's drifting quietly with lifted oars, and by the water above the edge of the vase that "does not flow over." The boat and the rose are images of the ego, now in contact with the source of fertility.

Harmony between opposed dimensions of personality, like that created by God with the separation of light and land (the "wooded island") from darkness and water (the lake) produces a Yeatsian Unity of Being, and the ooze or slime of earlier sections of "The Lost Son" sequence has been transformed, as by the moon's effects upon "the rotting sea" in "The Ancient Mariner." Spiritual value is thus symbolically represented as the harmonizing reconciliation between the limitlessness of "the whole air" and water (part 5), versus the small boat that drifts in this surround; between the unconscious childhood when "Death was not," when the poet "lived in a simple drowse" (part 4), and the mature perspective of this memory; between water and the light of this present intelligence. The boat of ego, like a rose in a vase, drifts on the surface between above and below, waking and sleep, where the unconsciousness of nature touches articulating consciousness and language.

Roethke's poetic heirs, such as Sylvia Plath (who seems to have learned her death/rebirth pattern largely from him), his student James Wright, Robert Bly, James Dickey, Margaret Atwood, and many others would probably agree with him that in the act of creation some "ghost comes out of the unconscious mind / To grope" the sill of consciousness ("The Dying Man"). In fact, the intention of probing this subterranean world through imagery of water, stones, and other geological and biological forms has become so pervasive as to constitute one of the poetic commonplaces of our time. In an essay entitled "Stone Soup: Contemporary Poetry and the Obsessive Image" David Walker has commented on the legacy of work such as Bly's 1962 *Silence in the Snowy Fields,* wherein the prevalence of the image of stones is bound up with "attention to the subconscious sources of darkness and dream." Articulating craftsmanship seems to Walker frequently surrendered in the effort to "find an entrance to the mysterious life" symbolized so often by stones. This recent version of the relation between the self and the object is, of course, simply another form of the romantic dynamic between observer and landscape (and the projected conscious and unconscious dimensions of personality) that we have traced. More than the later poets he influenced, Roethke grounded his quest into the unconscious in the work of the romantics and of their great modernist successors, especially Yeats and Eliot. Following his *The Far Field* of 1964, however, poetry of the 1960s and 1970s seemed too often marked by an impulse toward disavowal of the past, in conjunction with an attempt to explore the "deep image" through the verbal flux of a "new surrealism."

Chronology

1908	Theodore Roethke is born on May 25 in Saginaw, Michigan, to Helen Huebner Roethke and Otto Roethke, who runs the family business, the William Roethke Greenhouse.
1922	Otto sells his share in the greenhouse to his brother Charles.
1923	Charles commits suicide in February. Two months later, Otto dies of cancer.
1929	Theodore Roethke receives his bachelor's degree from the University of Michigan in Ann Arbor.
1930–31	Does graduate work at Harvard. Robert Hillyer encourages him to send out his poems.
1931–35	Roethke teaches at Lafayette College. He befriends Louise Bogan, Rolfe Humphries, and Stanley Kunitz.
1935	Teaches at the University of Michigan for two months. In November he suffers his first mental breakdown; remains in a sanitarium until January 1936.
1936	Receives master's degree from the University of Michigan.
1936–43	Teaches at Pennsylvania State College.
1941	Publishes *Open House*.
1943	On leave from Pennsylvania State College, he begins teaching at Bennington College. Becomes friends with Kenneth Burke who is also teaching at Bennington and living upstairs from Roethke.
1945	Receives a Guggenheim Fellowship.

1947   Leaves Bennington College and begins teaching at the University of Washington.

1948   *The Lost Son and Other Poems.*

1950   Awarded a second Guggenheim Fellowship.

1951   *Praise to the End!*

1952–53 Receives a Ford Fellowship. Marries Beatrice O'Connell, a former student, on January 3, 1953. *The Waking: Poems 1933–1953.*

1954   Mother dies in February. Roethke receives the Pulitzer Prize for *The Waking.*

1955–56 Is a Fulbright lecturer in Italy.

1958   *Words for the Wind* receives the National Book Award and the Bollingen Prize.

1959   Awarded a second grant from the Ford Foundation.

1960   Travels in Europe and is hospitalized at Ballinisloe for the month of August.

1961   Returns to the United States. *I Am! Says the Lamb.*

1963   Roethke dies suddenly on August 1. "Sequence, Sometimes Metaphysical" is published.

1964   *The Far Field* is published and receives the National Book Award.

1966   *Collected Poems.*

Contributors

HAROLD BLOOM, Sterling Professor of the Humanities at Yale University, is the author of *The Anxiety of Influence, Poetry and Repression,* and many other volumes of literary criticism. His forthcoming study, *Freud: Transference and Authority,* attempts a full-scale reading of all of Freud's major writings. A MacArthur Prize Fellow, he is general editor of five series of literary criticism published by Chelsea House. During 1987–88, he was appointed Charles Eliot Norton Professor of Poetry at Harvard University.

KENNETH BURKE is the author of such crucial works of theoretical and practical criticism as *Permanence and Change, The Philosophy of Literary Form, A Grammar of Motives* and *The Rhetoric of Religion.*

DENIS DONOGHUE is Henry James Professor of English and American Literature at New York University. His books include *Thieves of Fire* and *Ferocious Alphabets.*

ROY HARVEY PEARCE is Professor of American Literature at the University of California at San Diego. A Fellow of the American Academy of Arts and Sciences, his books include *The Continuity of American Poetry* and *Historicism Once More: Problems and Occasions for the American Scholar.*

BRENDAN GALVIN teaches at Central Connecticut State University and has published several books of poetry including *Seals in the Inner Harbor.*

JAMES DICKEY is generally acknowledged to be one of the major poets in contemporary American literature. In addition to such collections of verse as *Drowning with Others, Helmets,* and *Buckdancer's Choice,* he has also published two volumes of criticism, *Babel to Byzantium* and *The Suspect in Poetry.*

J. D. McCLATCHY teaches in the Department of Creative Writing at Princeton University. His poetry includes *Scenes from Another Life;* his criticism includes several essays on the work of James Merrill.

ROSEMARY SULLIVAN is Associate Professor of English at Erindale College, University of Toronto. She is the author of *Theodore Roethke: The Garden Master.*

JAY PARINI teaches in the Department of English at Middlebury College. He has published *Theodore Roethke: An American Romantic* as well as his own fiction and poetry.

THOMAS GARDNER teaches in the Department of English at Virginia Polytechnic Institute. He was Guest Editor for "American Poetry of the Seventies" in *Contemporary Literature.*

JAMES APPLEWHITE is Director of the Institute of the Arts at Duke University, where he teaches in the English Department. He is author of several volumes of poetry and has received writing fellowships from the National Endowment for the Arts and the Guggenheim Foundation.

Bibliography

Arnett, Carroll. "Minimal to Maximal: Theodore Roethke's Dialectic." *College English* 28 (1957): 414–17.

Auden, W. H. "Verse and the Times." *Saturday Review* 23 (1941): 30–31.

Benedikt, Michael. "The Completed Pattern." *Poetry* 109 (1967): 262–66.

Berryman, John. "From the Middle and Senior Generations." *American Scholar* 28 (1959): 384–90.

Blessing, Richard A. *Theodore Roethke's Dynamic Vision.* Bloomington: Indiana University Press, 1974.

———."The Shaking That Steadies: Theodore Roethke's 'The Waking.' " *Ball State University Forum* 12, no. 4 (1971): 17–19.

———."Theodore Roethke's Sometimes Metaphysical Motion." *Texas Studies in Literature and Language* 14 (1972): 731–49.

Bogan, Louise. "The Lost Son." *The New Yorker* 24 (15 May 1948): 118.

———."Praise to the End!" *The New Yorker* 27 (16 February 1952): 107–08.

Bogen, Don. "From *Open House* to the Greenhouse: Theodore Roethke's Poetic Breakthrough." *ELH* 47 (1980): 399–418.

Bowers, Neal. "Theodore Roethke: The Manic Vision." *Modern Poetry Studies* 11 (1982): 152–63.

Boyd, John D. "Texture and Form in Theodore Roethke's Greenhouse Poems." *Modern Language Quarterly* 39 (1971): 409–24.

Boyers, Robert. "A Very Separate Peace." In *The Young American Writers,* edited by Richard Kostelanetz. New York: Funk & Wagnalls, 1967: 27–34.

Brown, Dennis E. "Theodore Roethke's 'Self-World' and the Modernist Position." *Journal of Modern Literature* 3 (1974): 1239–54.

Burke, Kenneth. "Cult of the Breakthrough." *The New Republic* 159 (21 September 1968): 25–26.

Ciardi, John. "Comments on Theodore Roethke." *Cimarron Review,* no. 7 (1969): 6–8.

Davie, Donald. "Two Ways out of Whitman." *The Review,* no. 14 (1964): 14–19.

Davis, William V. "Fishing an Old Wound: Theodore Roethke's Search for Sonship." *Antigonish Review,* no. 20 (1974): 29–41.

Deutsch, Babette. "On Theodore Roethke's 'In a Dark Time.' " In *The Contemporary Poet as Artist and Critic: Eight Symposia,* edited by Anthony Ostroff, 36–40. Boston: Little, Brown, 1964.

Dickey, James. "Theodore Roethke." In *Babel to Byzantium: Poets and Poetry Now.* New York: Farrar, Straus, & Giroux, 1968: 147–52.

Eberhart, Richard. "On Theodore Roethke's Poetry." *Southern Review* 1, no. 3 (1965): 612–20.

Galvin, Brendan. "Theodore Roethke's Proverbs." *Contemporary Poetry: A Journal* 5, no. 1 (1972): 35–47.

Hamilton, Ian. "Theodore Roethke." *Agenda* 3 (1964): 5–10.

Heaney, Seamus. "Canticles to the Earth." *Listener* 80 (1968): 245–46.

Heyen, William. "The Yeats Influence: Roethke's Formal Lyrics of the Fifties." *John Berryman Studies: A Scholarly and Critical Journal* 2, no. 3 (1976): 32–51.

———, ed. *Prcfile of Theodore Roethke.* Columbus, Ohio: Merrill, 1971.

Kramer, Hilton. "The Poetry of Theodore Roethke." *Western Review* 18 (1954): 131–46.

Kunitz, Stanley. "On Theodore Roethke's 'In a Dark Time.' " In *The Contemporary Poet as Artist and Critic: Eight Symposia,* edited by Anthony Ostroff, 41–48. Boston: Little, Brown, 1964.

Kunitz, Stanley. "News of the Root." *Poetry* 73 (1949): 222–25.

Kusch, Robert. "The Sense of Place in Theodore Roethke's 'The Rose.' " *Concerning Poetry* 4, no. 4 (1982): 73–88.

La Belle, Jenijoy. *The Echoing Wood of Theodore Roethke.* Princeton: Princeton University Prcss, 1976.

Lane, Gary. *A Concordance to the Poems of Theodore Roethke.* Metuchen, N.J.: Scarecrow Press, 1972.

Lecourt, Jean-Philipe. "Theodore Roethke: The Inner Wilderness and the Barrier of Ideology." In *Myth and Ideology in American Culture,* edited by Regis Durand, 43–64. Villeneuve d'Ascq: Université de Lille III, 1976.

Lee, Charlotte I. "Roethke Writes about Women." *Literature in Performance: A Journal of Literary and Performing Arts* 1, no. 1 (1980): 23–32.

Lewandowska, M. L. "The Words of Their Roaring: Roethke's Use of The Psalms of David." In *The David Myth in Western Literature,* edited by Raymond-Jean Frontain and Jan Wojcik, 156–67. West Lafayette, Ind.: Purdue University Press, 1980.

Libby, Anthony. "Roethke, Water Father." In *Mythologies of Nothing.* Chicago: University of Illinois Press, 1984.

Liberthson, Daniel. *The Quest for Being: Theodore Roethke, W. S. Merwin, and Ted Hughes.* New York: Gordon, 1977.

Malkoff, Karl. *Theodore Roethke: An Introduction to the Poetry.* New York: Columbia University Press, 1966.

———. "Theodore Roethke: The Darker Side of the Dream." In *American Writing Today,* edited by Richard Kostelanetz, 171–81. Washington, D.C.: U.S. International Communication Agency, 1982.

Mazzaro, Jerome. "Theodore Roethke and the Failures of Language." *Modern Poetry Studies* 1 (1970): 73–96.

McLeod, James Richard. *Theodore Roethke: A Bibliography.* Cleveland: Kent State University Press, 1973.

McMichael, James. "Roethke's North America." *Northwest Review* 11, no. 3 (1971): 149–59.

Mills, Ralph J., Jr. "Theodore Roethke: The Lyric of the Self." In *Poets in Progress: Critical Prefaces to Ten Contemporary Poets,* edited by Edward Hungerford. Evanston, Ill.: Northwestern University Press, 1962: 3–23.

———. "Keeping the Spirit Spare." *Chicago Review* 13, no. 4 (1959): 114–22.

———. "Roethke's Garden." *Poetry* 105 (1962): 54–59.

———. *Theodore Roethke.* University of Minnesota Pamphlets on American Writers, no. 30. Minneapolis: University of Minnesota Press, 1963.

Molesworth, Charles. "Songs of a Happy Man: Theodore Roethke and Contemporary Poetry." *John Berryman Studies: A Scholarly and Critical Journal* 2, no. 3 (1976): 32–51.

Moul, Keith R. *Theodore Roethke's Career: An Annotated Bibliography.* Boston: G. K. Hall, 1977.

Nelson, Cary. *Our Last First Poets.* Urbana: University of Illinois Press, 1981.

Northwest Review 11, no. 3 (1971). Special Theodore Roethke Issue.

Pinsky, Robert. *The Situation of Poetry,* 118–29. Princeton: Princeton University Press, 1976.

Ramakrishnan, E. V. "The Confessional Mode in Theodore Roethke: A Reading of 'The Lost Son.' " *Indian Journal of American Studies* 11, no. 1 (1981): 58–65.

Ransom, John Crowe. "On Theodore Roethke's 'In a Dark Time.' " In *The Contemporary Poet as Artist and Critic: Eight Symposia,* edited by Anthony Ostroff, 41–48. Boston: Little, Brown, 1964.

Rosenthal, M. L. *The New Poets: American and British Poetry since World War II,* 112–18. New York: Oxford University Press, 1965.

Schott, Penelope Scambly. " 'I AM!' Says Theodore Roethke: A Reading of the Nonsense Poems." *Washington State University Research Studies* 43 (1975): 103–12.

Schwartz, Delmore. "Cunning and Craft of the Unconscious and Preconscious." *Poetry* 94 (1959): 203–5.

Scott, Nathan A. "The Example of Roethke." In *The Wild Prayer of Longing: Poetry and the Sacred,* 76–118. New Haven: Yale University Press, 1971.

Seager, Allan. *The Glass House: The Life of Theodore Roethke.* New York: McGraw-Hill, 1968.

———, Stanley Kunitz, and John Ciardi. "An Evening with Ted Roethke." *Michigan Quarterly Review* 6 (1967): 227–45.

Snodgrass, W. D. "The Last Poems of Theodore Roethke." *College English* 21 (1964): 5–6.

Staples, Hugh. "The Rose in the Sea-Wind: A Reading of Theodore Roethke's 'North American Sequence.' " *American Literature* 36 (1964): 189–203.

Stein, Arnold, ed. *Theodore Roethke: Essays on the Poetry.* Seattle: University of Washington Press, 1965.

Sullivan, Rosemary. *Theodore Roethke: The Garden Master.* Seattle: University of Washington Press, 1975.

Thurley, Geoffrey. *The American Moment: American Poetry in the Mid-Century.* New York: St. Martin's, 1978: 91–105.

Truesdale, C. W. "Theodore Roethke and the Landscape of American Poetry." *Minnesota Review* 8 (1968): 345–58.

Van Dyne, Susan R. "Self-Poesis in Roethke's 'The Shape of the Fire.'" *Modern Poetry Studies* 10 (1981): 121–36.

Vernon, John. "Theodore Roethke." In *The Garden and the Map: Schizophrenia in Twentieth-Century Literature and Culture*. Chicago: University of Illinois Press, 1973: 159–90.

Waggoner, Hyatt. *American Poets: From the Puritans to the Present*. Boston: Houghton Mifflin, 1968: 564–77.

———. *American Visionary Poetry*, 113–42. Baton Rouge: Louisiana State University Press, 1982.

Wesling, Donald. "The Inevitable Ear: Freedom and Necessity in Lyric Form, Wordsworth and After." *ELH* 36 (1969): 544–61.

Williams, Harry. *"The Edge Is What I Have."* Lewisburg, Pennsylvania: Bucknell University Press, 1977.

Winters, Yvor. "The Poems of Theodore Roethke." *Kenyon Review* 3 (1941): 514–16.

Wolff, George. "Syntactical and Imagistic Distortions in Roethke's Greenhouse Poems." *Language and Style* 6 (1973): 281–88.

———. *Theodore Roethke*. Boston: Twayne, 1981.

Acknowledgments

"The Vegetal Radicalism of Theodore Roethke" by Kenneth Burke from *The Sewanee Review* 58, no. 1 (January–March 1950), © 1950 by the University of the South. Reprinted by permission of the editor.

"Theodore Roethke" by Denis Donoghue from *Conoisseurs of Chaos* by Denis Donoghue, © 1964, 1984 by Denis Donoghue. Reprinted by permission of Columbia University Press.

"Theodore Roethke: The Power of Sympathy" by Roy Harvey Pearce from *Theodore Roethke: Essays of the Poetry*, edited by Arnold Stein, © 1965 by the University of Washington Press. Reprinted by permission of the University of Washington Press.

"Kenneth Burke and Theodore Roethke's 'Lost Son' Poems" by Brendan Galvin from *Northwest Review* 11, no. 3 (Summer 1971), © 1971 by the University of Oregon. Reprinted by permission.

"The Greatest American Poet: Theodore Roethke" (originally "The Greatest American Poet: Roethke") by James Dickey from *Sorties* by James Dickey, © 1971 by James Dickey. Reprinted by permission of Doubleday & Company, Inc., and Raines & Raines.

"Sweating Light from a Stone: Identifying Theodore Roethke" by J. D. McClatchy from *Modern Poetry Studies* 3, no. 1 (1972), © 1972 by J. D. McClatchy. Reprinted by permission.

"Wet with Another Life: 'Meditations of an Old Woman' " by Rosemary Sullivan from *Theodore Roethke: The Garden Master* by Rosemary Sullivan, © 1975 by the University of Washington Press. Reprinted by permission of the University of Washington Press.

"Blake and Roethke: When Everything Comes to One" by Jay Parini from *William Blake and the Moderns*, edited by Robert J. Bertholf and Annette S. Levitt, © 1982 by the State University of New York. Reprinted by permission of the State University of New York Press.

" 'North American Sequence': Theodore Roethke and the Contemporary American Long Poem" by Thomas Gardner from *Essays in Literature* 11, no. 2 (Fall 1984), © 1984 by Western Illinois University. Reprinted by permission.

"Death and Rebirth in a Modern Landscape" by James Applewhite from *Seas and Inland Journeys* by James Applewhite, © 1985 by the University of Georgia Press. Reprinted by permission of the University of Georgia Press.

Index

Modern Critical Views

Continued from front of book

Gabriel García Márquez
Andrew Marvell
Carson McCullers
Herman Melville
George Meredith
James Merrill
John Stuart Mill
Arthur Miller
Henry Miller
John Milton
Yukio Mishima
Molière
Michel de Montaigne
Eugenio Montale
Marianne Moore
Alberto Moravia
Toni Morrison
Alice Munro
Iris Murdoch
Robert Musil
Vladimir Nabokov
V. S. Naipaul
R. K. Narayan
Pablo Neruda
John Henry, Cardinal
 Newman
Friedrich Nietzsche
Frank Norris
Joyce Carol Oates
Sean O'Casey
Flannery O'Connor
Christopher Okigbo
Charles Olson
Eugene O'Neill
José Ortega y Gasset
Joe Orton
George Orwell
Ovid
Wilfred Owen
Amos Oz
Cynthia Ozick
Grace Paley
Blaise Pascal
Walter Pater
Octavio Paz
Walker Percy
Petrarch
Pindar
Harold Pinter
Luigi Pirandello
Sylvia Plath
Plato

Plautus
Edgar Allan Poe
Poets of Sensibility & the
 Sublime
Poets of the Nineties
Alexander Pope
Katherine Anne Porter
Ezra Pound
Anthony Powell
Pre-Raphaelite Poets
Marcel Proust
Manuel Puig
Alexander Pushkin
Thomas Pynchon
Francisco de Quevedo
François Rabelais
Jean Racine
Ishmael Reed
Adrienne Rich
Samuel Richardson
Mordecai Richler
Rainer Maria Rilke
Arthur Rimbaud
Edwin Arlington Robinson
Theodore Roethke
Philip Roth
Jean-Jacques Rousseau
John Ruskin
J. D. Salinger
Jean-Paul Sartre
Gershom Scholem
Sir Walter Scott
William Shakespeare
 (3 vols.)
 Histories & Poems
 Comedies & Romances
 Tragedies
George Bernard Shaw
Mary Wollstonecraft
 Shelley
Percy Bysshe Shelley
Sam Shepard
Richard Brinsley Sheridan
Sir Philip Sidney
Isaac Bashevis Singer
Tobias Smollett
Alexander Solzhenitsyn
Sophocles
Wole Soyinka
Edmund Spenser
Gertrude Stein
John Steinbeck

Stendhal
Laurence Sterne
Wallace Stevens
Robert Louis Stevenson
Tom Stoppard
August Strindberg
Jonathan Swift
John Millington Synge
Alfred, Lord Tennyson
William Makepeace
 Thackeray
Dylan Thomas
Henry David Thoreau
James Thurber and S. J.
 Perelman
J. R. R. Tolkien
Leo Tolstoy
Jean Toomer
Lionel Trilling
Anthony Trollope
Ivan Turgenev
Mark Twain
Miguel de Unamuno
John Updike
Paul Valéry
Cesar Vallejo
Lope de Vega
Gore Vidal
Virgil
Voltaire
Kurt Vonnegut
Derek Walcott
Alice Walker
Robert Penn Warren
Evelyn Waugh
H. G. Wells
Eudora Welty
Nathanael West
Edith Wharton
Patrick White
Walt Whitman
Oscar Wilde
Tennessee Williams
William Carlos Williams
Thomas Wolfe
Virginia Woolf
William Wordsworth
Jay Wright
Richard Wright
William Butler Yeats
A. B. Yehoshua
Emile Zola